HARVARD STUDIES IN ENGLISH

VOLUME II

THE ENGLISH MORALITIES
FROM THE POINT OF VIEW
OF ALLEGORY

BY

W. ROY MACKENZIE

THE ENGLISH MORALITIES FROM THE POINT OF VIEW OF ALLEGORY

BY

W. ROY MACKENZIE

ASSOCIATE PROFESSOR OF ENGLISH IN WASHINGTON UNIVERSITY

GORDIAN PRESS, INC.
NEW YORK
1966

Originally Published 1914
Reprinted 1966 by Gordian Press, Inc.

Library of Congress Catalog Card No. 66-29466

Printed in U.S.A. by
EDWARDS BROTHERS, INC.
Ann Arbor, Michigan

TO
WILLIAM ALLAN NEILSON
THIS BOOK IS GRATEFULLY DEDICATED

PREFACE

In beginning this work my aim was to throw some light on the allegorical methods employed in the Moralities. But I had not proceeded far on this quest before it became apparent that a proper presentation of the allegorical methods employed would necessarily include a thorough clearing away of the cobwebs of misapprehension which cling to most treatments of this species of drama, and a complete classification of the Moralities on the basis of allegorical structure. In my discussion of existing treatments of the Morality I have taken high ground, and I shall, without doubt, be most heartily criticized for assuming, from the start, the complacent attitude that I am right and everybody else is wrong. I plead, in my defence, that at the beginning of my study I used all these treatments, not as interesting bits of reading in themselves, but as prospective guides to a detailed investigation of the Moralities. The result was that each new guide led me into a new morass, and I soon reached the conclusion that I could do no worse, at least, by starting out to explore the country alone. The excuse for bringing in the results of my expedition I can state with a good deal of confidence. It is that the Moralities are, not a series of plays which have for the most part adopted allegory as a method of presentation, but a series of allegories presented in dramatic form. If this is granted it follows that the Moralities, before being considered as dramas or as chronological factors in a history of the drama, must be interpreted and classified as allegories.

There are a few points of obvious and general interest which the most casual student of the Moralities should have in mind at the beginning, and which are not out of place even in a preface.

First, and most important, is the reminder that the Morality, though usually exhibiting a most disgusting freedom of language in its scenes of vice, coupled often with a purely animal and sensual joy in the luxury of sin, had as its constant purpose a desire to edify. It was "a game wherein Vices fyght with Vertues," and it would hardly be consistent to demand that the Vices in this game should deport themselves like prigs, or display themselves as benevolent and clean-minded personifications of vile and abhorrent sins. The average Vice of the Morality has no such virtuous desire in mind. He shows himself in his true colors, and if these colors are often suggestive of mud and filth, we must at least admit that consistency is a jewel, and refrain from a desire to see our friend the Vice clothed in white and gold. Personally, I must confess to a base-born partiality for this rollicking incarnation of sin who skips merrily through so many scenes of the Moralities and interrupts so many doleful homilies. I am quite conscious now that I have shown this partiality — unconscious at the time — in the pages that follow, and the excuse that I must present is that I have not written this work primarily to inculcate morality.

The point, then, that we have almost lost sight of is that the Morality aims at being edifying on the whole, though it is not always so in details. At the close of the action virtue is triumphant, the representatives of vice are discomfited and driven from the stage, and Man, except in one or two cases, has obtained pardon and has attained strength to persist in a useful and moral life. This leads to the second point.

The question might arise, and as a matter of fact often does arise, What is this useful lesson that the Morality presents for the guidance of life? In the best-known class of Moralities, that in which the human hero is striven for by Virtues and Vices, Man regularly falls from grace, persists in sin during a great part of his life, and is usually reclaimed to virtue at the close of the action, when, in many cases, he has neared the end of his days. Do the Moralities, then, teach us to give free rein to our lusts and our dishonest desires through the prime of life and then to embrace virtue with a shrewd eye to the hereafter? Not so. In studying these plays we must never forget that Man is not presented as stalking in lordly fashion among Virtues and Vices and selecting from them companions at will, but that Virtues and Vices are presented as striving for the possession of Man. The latter is regarded as inclining to good rather than to evil; consequently, in nearly every case, the Vices have to resort to subterfuge in order to win his temporary companion-ship. The trick which they almost invariably practise is to in-troduce themselves by assumed names as Virtues; and, having once gained the favor of Man, they spur him on to vice and crime while deceiving him into the belief that he is leading the best possible kind of life. At last Man encounters the true Vir-tues and is reclaimed by them. Thus the spectator of these plays was put on his guard against the sins which have a spe-cious and pleasing aspect, and was taught to recognize the true virtues to be practised in the world.

It would be idle, however, to deny the probability of a purely dramatic reason for making the bulk of the action, in a great many Moralities, a picture of life in sin, since their only chance to provide amusement was through the representatives of vice. Consequently these vulgar and fun-provoking persons often oc-cupy the centre of the stage during the greater part of the play. One cannot but wonder at the constant employment of the phrase "bloodless abstractions," used sweepingly to designate the Morality actors, as if they were a set of sermonizing autom-atons. The Virtues, to be sure, may usually be thus described; but the Vices, on the contrary, are a troop of as virile, resource-ful, red-blooded scoundrels as one could wish to meet — or to avoid. The chief objection to be made in their case is that, from the point of view of allegory, they are often rendered entirely too many-sided and human to stand accurately for the abstractions which they are intended to personify. And, in consequence of this tendency to humanize the Vices, we frequently find that they are differentiated as actors on the stage rather than in accordance with the names that specify their characters. This, however, applies to scenes where the Vices foregather to compare sinful experiences, and scarcely ever to scenes where they appear as the tempters of Man.

I should like also to oppose the usual criticism that it is because of their allegorical structure that the Moralities are often insufferably dull. It is, on the contrary, when the allegory is temporarily neglected in favor of an uncalled-for literal explanation of events, or, as happens more frequently, for a lengthy homily, that the modern student must fight his desire to close the book. And even here one should regard the matter sympathetically, and with the realization that the persons for whom the plays were produced listened with patience and even with pleasure to sermons which inspire us only with impious and revengeful desires. We may admit, then, that these breaks in the allegory are displeasing to the person who turns nowadays to the Moralities in the hope of being amused, but what person with a sense for that which is true and appealing in literature can fail to recognize the beauty of the two Moralities, *Everyman* and *The Play of Wyt and Science* ? And these are two of the most finished and consistent allegories in existence.

Lastly, I wish merely to reiterate a point which I have mentioned in different parts of this work; that is, the admirable fitness of allegory for the presentation of a moral lesson by means of drama. Indeed, when one considers that a play, to merit the name, cannot be merely a sermon or a set of directions, one is forced to admit that, in drama, the allegorical structure is the most direct means by which a single and connected lesson can be taught for the guidance of life. There is no opportunity for the display of disturbing human passions and interests such as must enter into the play concerned with the fortunes of individual human beings. In the Morality, every character has his course of action decided by his name, so that, once given the proper set of characters, the lesson works itself out inevitably. In the pages that follow, and in more direct connection with the plays, this point has, I hope, been made clear.

This investigation in its first form was presented as a partial fulfilment of the requirements for the degree of Doctor of Philosophy at Harvard University. It was begun, and has been carried on, with the advice of Professor Neilson, from whom I have received, from first to last, the most sympathetic and helpful criticism. To Professor Kittredge, also, I owe the warmest thanks. His practical suggestions were of the greatest use to me in formulating those chapters in which my main conclusions are presented. Professors Neilson and Greenough have read the manuscript and proof throughout, and have given me many useful hints for revising and emending. And, finally, in the preparation of the entire work I have had the coöperation of my wife, and many of the conclusions that follow we have reached together by the way of discussion.

W. R. M.

Washington University, St. Louis

CONTENTS

THE ENGLISH MORALITIES FROM THE POINT OF VIEW OF ALLEGORY

CHAPTER I

THE SUBJECT DEFINED

The first impression that one receives in reading the existing treatments of the Morality is that of a curious discrepancy between the definitions presented and the plays which are grouped under the definitions. The chief criticism to be made — and it is a sufficiently damning one — is that many of these treatments restrict the type to such narrow limits that at best only two or three plays could be legitimately admitted; but the constructors of these limits, having thus appeased their desire for conservatism, proceed to admit many plays that could not be included under any definition that would not be too broad to warrant us in considering the Moralities as a separate class. It is of the first importance, then, that we should have some reasonable definition, applicable to the facts, and based upon the evidence of the plays themselves. If some of the present definitions were accepted literally we should have to consign the Morality, as a type, to the realm of hypothesis, and this might be a satisfactory solution of the problem if it were possible; but that Moralities do exist is attested by the very writers who, while they make the type theoretically non-existent, continue to discuss it as a real section of dramatic literature.

One of the prime causes of confusion is the attitude of some writers toward God and the Devil as actors in the Morality. Mr. Chambers, for instance, in his *Mediaeval Stage*, says: "The process of introducing abstractions into the Miracle plays does not seem to have gone very far. On the other hand the Moralities, *if God and the Devil may be regarded as abstractions*, admit of nothing else." [1]

I shall revert presently to the last part of this second statement. Just now I am concerned with the clause italicized. It seems that Mr. Chambers is suggesting that we regard supernatural powers as abstractions in order that the Morality may be defined with one sweep of the arm. Evidently he admits it without question himself. But would his admission, or ours, have anything to do with the case? It would seem that the necessary admission here should be from the author of the play and the people who saw it acted: and, to whatever realms of abstraction God and the Devil may have been consigned by modern metaphysics, we may be sure that to the people most concerned in the production of the Moralities they were real and living personages.

Professor Courthope, in his *History of English Poetry*, takes the same view of these supernatural figures. While discussing the Miracle Play, he says: "As its main object was to set before the people the scheme of redemption, the dramatist did not hesitate to place upon the stage impersonations of the most abstract conceptions of the mind. God, the nine orders of angels, the Devil and his rebel host, were all introduced in the pageants," [2] etc.

It is hardly necessary to argue that the theology of the fifteenth and sixteenth centuries did not present Jehovah and his great adversary as abstractions conceived by the human

[1] E. K. Chambers, *The Mediaeval Stage*, II, 153. (The italics are mine.)
[2] W. J. Courthope, *A History of English Poetry*, I, 398.

mind. To the persons who composed the Moralities, and to those who beheld them upon the stage, God was without doubt the mighty sovereign of Scriptural story; and the Devil was, just as truly, an actual personality who, "as a roaring lion, walketh about, seeking whom he may devour."

The matter is, after all, a very simple one. The playwright who believes in the actual existence of supernatural beings, or who accepts for dramatic purposes a belief in their actual existence, presents them exactly as he would present Achilles or Julius Caesar or King Henry the Fifth; and he knows also that, if his contemporaries are capable of a like belief, they will regard them in the same light. The skeptic may argue that these people are entertaining mistaken beliefs, but that does not affect the situation. He may discuss, as he frequently does, the reality of supernatural visitations in the days when people had certain well-defined theories of demonology; but if, for instance, the Elizabethans believed that a ghost could exist independently of a diseased mind, and if Shakespeare understood and shared this belief, it is entirely beside the point for the person who does not believe in ghosts to argue that the spirit of Hamlet's father was purely subjective — a conception of Hamlet's unsound imagination.

Instead, then, of admitting that God and the Devil are abstractions in the Moralities, I assume that they were, on the contrary, as real to the people who saw them on the stage as were Hamlet and his father's ghost to a later audience. If this is true, plainly the *dramatis personae* of the Morality must be capable of including more than personifications of abstract qualities.

But let us turn again to Mr. Chambers's statement that "the Moralities, if God and the Devil may be regarded as abstractions, admit of nothing else." I propose to show that the Moralities will admit of much else, but first I should like to refer to a few other treatments of the subject which avow, or take for granted, the same theory, and exclude all but abstractions.

Ward is quite clear upon the subject. In making his distinctions between Mysteries, Miracles, and Moralities, he says: " Lastly, Morals teach and illustrate the same religious truths, not by direct representation of scriptural or legendary events and personages, but by allegorical means, abstract figures of virtues or qualities being personified in the characters appearing in this species of play." [1]

This seems, at least, unambiguous ; but apparently Ward is troubled by doubts of its finality, for he presently adds a formal definition: " A Morality may be defined as a play enforcing a moral truth or lesson by means of the speech and action of characters which are personified abstractions — figures representing virtues and vices, qualities of the human mind, or abstract conceptions in general." [2]

This definition, as well as its precursor quoted above, evidently points to the same conclusion as does Chambers's statement, the only loophole for escape in Ward's case being the fact that he does not explicitly state that *all* the characters are personified abstractions. But if not stated, this is at least implied. And in contradistinction to this definition, the treatment of the Morality that follows is based almost entirely upon plays that contain important type figures, — as, indeed, it would have to be if it were based upon actual plays at all.

A more elusive definition is that presented by Collier: " A Moral, or Moral play, is a drama, the characters of which are allegorical, abstract, or symbolical, and the story of which is intended to convey a lesson for the better conduct of human life." [3]

The special characteristic of this definition is extreme vagueness. "Allegorical, abstract, or symbolical" : what steps can

---

[1] A. W. Ward, *A History of English Dramatic Literature*, I, 42.
[2] Ibid., p. 100.   [3] J. P. Collier, *History of English Dramatic Poetry*, II, 183.

one take to reduce this compound to its elements? Perhaps the author had a shrewd suspicion of the truth, and intended these terms to include characters, like the familiar human hero, that represent neither vices nor virtues; but one is tempted to suppose that he grouped the words simply as three synonyms, more inclusive than one term by itself. The word "symbolical" is especially troublesome. It means, in general, much the same as "allegorical," though possibly it is used here to indicate the type figures that embody the qualities by which they are dominated. On the whole, however, it is hard to avoid the conclusion that the three terms are grouped together for common protection. And undoubtedly the purpose is served, since it is impossible to characterize the statement as wrong. Still, as a definition it is vague and inadequate.

In order to show the kinds of characters that constantly appear in the Moralities, let us take as a specific instance the Morality of *Everyman*,[1] since it is better known than any other play of its class, and will serve as well as any other for an example. The following is a list of the *dramatis personae*:

Messenger	Kyndrede	Strengthe
God	Goodes	Dyscrecyon
Dethe	Good Dedes	Fyve Wyttes
Everyman	Knowledge	Aungel
Felawship	Confessyon	Doctour
Cosyn	Beaute	

Two of the characters, the Messenger and the Doctor, we may dismiss from the discussion, since they have no direct connection with the plot, but merely comment from the outside. All the other persons in the list are directly associated with the plot.

Everyman himself, the hero of the play, is identical with Mankind, Man, or Humanum Genus; that is, he is the representative of the human race, who appears under different names

[1] Dodsley, *Old English Plays* (ed. Hazlitt), Vol. III.

in many of the Moralities. We may regard Everyman as a
representative man without any decided bent in the direction
of either virtue or vice, but rendered as far as possible colorless in order to personate men in general; or we may regard
him as inclusive, that is, standing for all men with their possibilities for good and evil. The distinction, however, is very
hazy and, on the whole, is not worth striving for. The point
of importance is that Everyman is to be regarded, not as an
individual man, or as the representative of one class, but as
a *highly universalized type*, the representative of the whole
human race.

Let me make clear the signification of these terms. The individual man is, of course, easily understood. He is Tom Jones,
or William Robinson, or any person with a name applying
strictly to himself, though he may be broadened arbitrarily into
the representative of a class of men. The specialized type, or
representative of a class, is such a character as the lawyer, the
priest, or Jack Tar the sailor; that is, a human being confined
to some particular walk of life, or characterized by some idiosyn-
crasy. Then we pass, without crossing any distinct boundary,
to the universalized type, representing persons with more or less
universal tendencies. In this class are Mr. Worldly Wiseman
of the *Pilgrim's Progress*, and Greediness, in the Morality *All
for Money*, who stands for greedy men. The most highly universalized type of all is the Morality hero who represents the
entire human family.

The hero of *Everyman* is thus not the personification of an
abstract quality, but a type, and he does not in this respect
stand alone in the play. After being summoned to his pilgrimage by Death, he repairs to Fellowship and beseeches the
latter to accompany him. Fellowship refuses, and Everyman
has to leave him behind. What, pray, is Fellowship now?
Fickleness, possibly, but certainly no longer the abstract quality

of fellowship or friendship. The lament of Everyman himself
at this point indicates the exact nature of the figure Fellowship:

> It is said, in prosperity men *friends may find*
> Which in adversity be full unkind.
> Now whither for succour shall I flee
> Sith Fellowship hath forsaken me?[1]

That is, Fellowship does not personify an abstract quality, as
his name strictly interpreted would indicate, but represents
worldly friends with their capacities for fidelity or fickleness.
He also is a type — less highly universalized than Everyman —
of a kind very common in allegory. The Red Cross Knight,
for instance, in Spenser's *Faerie Queene*, is not the quality of
holiness, or, if so, why should he enter into intimate relations
with Duessa? He is rather the man striving for holiness, who
may at times, consistently with his character as a man, exhibit
tendencies in the opposite direction. Mercy, in Bunyan's *Pilgrim's Progress*, is not the quality of mercy personified, but
the woman of merciful disposition. It is entirely to misunder-
stand and over-simplify the methods of allegory to suppose that
its characters may not be designated by abstract names and at
the same time be types.

If we now permit Everyman to resume his speech he will
presently introduce two other type figures:

> To my kinsmen I will truly,
> Praying them to help me in my necessity:
> I believe that they will do so:
> For kind will creep where it may not go.
> I will go say: for yonder I see them go:
> Where be ye now, my friends and kinsmen [lo]?[2]

This appeal brings Kindred and Cousin to his side. After the
lines just quoted it is unnecessary to argue for their identity.
They are types — also less highly universalized than Everyman
— representing kinsfolk.

[1] Dodsley, III, 113.   [2] Ibid.

Thus we have, out of fifteen characters taking part in the action, one individual character — God ; and five more or less universalized types, — Everyman, Fellowship, Kindred, Cousin, and the angel. The rest are personified abstractions.

I have selected this play as exemplifying the sort of treatment one may expect to find in practically all of the Moralities. *The Play of Wit and Science*, and its later working over as *The Marriage of Wit and Science*, exhibit only personified abstractions ; but every other existing English Morality (with the possible exceptions of *Hyckescorner* and *New Custom* [1]) contains also types, or individuals, or both ; and a special warning is necessary against the conclusion that all abstract names appearing in the lists of *dramatis personae* must necessarily refer to personified abstractions in the plays.

Creizenach's definition of the Morality, though it fails to mention some of the chief points of the type, will now be seen to come nearer suiting the facts about the *dramatis personae* than any of the definitions already considered : "Mit dem Ausdruck Moralitäten bezeichnen die Literar-historiker diejenigen Dramen des ausgehenden Mittelalters und der Reformationszeit, in welchen die Träger der Handlung ausschiesslich oder vorwiegend personificierte Abstracta sind." [2]

The chief advantage of this definition is that it leaves the door ajar for the entry of the clamorous characters who recognize their eligibility, but who realize that they cannot consistently pose as "personificierte Abstracta." Its chief disadvantage is that it makes no mention of the prime object of the Morality, the presentation of some lesson for the guidance of life. Remove this from the Morality and you strip it of its essential quality, its reason for being. Creizenach, also, like every one else who has attempted to define the Morality, neglects to

---

[1] See the treatments of these two plays in Chapter IV.
[2] Wilhelm Creizenach, *Geschichte des neueren Dramas*, I, 458.

mention the important element of allegorical structure. Any sort of play may introduce allegory as an accidental embellishment, but these plays, written primarily to teach a moral lesson, involve the allegorical plot as their basis, since any other kind of plot is liable to produce a merely human interest in the spectacle of living characters in action, instead of centering the attention on a moral lesson. Any definition of this species, furthermore, which attempts to characterize the chief actors, should make explicit mention of the class of figures, exemplified by Everyman, who are the natural heroes of the plays. Such figures as God, Satan, and individual men and women need not be alluded to, since they rarely have any prominent part in the action. My definition, then, may take the following shape:

A Morality is a play, allegorical in structure, which has for its main object the teaching of some lesson for the guidance of life, and in which the principal characters are personified abstractions or highly universalized types.

Before we proceed to a detailed examination of the Moralities I should like to show by a brief examination of some of the plays that approach the border-line from opposite sides, how the above definition is to be applied throughout this discussion. During the second half of the sixteenth century the Morality made noticeable advances toward the drama of real life, and, in addition to this, various experiments were being made in the dramatic field; so that we find the materials of Comedy, History Play, and Tragedy combined in varying proportions with the older Morality. As a consequence of this mingling of forms a special confusion has arisen in denominating the plays of the period, and no two works on the subject can be found that follow the same method — or, indeed, any consistent method — in consigning plays to one group or another.[1] If my definition

---

[1] In the following chapter I illustrate the methods employed for the purpose by the different writers who have attempted a division.

is to contribute anything to the discussion, it must set up a standard, on technical grounds, by which to separate plays that are primarily Moralities from plays that are primarily Comedies, Histories, or Tragedies.

As an example of the historical play with distinct Morality features which is not a true Morality I shall take *Appius and Virginia*.[1] That the play contains an abundance of characters that make for allegorical action may be seen from the list of *dramatis personae*:

Virginius	Haphazard	Subservus	Justice
Mater	Mansipulus	Appius	Claudius
Virginia	Mansipula	Conscience	Rumour
Comfort	Reward	Doctrina	Memory

Some of the allegorical personages, especially Haphazard, on the side of vice, and Conscience, on the side of virtue, play intimate parts in the plot, and are not without effect on the action of the play. Haphazard, in fact, is the originator of the scheme by which Appius attempts the ruin of Virginia, and Conscience repeatedly warns Appius against the villainous action which the latter meditates.

But is this allegorical action vital to the play? The slightest outline will show that it is not. Appius at the very beginning is mad with love for Virginia. He simply makes use of Haphazard's clever scheme to serve his own preconceived ends, and refuses to listen to Conscience and Justice when they warn him against the act which he meditates. The play, in fact, is a picture of supposedly historical human beings, with varied human interests, acting with relation to each other, but in no sense dominated by the Vices and Virtues from whom they receive suggestions. The Morality, on the contrary, permits of no human action which is not the direct result of an attempt by Vices or Virtues to dominate the heart.

[1] Dodsley, Vol. IV.

It will now be seen that *Appius and Virginia* falls far short of the standard set up by the above definition. In the first place, it is not structurally allegorical; in the second, it fails to teach a specific lesson for the guidance of life, though there are here, as in most plays, abundant opportunities to deduce morals ; and in the third, it has real persons for its chief actors, while its allegorical characters are subsidiary and might be omitted without affecting the main plot. The play, then, does not fulfil any one of the three conditions, and must be classed as an historical play with Morality features.

It might be objected that the example I have chosen is, on the face of it, an historical play, and thus outside the realm of this discussion. The play, however, which I present in contrast, as a real Morality, is also based on an historical incident.

The *Conflict of Conscience*,[1] by Nathaniell Woodes, is founded on the story of Francis Spira, or Spiera, an Italian lawyer who abandoned the Protestant for the Catholic faith, and in remorse and despair committed suicide.[2] The author, however, has subordinated the personal element almost to the point of obliteration. The action is dominated by personifications of abstract qualities; and Philologus, the hero, though reminiscent of the Italian lawyer, is carefully broadened by the author into a universalized type. The Prologue gives two reasons for this, the second of which is extremely significant: first, comedy will not permit us to touch on the vices of one private man, and, second, if the play were written about an individual man the audience would fail to apply the moral to themselves. The Prologue goes on to explain the significance of the hero :

> But sith Philologus is nought else but one that loves to talk,
> And common of the word of God, but hath no further care,
> According as it teacheth them in God's fear for to walk,

[1] Dodsley, Vol. II.
[2] See Sleidan, *Vingt-neuf Livres d'Histoire*, Geneva, 1563, Liv. xxi.

If that we practise this indeed, Philologi we are.
And so by his deserved fault we may in time beware:
Now if, as author first it meant, you hear it with this gain,
In good behalf we will esteem that he bestowed his pain.[1]

I add a list of the *dramatis personae* in order that it may be compared with that of *Appius and Virginia*:

Prologue	Tyranny	Suggestion	Cardinal
Mathetes	Spirit	Gisbertus	Cacon
Conscience	Horror	Nuntius	Philologus
Paphinitius	Eusebius	Hypocrisy	
Satan	Avarice	Theologus	

Here, as in *Appius and Virginia*, appears the puzzling mixture of personified abstraction, type figure, and real person. Manifestly one must not be content with a reading of the list of *dramatis personae*. An examination of the play itself shows that the downfall of Philologus is accomplished by the direct persuasion of Vices, that is, personifications of evil qualities working in or upon the heart; and after his fall his state is so desperate that nothing but the direct intervention of God can save him. I shall elsewhere give a fuller interpretation of the allegory in the play, and for the present it will be sufficient to indicate its signification very briefly: The Christian who is readier to discuss God's word than to walk consistently in the fear of God may for a time resist the evil desires of his heart, but eventually he yields to the temptations of the world and to his own ambition for worldly prosperity. He stills the voice of conscience at first, but finally becomes convicted of sin; and then his remorse is so extreme that the comforts of religion make no impression upon him, until finally God intervenes directly to save his soul.

Let us sum up, then, the essential differences between the two plays. *Appius and Virginia* may be called a " tendenz "

---

[1] Dodsley, VI, 33.

play. There are abundant opportunities to draw morals from it, and, oddly enough, the moral which the author selects from the pack and presses upon his audience is, Let all true virgins take pattern from Virginia and lose their heads rather than their purity.[1] The play has a great deal of allegorical action at different parts, but this is incidental and forms no essential element of the plot. The *Conflict of Conscience*, on the other hand, though based on an historical tale, is allegorical in structure and teaches one direct and unequivocal moral lesson.

Other plays, however, that I shall have to reject, come nearer meeting the requirements and, indeed, have so much the appearance of Moralities that they are nearly always classed as such. Two important plays of this category are *The Nice Wanton* and *The Disobedient Child*. Each of them has the earnestness of purpose and the careful insistence upon a moral truth of the regular Morality. Each, in fact, would be a Morality if didacticism were the one requirement. They both, however, exhibit individuals and specialized types in their principal parts, and thus differ in a very essential point from the plays exhibiting personified abstractions and universalized types. Most of the action in both plays can be taken literally instead of allegorically, though the action is always for the enforcing of the moral, never for its own sake.

The play of *The Nice Wanton*[2] has the following list of *dramatis personae*:

The Messenger	Eulalia	Worldly Shame
Barnabas	Iniquitie	Daniel, the Judge
Ismael	Baily Errand	
Dalilah	Xantippe	

There are only two strictly allegorical names in the play, Iniquitie and Worldly Shame, and the latter takes scarcely any

[1] See the Prologue to the play.
[2] J. M. Manly, *Specimens of the Pre-Shaksperean Drama*, Vol. I.

part in the action. Iniquitie, who plays a fairly prominent part, is a specific character in all but name. He is a typical gallant, a man about town, who joins Ismael and Dalilah at one period of their downfall and becomes their boon companion. The characters that dominate the action are Barnabas, Ismael, and Dalilah, "three braunches of an yll tree." Barnabas is the good boy who goes to school, learns his lessons, and never fails to become edifying for the benefit of anyone who is unfortunate enough to come within hearing. At the end of the play he is a grown man, prosperous, and rejoicing in the prospect of many years to come in which to instruct his erring fellow-mortals. Herein consists half the moral. His brother and sister, Ismael and Dalilah, throw away their school-books, break away from the virtuous Barnabas, and presently take to throwing dice with their friend Iniquitie. By the end of the play Dalilah is " dead of the pockes, taken at the stews," and Ismael is " hanged in chaynes." The moral is complete.

Even such a slight outline as the foregoing cannot leave much doubt as to the purpose of the play. Indeed, the moral is insisted upon more steadily and more earnestly than in many of the full-fledged Moralities, but while the play lacks allegorical structure no amount of moral earnestness can retain it in the class.

A shorter account of *The Disobedient Child*[1] will suffice. The actors are these :

Prologue	The Woman Cook	The Devil
The Rich Man	The Young Woman	The Perorator
The Rich Man's Son	The Servingman	
The Man Cook	The Priest	

We are here still farther away from the sort of actors proper to the Moralities. The author evidently refrained from giving proper names to his characters in the fear that they might

[1] Dodsley, Vol. II.

become interesting in their own persons, and thus cause us to lose sight of the moral. If so, his object is only partly attained. The characters are to some extent dehumanized by their type names, but they are still actual people, influencing each other in various ways. Some interest is aroused in their fortunes, and some curiosity stimulated as to their ultimate fates. There is none of the inevitableness of Morality action, where all or most of the characters stand for, or are actuated by, some particular quality, in accordance with which they are bound to act. Here all the characters, except the Devil, may develop in any way the author chooses. Consequently the main interest is concentrated around these possibilities ; and the moral expressed at the end of the play seems to be entirely arbitrary, — a mere suggestion given by certain aspects of the story, instead of the inevitable lesson worked out when allegorical characters accompany each other throughout an allegorical plot. The Perorator, however, gives us his solemn assurance that

> By this little play the father is taught
> After what manner his child to use,
> Lest that through cockering he at length be brought
> His fathers commandment to refuse.[1]

In *The Nice Wanton* there was some semblance of allegorical action in the parts played by Iniquitie and Worldly Shame, but here there is no trace of it. The son is treated too indulgently by his father, acts badly, and suffers for it. It might have been more just to punish the father, but fortunately there is no need to go into that question here. The moral purpose is at least proclaimed. But the allegorical structure is lacking, and the play, though avowedly a moral play, is not technically a Morality.

At a later point in this work will be found a more careful discussion of the plays which, though possessed of Morality features, fall outside of the general class. For the present it is

[1] Dodsley, II, 316.

sufficient to explain the absence from my list of several plays usually classed as Moralities, but properly belonging elsewhere.

Finally, let us glance for a moment at one of the Moralities with a decided leaning towards the drama of real life, in order to show how far a play may go in that direction and still remain essentially a Morality. The important point here, as elsewhere in this introductory chapter, is to prove that the matter of division can be and ought to be arranged on technical grounds.

Like Will to Like, Quoth the Devil to the Collier[1] is the mouth-filling title of one of the later Moralities. The author's delight in full-sounding names did not stop short at the title-page, as the following list of characters will show:

The Prologue	Lucifer
Tom Tosspot	Ralph Roister
Hankin Hangman	Good Fame
Tom Collier	Severity
Hance	Philip Fleming
Virtuous Living	Pierce Pickpurse
God's Promise	Honour
Cuthbert Cutpurse	Nichol Newfangle, the Vice

The list hardly looks promising from the point of view of one arguing for the play as a Morality. But an examination of the plot and characters will show that it is mainly the author's genius for alliteration — with a suggestion of onomatopœia — that has led him, for the moment, into disguising some of the characters in a play conforming closely to the requirements of the Morality. Nichol Newfangle is the traditional Vice of the Moralities, the personification of "all sins generally." He is the godson of the Devil, and his only business on earth is to obtain victims for his godfather. The alliterative characters are a collection of types of the people who fall readily into the snares of sin, or, to speak allegorically, who obey the instructions

---

[1] Dodsley, Vol. III. The author is Ulpian Fulwel.

of Nichol Newfangle and come to grief thereby. Virtuous Living, on the other hand, resists the entreaties of Nichol, is commended by God's Promise, and is presently joined by Good Fame and Honour.

The play teaches that good living is commended by God and also leads to earthly happiness and honor, while evil living — of the various kinds illustrated by the dupes of Nichol — leads to earthly punishment and a future residence with the Devil. It is of the same type as *The Nice Wanton* in the lesson it teaches, though *The Nice Wanton* is a far more serious and — in the ordinary sense of the word — more moral play, holding faithfully to the didactic attitude, while the play under discussion is taken up largely with humorous scenes showing the vicious side of life in London. The essential difference is that in the one play the lesson is taught by means of a concrete illustration, in the other by means of allegorical action.

CHAPTER II

THE MORALITIES CLASSIFIED

Although several classifications of the Moralities have already been attempted, none of these has been made on any consistent basis. The only point of view from which it is possible to make a clear and complete division is, I am convinced, that of allegorical method; and with the exception of a partial classification, applied to a few of the Moralities, by Mr. R. L. Ramsay,[1] no such division seems even to have been thought of as yet. The plays have been treated either entirely on a basis of chronology, or else the treatments have been influenced mainly by chronological considerations. Dr. Ward's opinion indicates the general attitude towards the subject: "In the English Moralities it is not easy to draw a distinction between particular groups; and such signs of advance as they show would best be gathered from an attempt to survey them chronologically."[2] Professor Courthope in his treatment of the Moralities refers to Dr. Ward's statement, adding, "I am quite of this opinion";[3] and, in general, this attitude is frankly or tacitly assumed.

There is no objection to a chronological treatment of the Moralities, except when it is made the basis for a general and purely arbitrary classification. Mr. Pollard, for instance, makes two main divisions: (1) the earlier plays like *The Castle of Perseverance*, having to do broadly with human nature and human life; and (2) their later and inferior successors, shorter

---

[1] Robert Lee Ramsay, *Skelton's "Magnyfycence*," Introduction.
[2] Ward, I, 108.   [3] Courthope, II, 337.

and more specialized, usually referred to as Interludes, and exemplified by *Hyckescorner*.[1] It is almost unnecessary to comment on the misleading tendencies of this division. Such broad
and sweeping generalities reduce the chronological method to
absurdity; and Mr. Pollard goes on to heap up all sorts of
general statements on the strength of this purely arbitrary
distinction.

This, of course, is an extreme instance of the confusion that
may arise from an attempt to classify the Moralities on a purely
chronological basis, and I have encountered no other treatment
of the subject so open to criticism. Collier's division should be
mentioned in passing, though it is a good deal confused by the
fact that he makes a separate class for the Macro Moralities,[2]
which had not been published when he wrote, but were known
to exist in manuscript. His classes are:

1. Macro Moralities.

2. Printed Morals, the lesson enforced by which relates to
the vices and regeneration of mankind at large.

3. Such as convey instructions for human conduct of a more
varied character.

4. Pieces belonging to the class of Morals, but making approaches to the representation of real life and manners.

5. Interludes chiefly without allegory, and particularly those
of John Heywood.[3]

The classification is a fairly sound one as far as it goes, but
it indicates general tendencies in the plays without establishing
a basis for anything like an exact division. Furthermore, a close
study of Collier's treatment reveals the fact that he, too, was
influenced mainly by the chronological element in making his
distinctions. A much more detailed classification is attempted

---

[1] A. W. Pollard, *English Miracle Plays, Moralities, and Interludes*, pp. lii–liii.
[2] *The Castle of Perseverance; Wisdom, or Mind, Will, and Understanding;*
and *Mankind*.   [3] Collier, II, 199.

by Professor K. L. Bates, who divides the Moralities and semi-Moralities according to the following scheme:

I. Full scope Moralities (15th century)

II. Limited Moralities

    a. Dealing with temptations of youth

    b. Written in praise of learning

III. Transitional Moralities

    a. Written by professional poets

    b. Appeared in Shakespeare's boyhood

    c. Belated

IV. Early Comedies with Morality features

V. Early Tragedies with Morality features[1]

The weakness of such a division is at once apparent. It is not made from any particular point of view, but it is influenced partly by chronology, partly by the general character of the plays, partly by authorship, and partly by purely accidental circumstances; and these different influences come in arbitrarily at various points of the classification.

A method of division that, at a first glance, seems saner and more helpful is that of Professor Gayley, who treats the subject in his *English Representative Comedies*, and also, with more detail, in his *Plays of our Forefathers*. His classes, which he explains at some length in the latter work, I shall here indicate in the smallest possible compass:

I. Older Morals (produced before 1520)

    1. Plays interpretative of ideals in life, and relying on the fundamentally allegorical

    2. Plays that deal with the actual

II. Less-known survivals of the Moral Interlude

    1. School plays

    2. Controversial plays

---

[1] Katharine Lee Bates, *English Religious Drama*, Appendix. See Miss Bates's division for full lists of plays grouped under the different headings.

III. Artistic variations of the stock
    1. A few that show a decided advance in quality,
       even if not in kind
    2. A few Moral tragedies that might also be con-
       sidered [1]

But the classification, despite its plausible appearance, fails when it is applied to the plays which Professor Gayley himself groups under the different divisions, and would continue to fail with equal certainty no matter what grouping might be made. Professor Gayley gives no precise definition of the Morality, but before proceeding with his own classification criticizes Pollard for attempting to make arbitrary distinctions " between plays as earlier and later, longer and shorter, which in essential method were alike: that is, were allegorical." Thus he implies that allegorical method is the *sine qua non* of the Morality, and the main consideration in making a division. Then, as my summary shows, he makes his own first division include " Older Morals, produced before 1520," which indicates at the start that he, also, is not entirely free from the tendency to group the plays as " earlier and later."

Gayley's whole method of classification is of little use, since it does not treat the subject in any consistent fashion ; but it is likely to become positively misleading, since it throws the main emphasis upon characteristics which ought not to count in a general classification, no matter how important these characteristics may be in a detailed study of the plays.

The classification which follows is made purely on the technical basis of allegorical structure. According to it, every English Morality from the beginning down to the close of the sixteenth

---

[1] Charles Mills Gayley, *Plays of our Forefathers*, pp. 283 ff. See Professor Gayley's work for a detailed discussion and lists of plays. The classification given above is abridged from his work.

century[1] will be found to follow in its main plot some one of the following schemes:

I. *Conflict between Virtues and Vices*
   a. *For Supremacy:*
      Hyckescorner.   (1497–1512)
      Three Laws. By John Bale.   (1538)
      New Custom.   (Printed 1573)
      The Three Ladies of London. By R. W[ilson].
                                                         (1584)

   b. *For the Possession of Man*
      1. *Man Spiritual:*
         The Castle of Perseverance.   (*circ.* 1400)
         Mankind.   (1461–1485)
         Nature. By Henry Medwall.   (1486–1500)
         Magnyfycence. By John Skelton.   (1515–1518)
         Mundus et Infans.   (Printed 1522)
         The Thrie Estaites, Part I. By Sir David
            Lyndsay.   (Played 1540, and perhaps earlier)
         Lusty Juventus.   (1547–1553)
         Youth.   (1553–1558)
         Impatient Poverty.   (Printed 1560)
         Marie Magdalene. By Lewis Wager.
                                 (S. R. 1566. *circ.* 1560)
         Albion, Knight.   (1560–1565)
         The Trial of Treasure.   (Printed 1567)
         The Longer Thou Livest the More Foole Thou
            Art. By W. Wager.   (1571–1576)
         The Conflict of Conscience. By Nathaniell
            Woodes.   (Printed 1581)
      2. *Man Intellectual:*
         Interlude of the Four Elements.   (Printed 1519)

---

[1] A few Moralities that appeared in the seventeenth century were mere scholastic revivals of the old stock.

3. *Man Represented merely by One or More Personified Attributes:*

Wisdom, or Mind, Will, and Understanding.

(1480–1490)

Wyt and Science. By John Redford.   (*circ.* 1545)
Wealth and Health.   (S. R. 1557)
The Marriage of Wit and Science.

(S. R. 1569–1570)

The Marriage of Wit and Wisdom   (1579)

II. *Illustration of a Special Text:*

Like Will to Like, Quoth the Devil to the
    Collier. By Ulpian Fulwel.   (Printed 1568)
The Tyde Taryeth No Man. By George Wapull.

(Printed 1576)

All for Money. By T. Lupton.   (Printed 1578)

III. *The Summons of Death:*

The Pryde of Lyfe.   (*circ.* 1400)
Everyman.   (Printed before 1531)

IV. *Religious or Political Controversy:*

The Three Estaites, Part II.
Kyng Johan. By John Bale.   (Printed *circ.* 1548)
Respublica.   (1553)

CHAPTER III

ALLEGORICAL ELEMENTS IN THE MIRACLE PLAYS

The most important of the Miracle cycles, from the point of view of the student of Moralities, is that of Coventry.[1] Two of the important motives used in the early Moralities, the Summons of Death [2] and the so-called Debate of the Four Daughters of God,[3] are found here ; and, in addition to this, there is a general tendency throughout to introduce allegorical figures. The most noticeable of these figures is Contemplacio, the " exposytour in doctorys wede," who appears from time to time as a kind of Prologue to introduce the action, or to accompany it as chorus. I shall indicate the different appearances of this figure, and then go on to discuss the allegorical action more directly connected with the plays.

Contemplacio first appears to introduce Play VIII (*The Barrenness of Anna*).[4] Here he simply performs the part of Prologue, as he does at his next appearance in Play IX (*Mary in the Temple*). At the conclusion of the same play he comes out again to beseech the audience for patience and to announce the next performance.

[1] Usually referred to as " the so-called Coventry Plays," or " Ludus Coventriae." Gayley (pp. 205 ff.) uses the term " N——Town plays." Manly prefers the term " Hegge plays," and explains, " I have chosen to call the plays by the earliest known owner of the MS., for I see no reason to connect them with Coventry, and ' so-called Coventry plays ' is a clumsy expression." — *Specimens of Pre-Shaksperean Drama*, I, 31.

[2] Cf. the Moralities *Pride of Life* and *Everyman*.

[3] Cf. *Castell of Perseveraunce* and *Respublica*.

[4] The text used here is that edited for the Shakespeare Society by J. O. Halliwell.

As the introducer of Play XI (*The Salutation and Conception*), Contemplacio takes on more allegorical significance. He throws off the technical character of Prologue, laments the fallen state of man, and ends with a prayer to God for compassion.

In Play XIII (*The Visit to Elizabeth*), Contemplacio combines the duties of Chorus, Epilogue, and spiritual adviser. After Elizabeth and Zachariah go up to the temple to worship, he appears and instructs the audience as to "how the Ave was mad," adding:

> Who seyeth oure ladyes sawtere dayly for a ʒer thus,
> He hath pardon ten thousand and eyte hundryd ʒer.

He then proceeds to comment on the action behind the scenes, and brings the play to an end.

His next and last appearance is in the middle of Play XXIX (*King Herod*), where he fills up a gap in the performance, while the processions are moving into place. He greets the audience: "Sofreynes and frendys, ʒe must alle be gret with gode," and then explains what has gone before and what is to follow.

In all these appearances Contemplacio makes his address directly to the audience, and has no connection with any other character in the plays. He is, therefore, of no special allegorical significance.

As the other allegorical touches in the cycle are sporadic and have no connection with each other, I shall simply take them up in the order of the plays in which they occur.

In Play IX (*Mary in the Temple*), after the three-year-old Mary has nimbly ascended the "fiftene grees," the bishop gives her careful directions for the ruling of her life, and then bestows upon her an allegorical assemblage of maidens and priests to attend her:

> Our abydynge xal be with our maydenys ffyve,
> Whyche tyme as ʒe wole have consolacion.
>   *Maria.* This lyffe me lyketh as my lyve,
> Of her namys I beseche ʒou to have informacion.

> *Episcopus.* There is the fyrst Meditacion,
> Contryssyon, Compassyon, and Clennes,
> And that holy mayde Fruyssyon:
> With these blyssyd maydenes xal be ȝour besynes.
> *Maria.* Here is an holy ffelachepp, I fele
> I am not wurthy amonge hem to be:
> Swete systeres, to ȝou alle I knele,
> To recyue, I beseche, ȝour charyte.
> *Episcopus.* They xal, dowtere, and on the tothere syde se,
> Ther ben sevne prestys indede,
> To schryve, to teche, and to mynystryn to the,
> To lerne the Goddys lawys and Scrypture to rede.
> *Maria.* ffadyr, knew I here namys, wele were I.
> *Episcopus.* Ther is Dyscressyon, Devocion, Dylexcion,
>   and Deliberacion, —
> They xal tende upon ȝou besyly;
> With Declaracion, Determynacion, Dyvynacion;
> Now go ȝe, maydenys, to ȝour occupacion,
> And loke ȝe tende this childe tendyrly;
> And ȝe, serys, knelyth, and I xal gyve ȝow Goddys benyson,
> In nomine Patris et Filii et Spiritus Sancti!

Then follows the stage direction : " Et recedent cum ministris
suis omnes virgines, dicentes ' Amen.' "

The next allegorical scene, which occurs in Play XI (*The
Salutation and Conception*), is of uncommon significance. It is
based on the tenth verse of the 85th Psalm, " Mercy and Truth
are met together ; Righteousness and Peace have kissed each
other," a text which has been the basis for allegorical treatment
from the tenth century down.[1] In the present instance the
debate of the four sisters before the Trinity, and the consequent
annunciation by the angel Gabriel, occupy a full play.

Play XI is opened by Contemplacio,[2] and then the four sisters
argue before the Trinity on the proposed redemption of Man.
Truth maintains that when Adam sinned God had said that
Man should die and go to hell, and now he cannot be restored,

---

[1] For a discussion of this allegory, in all its phases, see Hope Traver, *The
Four Daughters of God*, Philadelphia, 1907.   [2] See p. 24, above.

since " twey contraryes mow not togedyr dwelle." If God breaks
his word now, she, Truth, will be lost to him. Mercy answers
that Man grieves greatly for his transgression and is pleading
for mercy, and reminds God that he has said that he will have
mercy on Man. Then Righteousness breaks in with :

> Mercy, me mervelyth what ȝow movyth,
> ȝe know wel I am ȝour syster Ryghtwysnes,
> God is ryghtfful and ryghtffulnes lovyth,
> Man offendyd hym that is endles,
> Therefore his endles punchement may nevyr sees;
> Also he forsoke his makere that made hym of clay,
> And the devyl to his mayster he ches,
> Xulde he be savyd? nay! nay! nay!

Mercy rebukes Righteousness for her revengeful spirit, pleads
the frailty of man, and again appeals to the endless mercy of
God. Peace then interposes, reminding her sister that

> It is not onest in vertuys to ben dyscension.

She admits that Righteousness and Truth have spoken reason-
ably, but still she is inclined to side with Mercy,

> ffor if mannys sowle xulde abyde in helle,
> Between God and man evyr xulde be dyvysyon,
> And than myght not I Pes dwelle.

Her advice is that the whole matter be referred to Christ, who
will judge in wisdom. They agree to this, and lay the case before "wysdam," or Christ, who is inclined to favor Man, but is
unwilling to lose Righteousness and Truth. He proposes, therefore, that heaven and earth shall be sought for one who is willing to die for the redemption of Man. This person, however,
must be without sin, so that hell will have no power to hold him.

Truth answers that she has sought through the earth, but
can find no man that is without sin from the day of his birth,
and Mercy adds that she has sought heaven and has found
none that has charity to suffer the deadly wound for Man. Then

Christ summons a council of the Trinity to see which of them shall restore mankind, and in this council he offers himself, since in his wisdom Man was created. When the matter is settled Mercy breaks out joyously,

> Now is the loveday mad of us fowre fynially,
> Now may we leve in pes as we were wonte :
> Misericordia et Veritas obviaverunt sibi
> Justicia et Pax osculatae sunt.

Then the sisters kiss each other, and Gabriel is sent to make the announcement to the Virgin Mary.[1]

The next appearance of allegorical characters is in Play XIV (*The Trial of Joseph and Mary*), where the two chief accusers of Joseph and Mary are Backbiter and Raise-Slander. They have no object in making their accusations, but are actuated by innate viciousness; and their language and deportment are so exactly like those of the regular Vices in the Moralities that it

---

[1] Hone suggests as the immediate source for this scene the " Council of the Trinity " in the English *Speculum Vitae Christi* (*Ancient Mysteries Described*, 1823, pp. 73–76). Courthope (*History of English Poetry*, 1895, I, 415) states that it was borrowed from Grossteste's *Chateau d'Amour*. Hope Traver (*The Four Daughters of God*, pp. 126, etc.) compares the scene with a version of the allegory found in the 14th century prose treatise, *The Charter of the Abbey of the Holy Ghost* (C. Horstmann, *Richard Rolle of Hampole*, 1896. It is doubtful whether Rolle is the author) which offers some special resemblances. Miss Traver makes extended use of parallel passages to show these resemblances. She concludes that both these versions of the allegory ultimately belong to the group going back to the *Meditationes Vitae Christi*, by Cardinal Bonaventura of Padua (*Sancti Bonaventurae . . . Opera*, London, 1668, VI, 335–336) and that either the *Salutation* scene must derive directly from the *Charter*, or both the *Charter* and the *Salutation* scene must be using a common source which is itself in turn derived from Bonaventura. In the *Charter* the allegory of the Four Daughters has been thrust into another allegory, and in the process somewhat disarranged, whereas in the *Salutation* scene the events follow the regular order; also, the *Charter* does not introduce the annunciation of Gabriel, which appears in Bonaventura, and also in the *Salutation* scene. Miss Traver concludes: " In spite, therefore, of the resemblances between these two versions at many points, it is difficult to believe that the *Salutation* was derived from the *Charter*."

will be worth while to quote a considerable part of their speech.
Raise-Slander, the *primus detractor*, comes out first and introduces himself to the audience:

> A! A! serys, God save ȝow alle.
> Here is a fayr pepyl in good ffay;
> Good seres, telle me what men me calle,
> I trowe ȝe kannot, be this day;
> ȝitt I walke wide and many way,
> But ȝet ther I come I do no good,
> To reyse slawndyr is al my lay,
> Bakbytere is my brother of blood.
>
> Dede he ought come hedyr in al this day,
> Now wolde God that he were here!
> And be my trewthe I dare wel say,
> That if we tweyn togedyr apere,
> More slawndyr we to xal arere,
> Within an howre thorweouth this town,
> Than evyr ther was this thousand ȝere,
> And ellys I shrewe ȝow both up and downe.
>
> Now by my trewthe I have a syght
> Evyn of my brother, lo! where he is:
> Welcom, dere brother, my trowthe I plyght,
> ȝowre jentyl mowth let me now kys.

> *Secundus detractor.* Grammercy, brother so have I blys,
> I am ful glad we met this day.
> *Primus detractor.* Ryght so am I, brothyr, i-wys,
> meche gladder than I kan say.
> But ȝitt, good brother I ȝow pray,
> Telle alle these pepyl what is ȝour name;
> ffor if thei knew it, my lyf I lay,
> They wole ȝou wurchep and speke gret fame.
> *Secundus detractor.* I am Bakbytere that spyllyth alle game,
> Bothe kyd and knowyn in many a place.
> *Primus detractor.* Be my trowthe I seyd the same
> And ȝet sum seyden thou xulde have evyl grace.
> *Secundus detractor.* Herk, Reyse-sclaundyr, canst thou owth telle
> Of any newe thynge that wrought was late?

> *Primus detractor.* Within a shorte whyle a thynge befelle,
> I trowe thou wylt lawh3 ryght wel therate,
> ffor be trowth, ryght mekyl hate,
> If it be wyst, therof wyl growe.
>   *Secundus detractor.* If I may reyse therwith debate,
> I xal not spare the seyd to sowe.

Then Raise-Slander tells his brother of the impending trial, and the pair plan to make it as hard as possible for Joseph and Mary. Through the ensuing scene they endeavor to prove Mary guilty, and scoff openly when she is proved innocent by the drink of purgation. Then the bishop presiding at the trial compels Raise-Slander to test the drink himself. This second test is attended with dire results to Raise-Slander, who feels as if his head were on fire, and who gets no relief until he begs Mary's pardon.

The quotation given above will show how closely these two characters are related to the traditional Morality Vices, especially in their manner of introducing and explaining themselves to the audience. Also, like the usual Vices, they are "brothers of blood" and have no settled abode, but simply appear in the places where they can do most harm. They are the natural enemies of goodness, here embodied in the earthly father and mother of Christ.

No other allegorical elements appear before Play XIX (*The Slaughter of the Innocents*), where occurs the well-known Summons of Death motive.[1] After the slaughter of the children Herod seats himself at a feast with his knights and soldiers, exulting in the belief that his rival is slain. " I was never merrier since I was born ! " he exclaims. " In joy I begin to glide ! "

At this moment Death enters, looking for the king whom he has heard " make preysying of pride." He announces :

> I am Dethe, Goddys masangere !
> Allemyghty God hath sent me here,
> 3on lordeyn to sle, withouten dwere,
> ffor his wykkyd workynge.

[1] See Creizenach, I, 461–462, and Chambers, II, 153.

While Death, in the background, is boasting of his power and exulting over his intended victim, the unconscious Herod continues to exhort his knights to be merry and glad. He assures them repeatedly that his rival must be dead, and, in a burst of gaiety, orders the minstrel to "blowe up a mery fytt," when suddenly Death approaches and strikes him down : "Hic dum buccinant mors interficiat Herodem et duos milites subito, et diabolus recipiat eos." When the Devil has borne his victim off, Death delays, exhorts his hearers to be warned by the death of Herod, and moralizes on his own omnipotence.

This ends the allegorical action in the Coventry Plays; but there are a few other passages to which attention should be called.

In Play XXV (*The Council of the Jews*), Lucifer makes a long speech in the course of which he renames the Deadly Sins :

> I have browth ʒow newe namys, and wyl ʒe se why
> ffor synne is so plesaunt to eche mannys intent,
> ʒe xal kalle pride oneste, and nateralle kend lechory,
> And covetyse wysdam there tresure is present;
>
> Wreth manhod, and envye callyd chastement;
> Seyse nere sessyon, lete perjery be chef;
> Glotonye rest, let abstynawnce beyn absent;
> And he that wole exorte the to vertu, put hem to repreff.
>
> To rehers al my servauntes my matere is to breff,
> But alle these xal everyth the dyvicion eternal;
> In evyrlastynge peyne with me dwellyn thei xal.

This trick of changing names is practised by the Vices in almost all of the Moralities where they attempt to delude man and lead him into a life of sin. The allegorical interpretation of all these changes is neatly summed up by Lucifer in this speech, — "ffor synne is so plesaunt to eche mannys intent."

It is of very little allegorical significance that in Play XLI (*The Assumption of the Virgin*) Christ speaks under the name of Sapientia. Christ is frequently referred to as Wisdom or

Sapientia, as in the Salutation scene already discussed, and in the Morality of *Wisdom, Who is Christ.*

In the final play of the cycle (*The Doomsday*), specific mention is again made of the Seven Deadly Sins, when the devils are claiming the souls of the damned because of their adherence to the Sins. I shall transcribe the passage, since I shall have occasion to refer to it again :

> *Secundus diabolus.* I fynde here wretyn in thin fforhed,
> Thou were so stowte and sett in pryde,
> Thou woldyst nott ȝeve a pore man breed,
> But ffrom thi dore thou woldyst hym chyde.
>
> *Tertius diabolus.* And in thi face here do I rede,
> That if a thryfty man com any tyde,
> Drynk from hym thou woldyst evyr hyde ;
> On covetyse was alle thy thought.
>
> *Primus diabolus.* In wratthe thy neybore to bakbyte,
> Them for to hangere was thi delyte,
> Thou were evyr redy them to endyte ;
> On the seke man rewyst thou nought.
>
> *Secundus diabolus.* Evyr more on envye was alle thi mende,
> Thou woldyst nevyr vesyte no presoner ;
> To alle thi neybores thou were unkende,
> Thou woldyst nevyr helpe man in daunger.
>
> *Tertius diabolus.* The synne of slauthe thi soul xal shende,
> Masse nore mateynes woldyst thou non here,
> To bery the deed, man, thou woldyst not wende,
> Therfore thou xalt to endles ffere :
> To slowthe thou were ful prest.
>
> *Primus diabolus.* Thou haddyst rejoyse in glotonye,
> In dronkesheppe and in rebawdye,
> Unherborwyd with velonye
> Thou puttyst from here rest.
>
> *Secundus diabolus.* Sybile Sclutte, thou ssalte sewe,
> Alle ȝour lyff was leccherous lay ;
> To alle ȝour neybores ȝe wore a shrewe,
> Alle ȝour plesauns was leccherous play, etc.

The only one of the Sins not mentioned by name is lechery. But lechery is not forgotten, as the last accusation will testify.

The other cycles may be passed over with scarcely more than a word. There is one short passage from the Chester cycle[1] which I should like to quote, as showing, not a disposition toward allegory, but on the contrary a deliberate avoiding of it when allegory might easily have been indulged in.

In Play XII (*The Temptation*), the expositor explains how Christ overcame the devil:

> Loe! Lordinges, God's righteousness,
> as St. Gregorie makes mynde expresse,
> since our forefather overcomen was
> by three thinges to doe will.

> Gluttony, vayne glorye there be twooe,
> Covetousness of highnes alsoe,
> by these three thinges, without moe,
> Christ hath overcome the devill.

The expositor goes on to contrast with this the experience of Adam, who was tempted in gluttony, in vainglory, and in avarice. His object is to show that Adam and Christ were tempted in the same ways, but while Adam fell Christ was victorious. The vices which might have been represented as assailing them allegorically are carefully described as " these three thinges."

In the *Juditium*, the concluding play of the Townley Mysteries,[2] there is a conversation among the demons where four virtues and the Seven Deadly Sins are personified. The demons are reckoning up their rolls for Doomsday:

> *Secundus daemon.*   Thise rolles
>   Ar of bakbytars,
>   And fals quest-dytars
>   I had no help of writars
>   But thise two dalles:
> Faithe and trowthe, maffay, have no fete to stande,
> The poore pepylle must pay if oght be in hande,
> The drede of God is away and lawe out of lande.

---

[1] The text used is that of the New Shakspere Society, ed. T. Wright, 1843.
[2] The text used is that published by the Surtees Society, 1836.

Later on Tutivillus makes his contribution, and presently comes
to the Deadly Sins :

> Yit of the synnes seven som thyng specialle,
> Now nately to neven, that ronnys over alle,
> Thise laddes thai leven as lordes rialle,
> At ee to be even picturde yn palle
> As kynges.
>
> . . . .
>
> Of ire and of envy fynde I herto
> Of covetyse and glotony and many other mo,
> Thai calle and thai cry " go we now, go,
> I dy nere for dry," and ther syt thai so
> All nyghte
> With hawvelle and jawvelle,
> Synging of lawvelle,
> Thise ar howndes of helle,
> That is thare right.

This is the only allegorical passage in the cycle, and it is
interesting to compare it with the Coventry *Doomsday*,[1] where
there is no attempt to personify the Sins.

There remain the two Digby plays, *St. Paul* and *Mary
Magdalene*.[2] The *Conversion of St. Paul*[3] does not contain
allegorical action, but in the speeches of Belial and in the sermon of the converted Saul the Seven Deadly Sins are personified, and also, on the side of vice, Sin and Folly, — regarded
as synonymous with Pride, the chief of the Sins, — and Vanity,
Vainglory, and False Idleness. On the side of virtue are Humility
and Pity. These personifications are treated with a considerable
amount of detail, but the general method of handling is much
the same as that illustrated in the foregoing paragraphs.

In *Mary Magdalene*[4] the allegorical element is more important, — so much so, indeed, that the play has been sometimes

---

[1] See p. 32, above.

[2] The Digby MS. is assigned to the last decade of the fifteenth century.

[3] Ed. Furnivall, for the New Shakspere Society. In Manly, Vol. I.

[4] The text used is that in Furnivall's edition.

classed as a Morality. It is usually, however, referred to as a Morality-Mystery, which is a much safer classification. The main interest of the play is in the conversion of Mary and in her subsequent journey to convert the heathen King of Marcylle; so, with Dr. Ward's convenient distinction [1] in mind, I prefer to call it a Miracle play with Morality features.

After some introductory scenes dealing with the family of Mary and the death of her father, the Morality element begins with a council of the three kings, — the World, the Flesh, and the Devil.[2] First appears the World, vaunting his power, and attended by Pride and Covetousness; then Flesh and his spouse Lechery, his knight Gluttony, and his friend Sloth; and, lastly, Satan with his attendants Wrath and Envy. Satan tells his followers of his desire to bring "mannes soule to obeysauns." Wrath answers:

> With wrath or wyhylles we xal hyrre wynne.

The three unite to plot the downfall of some woman, without mentioning any name, — a singularly abrupt way of introducing Mary as the intended victim. Satan summons his brother kings to a council, and they lay their plans for Mary's ruin.[3] Lechery is selected to seduce her, and sets out to perform her task.

[1] Ward, I, 41, makes the distinction that Mysteries deal with gospel events only, while Miracles are concerned with incidents derived from the legends of the Saints of the Church. The distinction is a convenient one, though there is no evidence that it was actually used.

[2] These three characters are referred to also as the King of the World, the King of the Flesh, and the Prince of Devils.

[3] The three kings, as they come out, proclaim their power over the world and man in general; and the Devil expresses his desire to corrupt man. After this the sudden introduction of a particular person to strive for is exceedingly abrupt. The author evidently feels it to be so; and later, at the council, Mundus gives a good reason for directing their combined efforts at Mary:

> Sertenly serys, I yow telle,
> yf she in vertu stylle may dwelle
> she xall byn abyll to dystroye helle
> but yf your counsyll may othyrwyse devyse.

At the beginning of the next scene is the stage direction : " Her xalle þe VII dedly synnes bi-sege þe castell tyll they a-gre to go to Jerusalem.[1] Lechery xall entyr þe castell with þe bad angyl," etc. Within the castle, Lechery finds Mary lamenting the death of her father. She begins by artfully prais- ing Mary's beauty, and Mary, accepting the bait at once, gives her a warm welcome. Lechery comforts her, and advises her to forget her grief by amusing herself. This advice pleases Mary, and she prepares to accompany Lechery on a journey. Lazarus bids her an affectionate farewell, and the pair set out for Jerusalem.

After the arrival at Jerusalem, Lechery takes her companion to a tavern and orders the taverner to bring out the best wine. Curiosity, a gallant, enters, exulting in his fine clothes and long- ing for some pretty girl to amuse himself with. Lechery whispers to Mary that this is the man for her, and Mary asks the taverner to call him in. Curiosity[2] comes and begins at once to make love to Mary, who is soon persuaded to return his affection and protests that she will go to the end of the world for his sake. He invites her to go and dance, and they retire together.

In the next scene the Bad Angel reports to the three kings that Mary has been seduced by Curiosity. The Devil bids Lechery (who has come back in the meantime) to return to Mary and keep her in sin; then the three kings, having accom- plished their object, take their leave and depart with their respective trains.

---

[1] Nothing more is made of this siege of the Castle of Maudleyn. It would, of course, be represented in acting, but has no place in the dialogue.

[2] It is possible, of course, to read allegorical significance into the figure Curiosity. He seems to be the personification of fastidiousness or nicety, espe- cially in matters of personal adornment, — a common mediaeval application of the word. In that case the play teaches that Mary's downfall began in an in- ordinate desire for finery. This view, it is to be noticed, is taken in the later play presenting Mary as its heroine. See pp. 111 ff., below.

Then follow three short scenes. The first shows Mary in an arbor, waiting for her lover; in the second Simon the Leper announces that he has ordered a grand dinner and wishes that he could get the great Prophet to come; in the third the Good Angel rebukes Mary for her sin, and Mary at once repents and resolves to seek Christ.

After this Jesus appears with his disciples and enters the house of Simon the Leper. Mary follows with a box of ointment, washes the feet of Christ, and dries them with her hair. Then Christ forgives Mary her sins and bids her depart in peace. Seven devils (regarded, of course, as the Seven Deadly Sins) leave her, the Bad Angel enters into Hell with noise of thunder, and the Good Angel rejoices.

In the next scene the Devil howls with rage at losing Mary, and orders the Bad Angel and the Seven Deadly Sins to be beaten for their carelessness.[1]

This ends the allegorical portion of the play. The remaining scenes, to which the part discussed is really preliminary, are taken up with the miracles performed by Mary on her mission to convert the heathen King of Marcylle.[2]

It will now be seen that, outside of the Coventry cycle and *Mary Magdalene*, the allegorical elements in the Miracle plays are practically negligible. As to the question of the relationship between these plays and the Moralities, much light might be looked for from the solution of the problem of the origin of the plays now commonly associated with Coventry. The theory that allegorical elements were taken from the Miracles and developed into the Morality has been made the basis for much unwarranted

---

[1] This punishment also takes place in the *Castle of Perseverance*, with which play this portion of *Mary Magdalene* has a good many points in common.

[2] The present play follows pretty closely the version of the story in the *Legenda Aurea* of Jacobus a Voragine (c. 1275). The latter work was published by Caxton in 1483, under the title of *The Golden Legend*, in a free English translation made with the help of an older French version.

generalization.[1] Whatever influence the Mysteries exerted upon the Moralities — and with two types of drama so closely allied in the dissemination of religious instruction it would be unreasonable to deny the older form some influence on the younger — it seems much more probable that, as far as allegorical treatment is concerned, the Moralities influenced the Mysteries. The only certain relationship here, then, is in the general purpose of disseminating religious and moral instruction through the medium of drama, and the actual sources from which the Moralities drew their distinctive methods of presenting this instruction must be sought elsewhere. In the non-dramatic literature of mediaeval and early modern times there is a large body of allegorical work written with the same didactic purpose, and recent research is making it more and more apparent that this was the source from which the Moralities drew not only their general method but also many of the specific details of their presentation.

[1] See, for instance, Collier, II, 184, and Symonds, *Shakspere's Predecessors in the English Drama*, pp. 145 ff.

CHAPTER IV

MORALITIES DEALING WITH THE CONFLICT BETWEEN VIRTUES AND VICES FOR SUPREMACY

The conflict between Vices and Virtues is the theme of the greater number of Moralities, and in most of the plays of this class the struggle is for the soul of Man. An older form of the conflict, however, is still represented by a few plays coming under my division I, a.[1] But even in these plays, which preserve the general formula of "Conflict for supremacy," the manner of carrying on the conflict is very different from that in the oldest known treatment of the theme, the *Psychomachia* of Prudentius[2] (about 400 A.D.), where the struggle took the form of a series of Homeric single combats. It is quite possible that this primitive mode of battle may have been used in the two lost English plays of the Paternoster and the Creed,[3] but in the extant Moralities the Virtues and Vices combat each other by means of argument; or, more properly, the Virtues argue while the Vices abuse and revile them.

The first play of this class is *Hyckescorner*,[4] which, like the earlier Morality *Mankind*, was written to amuse as well as to chasten. The stage is held during a great part of the play by Imagynacyon, Frewyl, and Hyckescorner, of whom the first two, at least, are personifications of human characteristics. But when

---

[1] See p. 22, above.   [2] See Creizenach, I, 463.

[3] Ibid., III, 495; also Ward, I, 97; Pollard, p. xlii; and Ramsay, *Skelton's "Magnyfycence,"* pp. cli–clii.

[4] Manly, Vol. I. The play was printed about 1530. Gayley (p. 283) dates the composition between 1497 and 1512.

they are not in actual contact with their enemies, the Virtues of the play, Imagynacyon and Frewyl are a pair of light-hearted rascals fresh from the streets of London.

Yet these lighter scenes are no more essential to the plot than are the humorous scenes in a tragedy. The moral is the thing. Here, as in most of the Moralities, the allegory refers to a struggle within the heart of man. This general statement about the Moralities as a whole will not, however, apply to the remainder of the subclass now under consideration; since of the four plays forming the group all except *Hyckescorner* deal with forces — good and evil — operating at large in the land, and not confined within the compass of the heart of man. In *Hyckescorner* all the personifications represent characteristics of men, and the play is separated from Class I, b only by the fact that Man himself is not presented in the action.

The play opens with a lengthy discussion on the subject of the Redemption, by Pyte, Contemplacyon, and Perseveraunce, who proceed to a hearty condemnation of the social and religious evils of the day, and retire somewhat dispirited. But the atmosphere is soon brightened by the appearance of Frewyl, who enters in high glee, and is reduced to soberness only when he discovers that his pocket-money has disappeared. He calls impatiently for Imagynacyon, who presently enters in a state of momentary dejection because he too has been robbed of his pocket-money, and has received, into the bargain, a "payre of sore buttockes." But these two irrepressibles cannot remain downcast very long, and they soon fall to recounting gleefully their adventures about town and their plans for stealing more money in order to continue their patronage of the taverns and stews.

Suddenly Frewyl bethinks him of their friend Hyckescorner, who ought to be in this merry company. The pair set up a shout, and in a moment Hyckescorner is heard outside, yelling nautical directions. He apparently gets his ship satisfactorily moored, and then joins his friends, who listen open-mouthed to his tales of strange lands and adventures. The three finally decide to stroll out and enjoy the pleasures of the town; but as they are departing Frewyl and Imagynacyon get into a quarrel, and Hyckescorner, interfering in the interests of peace, gets a sound drubbing from Imagynacyon. Just at this moment, however, Pyte enters, and the three rascals at once make common cause against him. Frewyl runs for a "payre of gyves," the other two pick a quarrel with Pyte, and, Frewyl appearing again at the proper moment with his "medycyne for a payre of sore shynnes," they clap Pyte into the stocks and proceed on their errand.

Pyte now compels the audience to share in his misery by forcing them to listen to a long and lugubrious sermon on the text,

> We all may say weleaway
> For synne that is now-adaye;
> Loo, vertue is vanysshed for ever and aye:
> Worse was hyt never!

But at last Contemplacyon and Perseveraunce enter and put an end to the sermon by setting Pyte free. Pyte rushes out in a fury of zeal to convert his persecutors, and his two companions are presently joined by Frewyl, who stumbles upon them by mistake. He attempts to retreat, but is seized and borne down by a torrent of arguments from Contemplacyon and Perseveraunce, finally convinced of his wickedness, and brought to repentance.

At this juncture Imagynacyon enters in a state of lively satisfaction over the fact that he has been made "controller of all the houses of lechery." Announcing the glad news to Frewyl, he is almost struck dumb by the latter's rejoinder,

> God graunte the waye to heven I maye fynde,
> For I forsake thy company.

Recovering himself, however, he turns furiously upon the two responsible for Frewyl's disaffection; but they, reinforced by Frewyl, beat down his arguments, and finally convict him of sin also. The converted sinners are given new coats to symbolize their change of character, and Imagynacyon's name is changed to Good Remembraunce. Perseveraunce gives them instructions for the guidance of their new life, and so the play ends.

The interpretation of the play is rendered somewhat more difficult by the presence of Hyckescorner himself, who is obviously the chief Vice, and whose name would indicate that he is, as usually interpreted, a type character rather than a personified abstraction. It is impossible to prove conclusively that he is either the one or the other, but the only bit of direct evidence that the play affords would seem to give him the latter character. Frewyl and Imagynacyon are waiting for him to join them, and Frewyl asks, " Ye, but where is Hyckescorner now?" " Some of these yonge men," answers Imagynacyon, alluding to the audience, " hath hydde hym in theyr bosomes, I warraunt you." [1] This may be a mere joke at the expense of the audience, but if it is taken at its face value it would indicate that Hyckescorner is stupid scoffing rather than the stupid scoffer; and though there is no other direct evidence of this in the play, neither is there any evidence to the contrary. Therefore it is better to exonerate the author from the blame of creating such an unnecessary confusion in a play of this allegorical structure as to introduce one type figure along with his abstractions,[2] and

[1] P. 396.

[2] It is, of course, not necessary that type figures should be barred from a play of this class. In such a play as *The Three Ladies of London*, with its more pretentious list of *dramatis personae*, types are introduced easily and naturally on both sides, good and evil. But in *Hyckescorner* the list is simplified as much as possible, and to introduce a type figure to assist the Vices in their war against the Virtues would seem to be a complication out of harmony with this evident desire to simplify.

to regard Hyckescorner as standing for stupid scoffing against God's word and piety of life. The other characters are unequivocal. They are all personifications of abstract qualities; Pyte, Contemplacyon, and Perseveraunce on the side of virtue, and Imagynacyon and Frewyl on the side of vice.[1]

Leaving out of account the realistic embellishments, which have nothing to do with the main plot, we can interpret the allegory thus: The will, which is free, arrays itself in opposition to the sense of divine goodness ("pity" is here used in the wider signification of mercy or goodness) which struggles for recognition in the heart. The heart is further seduced by evil imaginings and by stupid jeers at piety of life, and the knowledge of divine goodness is rendered inoperative. But, by the contemplation of God's mercy and perseverance therein, the heart is relieved from the domination of vicious thoughts. The worship of divine goodness again operates, the will is brought into harmony with the will of God and travels only in the paths of religion, while the evil imaginings of the heart are changed to grateful recollections of God's goodness.[2]

The Comedy Concerning Three Laws,[3] written by Bishop Bale (1538), is placed in this class by its allegorical plot; but in purpose it is first and foremost a vicious attack on the Roman Catholic Church such as only the "bilious Bishop" was capable of. Most of the late Moralities were written by Protestant sympathizers,[4] but none of the other authors was carried so far by his sympathies as was Bishop Bale.

[1] See note 1, p. 50, below.

[2] It will readily be seen that Imagynacyon and Frewyl are not out-and-out Vices, though they are virtually that throughout most of the action. They are neither essentially good nor essentially bad. Thus, the logical result of their defeat by the Virtues is a conversion in their characters.

[3] In *The Dramatic Writings of John Bale*, ed. by John S. Farmer, 1907.

[4] Cf. Creizenach, III, 35 ff., 515. This statement means only that most of the plays were Protestant in their sympathies, not necessarily that they were controversial plays.

For the present we may turn, with thankful hearts, from the bitter and revolting invective against Catholicism. Though it is most evident that the grim Bishop considered this the first reason for the existence of the play, yet from our present point of view we can ignore it completely and concern ourselves only with the allegorical plot, which he was careful to preserve. Here the struggle goes on in the land at large, and, allegorically, is not to be interpreted as raging within the heart of man.

The play is almost devoid of action, and is taken up chiefly with gleeful speeches on the part of the different Vices, to show their popularity in the Catholic Church. The Prolocutor indicates the general course of the play; then, in the first scene, Deus Pater addresses the three laws, Naturae Lex, Moseh Lex, and Christi Lex, and gives each his commission with regard to men:

> Thou, law of Nature, teach thou him, first of all,
> His Lord God to know, and that is right to do:
> Charge and enforce him, in the ways of us to go.
> Thou, law of Moses, and Christ's law finally,
> Raise him and save him, to our perpetual glory.

The three laws profess their loyalty to God, then leave to carry out the divine commands.

The next scene is headed *Naturae Lex Corrupta*. Naturae Lex appears on earth and proclaims his intention to act according to God's will. Then Infidelitas, the chief Vice of the play, enters and engages him in a long argument, throughout which Infidelitas employs the regular abusive and scurrilous language of the Vice, while Naturae Lex responds, as the Virtues always do, with dignity and high disdain. Finally Naturae Lex leaves in disgust, and Infidelitas summons two of his followers, Sodomismus and Adolotria, and instructs them to corrupt men in order to overcome Naturae Lex. After a long conversation, in which the unsavory doings of the Catholic clergy are recounted with great zest, the two minor Vices go out to perform their work. Infidelitas tells the audience what they are doing, and retires. Then Naturae Lex comes in lamenting, and disfigured by leprosy. He himself has not sinned; but men have become corrupted, and that has brought the disease upon him.

The next scene — *Moseh Lex Corrupta* — follows the same scheme. Moseh Lex encounters Infidelitas just as his predecessor has done, and then goes about his work. This time Infidelitas summons Avaritia and Ambitio, and sends them out to undermine the labors of Moseh Lex, who finally arrives on the scene " stark blind."

The last encounter — *Christi Lex Corrupta* — is slightly varied. After the argument and separation between Christi Lex and Infidelitas, the latter summons Hypocrisis and Pseudo-doctrina to perform his work; and while the three are smacking their lips over the scandals of the Romish Church, Christi Lex comes on them. The three Vices at once overcome him, and Infidelitas sends him out under the guard of his two henchmen to be burned at the stake.

In the last scene Deus Pater interferes to save his laws. He rebukes Infidelitas sternly, then strikes him with fire. Infidelitas disappears in a blaze, screaming that he is doomed to hell. Then Deus comforts his three laws, and restores them to their original state.

The interpretation runs as follows: God has framed three laws for the guidance of man, — the law of nature to lead him in the paths of virtue, and the laws of Moses and of Christ to instruct him in true religion and to bring him at last into heaven. These laws are proclaimed among men so that all may understand them. But the people are unfaithful to these laws. They practise unnatural vices and give themselves over to idolatry, thus perverting the law of nature; they are greedy and ambitious, and render the law of Moses of no avail; and by their hypocrisy and their leaning toward false beliefs they are led to forget the teachings of Christ. But eventually God will appear in his wrath and will sweep away this unbelief which corrupts the hearts of men; and then his beneficent laws will be used for the guidance of the people.

Of the three leading personifications that dominate scenes ii, iii, and iv, Naturae Lex is infected with leprosy in the first; in the second Moseh Lex is made " stark blind "; and in the third Christi Lex is sent out to be burned. But it is important to notice that none of these personifications is corrupted in the sense of giving himself over to a life in sin. In that case the allegory would break down, since it is impossible for a virtue or a conception essentially good to be anything but good. It may be rendered inoperative — as the laws are — by the prevalence of vice, but must always retain its essential quality. In the play last considered, two personifications, Frewyl and Imagynacyon, are Vices at their first appearance and are finally converted into Virtues ; but that is because the powers of free will and imagination are neither essentially good nor essentially bad, but are good or bad according as they are directed, and this is carefully explained in the play.

New Custom[1] is more avowedly a controversial play than *The Three Laws*, though it lacks the bitterness of the latter. The purpose behind the allegorical teaching is plainly advertised in the list of *dramatis personae*, where each abstraction is made to stand also for a type, as " Perverse Doctrine (an old popish

[1] Dodsley, Vol. III. The play was printed in 1573, but was probably written some years earlier. Fleay (*History of the Stage*, p. 64) conjectures that it was " probably altered from one [*i.e.*, a Morality] of Edward VI's time as the controversy about square caps is alluded to in it as contemporary. This question was raised by John Rogers and Richard Hooper in 1550. In its present state the Morality is of the time of Elizabeth, but as the revival of old Moralities is mostly met with very early in her reign, and very few actors — four — are required in this one, I would date it 1562–1563, near *King Darius*, which is so like it in its anti-papistry."

priest)," and so on. The play, consequently, falls in the present class on account of the nature of its plot, but has affiliations with Class IV on account of its pronounced controversial spirit.

Though the characters here, as in the play preceding and the play following, all represent forces operating in the land rather than in the heart of man, they cannot be said to exclude the latter idea, since all so-called national virtues are in reality virtues practised by the people of the nation. The distinction is, of course, a rather hazy one, but it is worth insisting upon, as it seems to have been felt in that age of literary abstractions, and as it was responsible for two very different attitudes in the Moralities.

After the Prologue explains the purpose of the play, and deprecates any displeasure that may arise in the audience, Perverse Doctrine and Ignorance enter with bitter complaints that "the world was never in so evil a state." The young people, instead of "playing at quoits or nine-holes, or shooting at butts," are busying their immature brains with theology, the proper concern of older and wiser heads. Perverse Doctrine is particularly aroused over the case of a young fellow who has lately been preaching in London. "But," he exclaims irascibly,

> If I had had the boy in a convenient place,
> With a good rod or twain, not past one hour's space,
> I would so have scourged my merchant that his breech should ache.

Ignorance is in full accord with the sentiments of Perverse Doctrine, and — rather paradoxically, since he is supposed to be "an old Popish priest" — states that he is "the *mother* of true devotion." The pair vow vengeance on New Custom, the young minister who is undermining their power, and, for the better accomplishing of their purpose, change their names, — Ignorance to Simplicity, and Perverse Doctrine to Sound Doctrine. With this precaution they feel secure in the belief that they "may go in any place and never be blamed."

At this point the object of their hatred appears, giving utterance to a soliloquy on the ignorance and wickedness of the Catholic Church. The choleric Perverse Doctrine, after standing this as long as he can, bursts in upon the speaker in a towering rage. New Custom retorts with that superior placidity always assumed by a Virtue in conversation with a Vice, and informs Perverse Doctrine that he is the elder of the two, and has a perfect right to his opinions. "What," exclaims Perverse Doctrine,

> Older than I!
> The young knave, by the mass, not fully thirty,
> Would be elder than I, that am above sixty!

New Custom assures him, with unabated suavity, that he is "a thousand and a half" years old.[1] After a protracted argument the disputants separate, and in the next scene New Custom enters conversing with his friend Light of the Gospel, who addresses him as Primitive Constitution.

Ignorance, Perverse Doctrine, and his sister Hypocrisy then lay their heads together to plan the downfall of their two enemies. Cruelty and Avarice enter opportunely while they are at their counsels, and are engaged as confederates. In order to "delude the people in every place" Cruelty's name is changed to Justice-with-Severity, and Avarice's to Frugality.[2] After a song to celebrate their compact the Vices depart on their mission.

---

[1] This is a natural confusion resulting from the double aspect of the play, — a contest between Virtues and Vices for supremacy, and a controversy between Catholic priests and Protestant clergymen. Perverse Doctrine as the priest is "above sixty," but as the Vice is as old as the Catholic faith. New Custom as the clergyman is "not fully thirty," but as the Virtue representing the Protestant religion is — or maintains that he is — fifteen hundred years old.

[2] It is to be noticed, always, that the constant changing of names on the part of the Vices is to delude the people, who, in this case, are behind the scenes, but on whose preference the victory depends. The Virtues, except in one or two cases, which may be regarded as irregular, are not deceived, and it is not intended that they should be.

But Perverse Doctrine, the most fiery of the conspirators, is soon to be coerced into an utter revolution of character. He stumbles accidentally upon a conference between New Custom and Light of the Gospel, and tarries a little too long to gloat over the destruction that he has prepared for them. They seize and compel him to listen while they heap argument after argument upon him. Perverse Doctrine is at first rebellious and abusive, then becomes passive, and finally is won over to the other side. His name is changed to Sincere Doctrine, and he is reassured and instructed successively by Edification, Assurance, and God's Felicity. Then the play ends with a prayer for Queen Elizabeth.

In interpreting this Morality one must remember that the so-called New Custom is not New Custom at all, but Primitive Constitution. He is known by the former name to his enemies and to strangers, but his friend Light of the Gospel addresses him as Primitive Constitution throughout, and he himself explains this toward the end of the play, while addressing the vanquished Perverse Doctrine. The interpretation should run as follows: The original constitution of God's church has been forgotten, and men, owing to their ignorance, have taken up with false doctrines. When, after many years, the old faith is introduced again, the believers in these false doctrines refuse to recognize the original doctrines of their religion, and denounce them as innovations. They have become hypocritical and avaricious, and, animated by the cruelty which is a natural result of their false worship, they prepare to destroy the followers of this new faith. But this supposed new doctrine is the one countenanced by God's word. When the adherents of the false belief have proof of this thrust upon them in the written word of the Bible, and understand that the religion they had supposed to be an innovation is really the original faith of their church, they are no longer able to combat the true belief, but are converted.

With this interpretation in mind it will be seen that the action of the play is not so haphazard as it at first appears. The conversion of Perverse Doctrine, which seems at first to happen quite by chance, and to be not only unnecessary, but even undesirable (from an allegorical point of view), is really necessary to signalize the complete victory of New Custom, or Primitive Constitution. That is, the only complete victory that one can gain over one's religious opponents is to succeed in converting them. I am not arguing for this scene as a merit in the play as a play. It is rendered necessary only by the controversial nature of the allegory. From an artistic point of view the conversion of Perverse Doctrine is a blemish in the allegory, since, technically, a Vice should always remain a Vice.[1] The changing of Perverse Doctrine to Sincere Doctrine is the deliberate converting of a Vice to a Virtue, and is very different from the changing of Imagynacyon (in *Hyckescorner*) to Good Remembraunce. In the present play the author sacrifices technical consistency to religious zeal, and both the drama and the allegory suffer in consequence.

The Three Ladies of London,[2] by R. Wilson, is a much more pretentious allegory than any we have yet considered. It represents the gradual spread of evils, religious, political, and social,

---

[1] Neilson has noted that in allegory a personification easily retains his essential character *as long as he is active.* But as soon as he becomes passive he is likely to be persuaded, cajoled, or bullied into a complete revolution of character, as if he were a type figure instead of the personification of an abstract quality. In the conversion scene Perverse Doctrine is regarded as the typical adherent of a false faith (or, in the controversial aspect of the play, as a typical Catholic) and not as that false faith itself (or Catholicism).

[2] Dodsley, Vol. VI. The play is dated 1584, but Fleay (*History of the Stage*, pp. 39–40) suggests an earlier date of composition: "'*The Jew*, representing the greediness of worldly chusers and bloody minds of usurers' (*School of Abuse*) was acted before 1579 (in the Bull Theatre). Surely this was the play of the *Three Ladies of London*, in which Gerontus, a Jew of Venice, is the chief human character; the others are mostly allegorical personifications. It is devoted to the subject of the greed of the followers of Lady Lucre, and in it

and the gradual loss of virtue. In the last scene of the *Three Ladies*, Lucre, the leader of the Vices, and Love and Conscience, the chief representatives of goodness—who have been overcome and corrupted by Lucre and her band—are indiscriminately sentenced to punishment. This is an obviously unsatisfactory conclusion. The author himself felt that the play was unfinished as it stood, and about ten years later he came out with a sequel, *The Three Lords and Three Ladies of London*, in which the three ladies, good and bad, are indiscriminately restored to happiness. This later play was, partly at least, inspired by the recent victory over the Spanish Armada,[1] as the chief scene is a mimic battle between the three Lords of London and the three Lords of Spain. It has got so far away from the traditional Morality scheme, and is so late in the period, that it must be regarded as merely an artificial revival. It is allegorical throughout, but lacks the moral element and singleness of purpose which characterize the orthodox Morality. We can detect, in fact, three distinct purposes : first, to reëstablish the three Ladies of London in a condition of prosperity; second, to celebrate the English victory over the Spaniards; and third, to show the superiority of London over other parts of England. Obviously the play cannot be regarded as a Morality, in spite of the fact that the play to which it is a sequel is one.

Usury murders Hospitality. But this play was written by R. W(ilson), and if its identity with *The Jew* be admitted, must have been acted by Leicester's men." Fleay goes on to conjecture that 1584, or the twenty-seventh year of Elizabeth's reign, given on the play as the date, was the date of publication, not of performance.

The evidence for this identification seems to me quite insufficient. Fleay's statement that Gerontus, the Jew, "is the chief human character" is misleading. The part played by Gerontus is almost negligible. All he does is to dun Mercatore (an Italian merchant who *is* "the chief human character") for an unpaid bill, and then generously forgive him the debt rather than have Mercatore resign his faith and "become a Mahomet."

[1] The play, which is to be found in Dodsley, Vol. VI, was printed in 1592, but, as the editor suggests, it may have been written about two years earlier.

The Three Ladies of London itself comes so late in the period that it has decided leanings toward the drama of real life. Not only are a great many type figures introduced, — of a kind familiar in London, and not very highly universalized, — but the abstractions themselves who carry the burden of the action are all dressed on the stage to represent familiar types. Furthermore, the play has constant reference to conditions in London. These attributes all raise the question of the eligibility of the play to appear as a Morality, but it emerges from the test with the three main requisites uppermost : it has the allegorical structure, it represents the sort of actors proper to a Morality, and it teaches a lesson for the guidance of life. This last may be expressed in one statement, — When love and conscience are subordinated to greed for gain the land suffers in consequence.

The play opens with the complaints of Love and Conscience that all men are now attached to Lady Lucre, and that her followers have little liking for Love and Conscience. Fame exhorts them to stand firm, and promises them a " triple crown " if they establish their supremacy over Lucre. The two ladies, however, continue to suffer from low spirits, and Fame leads them out to provide chaste amusement for their recreation.

Dissimulation comes upon the scene, " having on a farmer's long coat and a cap, and his poll and beard painted motley." He is not willing, however, to run any risk of being mistaken for a mere farmer, and explains himself to the audience :

My name is Dissimulation, and no base mind I bear,
For my outward effects my inward zeal do declare ;
For men do dissemble with their wives, and their wives with them again,
So that in the hearts of them I always remain.

He is soon followed by Simplicity attired like a miller, and by Fraud in the guise of a ruffian. Simplicity ventures to give Fraud some good advice and narrowly escapes a sound thrashing in consequence. Then Simony and Usury come in, hand in hand, and a grand reunion takes place, in which, for some reason, the luckless Simplicity is not included.

Love and Conscience reënter, and the four rogues, Fraud, Dissimulation, Usury, and Simony, at once ask to be admitted to their service, but are rejected. Then Simplicity takes heart of grace, applies, and is accepted; whereat he waxes bolder and expresses a wish to be Love's " good-man." But this is too much. He is informed that " Love may not marry in any case with Simplicity," and he is fain to content himself with the humbler rôle of servant. Love and Conscience depart, taking their new follower with them.

The rejected petitioners see Lady Lucre coming toward them, and at once greet her with an application for favor and service. Usury says he has come from the service of old Lady Lucre in Venice on purpose to enter that of young Lady Lucre, and is assured that he may live even more pleasantly in England than in Venice. Lucre accepts them all, making Dissimulation her steward, Fraud her rent-gatherer, Usury her secretary, and reserving Simony for " such matters as are ecclesiastical."

Mercatore, dressed like an Italian merchant, comes looking for Lady Lucre. Dissimulation agrees to present him for a consideration. Mercatore pays his fee, is introduced, and is well received by Lucre, who tells him that he must not be over-squeamish about his business affairs if he wishes to win her.

Artifex comes and pleads with Dissimulation and Fraud to introduce him to Lucre, but since he neglects to pay his fee the promised introduction never comes. He is followed by a lawyer who is on the same errand. The latter shows himself much more apt to win the good offices of Fraud and Dissimulation, and he is presently led inside to where Lucre has retired.

Simplicity has a cousin Sincerity, who has studied in both Oxford and Cambridge, but lacks a benefice. He comes to his cousin, who refers him to Conscience for help. Conscience recognizes his qualifications and wishes to help him, but her power in such matters has of late become very slight. He then presents his credentials to Lucre, who looks them over, but says that her servant Simony has charge of all such matters. Dissimulation here joins in to inform her that there is one living which she may bestow without Simony's consent, the parsonage of St. Nihil. This is accordingly presented to Sincerity, and Simplicity is highly elated over his cousin's good fortune until the latter informs him that Nihil means nothing.

Meanwhile Love and Conscience have been sinking deeper and deeper in poverty, owing to the machinations of Lucre and her followers. Usury now tells Conscience that she may have her house for another quarter for forty pounds (the old rent was ten pounds a year), and then will have to leave. Presently Simplicity appears with the gowns of Love and Conscience, which are all they have left to send for the quarter's rent. He meets Dissimulation, and the latter shows that he has a new plan for overpowering Love, since he sends her gown back to her with some gold in addition. Conscience's gown, he says, may go to Usury, and her skin with it.

Hospitality, who has appeared once before to invite Conscience to a simple dinner on "bread and beer, one joint of meat, and welcome," now comes in, closely followed by Usury, who sets on him to murder him. Conscience runs in and tries to prevent the crime, but she is helpless, and poor Hospitality is dragged out to his death, crying dolefully, "Farewell, Lady Conscience; you shall have Hospitality in London nor England no more."

Conscience is finally reduced to selling brooms for a living. While she is engaged in this business Lucre comes along, buys the brooms, and makes Conscience an offer, to the acceptance of which Conscience is driven by her poverty. According to the terms of the offer Conscience must keep a cottage to which

Lucre may resort when she wishes "with familiar friends to play," since her own house is watched by constables and spiteful neighbors. Lucre sends Usury for her "box of all abomination," and, dipping her fingers in the box, spots Conscience's face over. Then Conscience goes to her new position.

Dissimulation now takes advantage of the poverty of Love to seduce her into a marriage with him. Soon her head swells monstrously, and she is compelled to wear a "vizard." The Virtues are now completely overcome.

The final scene depicts the trial of Love, Conscience, and Lucre before Judge Nemo. Lucre is convicted of adultery and of conniving at the murder of Hospitality. She is condemned to a place of darkness, to be burned forever in a lake of fire and brimstone. Love is sent along with her, to pine in endless pain, because she has sold herself to Lucre; and Conscience is sent to prison till the day of general session.

The characters, in the main, are easily interpreted. The personifications all represent forces operating in the land at large — with a more specific application to London. On the side of virtue, Love and Conscience are forces for good, and Fame is the reward accompanying them. Sincerity and Hospitality are Virtues. On the side of vice, Lucre is money with an evil connotation. Dissimulation, Fraud, Simony, Usury, and Cogging are vices practised throughout the land. Nemo is an Agent of Retribution, and Diligence, or Serviceable Diligence, appearing simply as a constable — as he does in many of the Moralities — is a negligible figure. Simplicity is not a vicious character, neither is he uncompromisingly good. His virtue is of a negative kind, and he occupies a position much like that of the clown in the drama of real life.

Several type figures are introduced to point the moral. These are Mercatore, the merchant; Artifex, the artificer; Peter Pleaseman, the parson; Wily Will; Tom Beggar; and the Lawyer. Gerontus the Jew and the Judge of Turkey are individuals. These figures, as the outline has shown, bear only a slight part of the action.

To go carefully into the interpretation of the allegory would be to do very little more than repeat the outline of the play. In order to present the underlying significance a very general interpretation will be clearer and more useful: When love and conscience are subordinated to greed for money, all sorts of evils result. This greed becomes manifest not only in business and professional activities, but also in religion. As easy methods of accumulating money rapidly, fraud and usury are practised, and simony becomes a regular practice in the Church. The old spirit of hospitality cannot exist while each man is seeking to rob his neighbor. At length the better feelings of men — love and the promptings of conscience — are completely overcome and cease to have any part in the dealings of life. Then comes retribution.[1] The constant struggle for money at all costs has driven out the tendencies which make for general peace and happiness, and the land is plunged in misery and remorse.[2]

[1] The play is not clear, at this point, as to the source of vengeance. We should expect the arrival of some such figure as Despair.

[2] The punishment, also, is very indefinite. It may represent national calamity, or simply general remorse for evil deeds. The play, as I have shown, does not come to a logical conclusion, and we must conjecture either that it was hurriedly finished, or that it was deliberately left in an unfinished condition in order to leave opportunity for a sequel.

CHAPTER V

MORALITIES DEALING WITH THE CONFLICT BE-
TWEEN VIRTUES AND VICES FOR THE POSSESSION
OF MAN

The bulk of the English Moralities depict a struggle between personified virtues and vices to win the favor of Man. This, when translated into literal terms, refers to the eternal struggle in the human soul between evil passions and impulses for good. I have made three subdivisions of this motive: 1. Man Spiritual (where the struggle is for the human soul). 2. Man Intellectual (where the struggle is for the human mind). 3. Man represented merely by one or more personified attributes.

The demands for condensed expression in a table of classification may have left some obscurity in the phrasing of the first two subdivisions. In both of them Man appears in person, and the struggle takes the form of repeated attempts on the part of the personified virtues and vices to obtain his favor and companionship. In the first he is approached, on the one hand, by Vices who tempt him to renounce piety and live in sin, and, on the other, by Virtues who urge him to live in the fear of God. In the second the Vices tempt him to an existence of idleness and ignorance, as against the Virtues, who strive to win him over to a life of study. In the third subdivision the distinction lies in the fact that Man himself does not appear as the object of strife, but, instead, some attribute or attributes of Man personified, occupying the same position with relation to the Virtues and Vices as does Man himself in the first two subdivisions.

In the last analysis this plot is the same as that in the class considered in the previous chapter, since all struggles between good and evil may be said to have their battle-ground in the nature of Man. But the difference, technically, between the allegory where Man is present in the body to be won or lost, and the allegory where he is dimly understood but not specified as the prize, is an essential one. In the former, Man, or a personification representing Man, is the central figure on the stage, and victory falls to that side which ultimately proves more attractive to him; in the latter, we are interested in the fortunes of abstract good and evil, and the more interested we become in the strife the less likely are we to remember that Man is the spoil of the victor.

1. Conflict for the Possession of Man Spiritual

This subdivision is the most important section of the English Moralities. In the main, it is taken up with the struggles of Virtues and Vices to obtain the favor of Man. But another aspect of this strife, which is not so apparent, must also be taken into consideration here. This is the enmity of the three great powers — the World, the Flesh, and the Devil — towards Man, an aspect of the allegory influenced by Paul's exhortation to the Ephesians to " put on the whole armor of God " against the attacks of the devil.[1] This motive appears with the more important one in *The Castle of Perseverance*, which, with the possible exception of the *Pryde of Lyfe*, is the earliest existing English Morality.

The Castle of Perseverance[2] is not only one of the earliest of the existing Moralities; it is one of the finest of its class. While most of the Moralities are disfigured, from an artistic

[1] Cf. Creizenach, I, 464.

[2] Edited by F. J. Furnivall and Alfred W. Pollard for the Early English Text Society, London, 1904. The play is usually dated about 1400, but Pollard here places it about 1425.

point of view, by constant attempts to appeal to the vulgar class of spectators, this play holds itself sternly, from beginning to end, to the allegorical struggle in the soul. This gives it a solemnity and an earnestness of purpose not attained by any other Morality except *Everyman*.

The two Vexillatores give a full account of the play that is to follow; and a part of this explanation, which I shall quote, shows how closely the two motives are mingled here, the old combat of the Seven Deadly Sins against the Seven Cardinal Virtues, — first presented in the *Psychomachia*, and presented here as there in a series of single combats, — and the rivalry of the Virtues and the Vices for the favor of Man:

> The Castel of Perseverans, wanne Mankynde hath tan
> Wel armyd with vertus, & overcome all vycys,
> There the Good aungyl makyth ful mery thanne
> That Mankynde hath overcome his gostly enmys.
> The Badde Aungyl mornyth that he hath myssyd man:
> He callyth the Werld, the Fende, & the foule Flesch, I-wys,
> & all the sevene synnys to do that they canne
> to brynge Mankynd a-geyn to bale out of blys,
> > With wronge.
> Pride a-saylyth Meknesse with all his myth:
> Ire, a-geyns Paciensse, ful fast ganne he fyth:
> Envye, a-geyn Charyte strywth ful ryth:
> but Covetyse a-geyns Largyte fytyth over longe.
> Coveytyse, Mankind euere covytyth for to qwell:
> he gaderith to hym Glotony, a-ȝeyns Sobyrnesse:
> Lecherye, with Chastyte ffytith ful fell,
> & Slawthe in Goddys seruyse, a-geyns Besynesse.
> Thus vycys a-geyns vertues fytyn ful snelle;
> every buskith to brynge man to dystresse:
> but Penaunce & Confescion, with Mankynd wyl melle;
> The vycys arn ful lyckely the vertues to opresse:
> > sann dowte;
> Thus in the Castel of good Perseverance
> Mankynd is maskeryd with mekyl varyaunce;
> The Goode Aungyl & the Badde be euere at dystaunce:
> The Goode holdith hym Inne: the Badde wolde brynge hym owte.

Before the appearance of Humanum Genus, or Mankind (I shall use the English names, which are those employed in the dialogue), the three kings, the World, the Flesh, and the Devil, speak from their respective scaffolds. The World boasts of his power over the nations, procured for him by his "tresorer, Syr Coveytyse." The Devil tells of his anxiety to have Mankind destroyed, and proclaims his intention of staying to effect this destruction. Lastly, the Flesh glories in the power of his followers, Glotony, Lechery, and Slawth, who are able to trick Mankind.

Then Mankind enters, newly born and naked, attended by his Good Angel and his Bad Angel. He laments his poverty and proneness to sorrow, and prays to Christ that he may follow his Good Angel. The two attendants, realizing that Mankind must now choose his way of life, present their respective arguments to him; and, lured by promises of wealth and ease, he decides to follow his Bad Angel.

The World, on his scaffold, addresses his followers, Lust, Lyking, and Foly. They all agree that the only real happiness obtainable on earth is in their service. Then the Bad Angel enters with Mankind, introduces him, and instructs the Vices how to look after him so that he may go at last to Hell with them. The Vices gladly take Mankind into their fellowship, and tell him of the riches and pleasures they have in store for him. The World extends a hearty welcome and gives Mankind a place on his scaffold.

Bacbytere enters with a lengthy explanation of his character. The World and his followers go on with their plans for Mankind, whom they will not abandon till he hangs high in Hell. The Good Angel makes an attempt to warn Mankind of his danger, but is abused and driven away by the Bad Angel. On the advice of the World, Mankind takes Bacbytere with him and goes to Coveytyse to receive the riches that have been promised him. Bacbytere (or Bacbytynge) introduces Mankind to Coveytyse, who receives him lovingly, gives him a seat on his scaffold, and proceeds to offer careful instructions about the way he is to act toward his fellow-men. Mankind is an apt pupil, and readily promises his instructor,

> where-so that I fare, be fenne or flod,
> I make a-vow, be Goddys blod,
> of Mankynde, getyth no man no good,
> but if he synge " si dedero."

Then Coveytyse calls the attendants of the Flesh and the Devil and presents them to Mankind, and the Devil himself appears and instructs his followers, Pryde, Wrathe, and Envy, to stick by Mankind so that he may be bound fast in Hell when he dies. Mankind is now thoroughly under the influence of the World, the Flesh, the Devil, and the Seven Deadly Sins, and is ready to follow their advice implicitly. The Good Angel mourns and is again ridiculed by the Bad Angel.

Schryfte appears and asks the Good Angel why he weeps, and the latter says it is on account of the disaffection of Mankind. Schryfte goes to try his powers of persuasion, but Mankind puts him off with

> thou art com al to sone;
> therfore, Schryfte, be thi fay,
> goo forthe tyl on Good Fryday!
> tente to thee thanne, wel I may;
> I have now ellys to done.

But Penance joins forces with Schryfte, and their arguments reduce Mankind to sorrow for his misdeeds. He calls on God for mercy and renounces his sins. Schryfte tells him he must avoid Foly and confess all his sins, which he does, receiving absolution from Schryfte.

Feeling his weakness in the presence of temptation, Mankind wishes to be sheltered from the attacks of the Seven Deadly

Sins, and Schryfte sends him to the Castle of Perseverance, where the Seven Cardinal Virtues are waiting to receive him. Each gives her counsel in turn, and Mankind solemnly promises to abide by his instructions.

The Bad Angel sends Bacbytynge to warn the World, the Flesh, and the Devil of Mankind's desertion, and to summon them to the Castle. Bacbytynge delivers his message to each of the kings, and each has his attendants soundly flogged for their carelessness, to the intense joy of Bacbytynge, who takes a strictly impartial delight in misery, wherever he can find it. Then the powers of evil make ready to storm the Castle. Mankind, in his stronghold, hears of the coming attack and prays to Christ for strength. Then his Good Angel summons the Virtues to defend him.

The Seven Deadly Sins, under the leadership of their captains, the World, the Flesh, and the Devil, approach the Castle and order the Virtues to surrender Mankind. The demand is refused, and after several threats and arguments the assault begins. The Virtues shower down roses (the emblems of Christ's passion) upon the assailants, and repulse them in a series of single combats. The followers of the Devil advance first, and Pryde is beaten back by Meknesse, Envye by Charyte, and Wrathe by Paciensse. After the last-mentioned encounter Wrathe emerges crying,

> hyr rosys fel on me so scharpe
> that myn hed hangyth as an harpe:
> I dar neyther crye nor carpe,
>   sche is so pacyent,

—a sufficiently striking example of the effort to make allegorical action intelligible by the addition of literal comment.

Flesh then urges on his followers, Glotony, Lecherye, and Slawthe; but they are in turn repulsed, Glotony by Sobyrnesse (or Abstinence), Lecherye by Chastyte, and Slawthe by Besynesse (or Industry).

As a last resort the World calls on his attendant Coveytyse to bear his banner to the front. Coveytyse advances and invites Mankind to leave the Castle and come with him. Largyte (Generosity) curses Coveytyse and orders him off; but he bids her hold her tongue, and renews his invitations to Mankind, who says that he is growing old, and finally agrees to leave the Castle and go with Coveytyse. As he departs, Meknesse, speaking for the Virtues, explains that Mankind has a free will and that it is no fault of theirs if he leaves them. Then the Virtues all lament Mankind's unfortunate choice.

Coveytyse now instructs Mankind, promising him land and riches if he will guard them carefully and give nothing to the poor. Mankind readily agrees to all the conditions of Coveytyse. But presently Dethe enters, explains his mission, then goes and lays his stroke upon Mankind:

> now I kylle thee with myn knappe!
> I reche to thee, Mankynde, a rappe
> to thyne herte rote.

Mankind appeals to the World for help, but the World calls to a boy and turns Mankind's property over to him. Mankind reproaches the World and Coveytyse, laments bitterly that he must go and leave all his riches to this boy whom he does not know, and dies.

The Soul appears from under the bed where Mankind has breathed his last, and reproaches the Body. He then appeals to the Good Angel, who says that he must go to Hell unless Mercy will save him; but the Bad Angel insists that the Soul must go to Hell with him.

Finally the Four Daughters of God, Mercy, Rytwysnes, Pes, and Trewthe, enter and contend for the Soul. Mercy and Pes are eager to rescue him from the clutches of the Devil, but Rytwysnes and Trewthe argue sternly and logically that Mankind has damned the Soul by his own free will. The sisters carry their debate before the throne of God, who at last decides in favor of Mercy and Pes, and sends his daughters to take Mankind from the Devil. They conduct Mankind before the throne, and he is given a seat on the right hand of God.

The allegory, which is a picture of Man's progress through life, is simple and easily interpreted. Man is born into the world naked, defenceless, and innocent. Early in life he has to decide between good and evil courses, and, lured by the prospect of pleasure and worldly profit, he chooses the latter. Then he gives free rein to his lusts and appetites, and indulges in every kind of folly. But while engaged in this evil life he comes under the influence of religion. At first he hardens his heart, but the truths of religion are so impressed on him that he becomes filled with remorse for his past wickedness and cries to God for mercy. Then he confesses his sins, gets absolution, and resolves upon a better life. For many years he lives up to his purpose. His evil desires never leave him; but, strong in the practice of virtue, he is empowered to resist them. At length he grows old, and while the lusts of his flesh have steadily grown weaker, he is becoming more prone to avarice, the peculiar vice of old age. His love for money finally becomes too strong to be resisted, and in his last years he indulges to the full his pleasure in hoarding riches. Death overtakes him while he is thus engaged; and he has the bitter experience of realizing, in his last moments, that a stranger is to enjoy his wealth, while he must appear before God with only the record of his deeds upon earth. His soul appears before the judgment seat. In strict justice God cannot pardon him; but God's mercy is greater than his desire for justice, and the soul is received into heaven.

The Castle of Perseverance is one of the few Moralities that depict the whole life of Man from infancy to old age or death;[1]

---

[1] Cf. Brandl, *Quellen des weltlichen Dramas in England vor Shakespeare*, p. xl.

and as a natural consequence of this wider view of the hero's career it presents more stages than are usually found in plays of this class. The normal scheme of the Morality with a human hero may be said to include the following stages: State of Goodness—Fall from Grace—Life in Sin—Repentance and Pardon. *The Castle of Perseverance*, in effect, doubles this scheme, presenting the stages, State of Goodness — Fall from Grace — Life in Sin — Repentance and Pardon — Life of Goodness — Second Fall from Grace — Life in Sin — Final Repentance and Pardon. These stages, in different Moralities, are shifted and repeated in various ways, though on the whole the simple scheme of four stages is usually adhered to. Most of the Moralities in which Man is the hero depict, not the whole life as in *The Castle of Perseverance*, but one crucial period of temptation and struggle. Of the latter type is the play next to be considered.

Mankind[1] belongs to the same allegorical class as *The Castle of Perseverance*, but otherwise it has almost nothing in common with the latter play. *The Castle of Perseverance* is pure in tone, with almost the sternness and severity of Greek tragedy. *Mankind* is remarkable mainly for the coarse jokes and vulgar antics of four rascals, like the Imagynacyon and Frewyl of *Hyckescorner*, thinly veiled as personifications. The author is quite conscious of the fact that he is writing a Morality, and takes care to preserve the traditional form and to insist on his moral; but the religious teaching of the play is stilted and unnatural to the last degree, while the mad pranks of Mischeff and his crew are pictured with a zest and unction which must have gone far toward making the play a favorite with those who loved a joke more than a sermon.

[1] Between 1461–1485. In Manly, Vol. I. For a discussion of possible sources for the play see Mabel M. Keiller, "The Influence of Piers Plowman on the Macro Play of Mankind," *Publications of the Mod. Lang. Assoc.*, Vol. XXVI, No. 2, and W. R. Mackenzie, "A New Source for *Mankind*," ibid., Vol. XXVII, No. 1.

Mankind begins with a very stilted speech from Mercy on the Redemption. Presently relief appears in the person of Mischeff, who mocks and teases Mercy most unmercifully. The dignified soliloquizer expostulates,

> A-voyde, goode brother! ye ben culpable
> To interupte thus my talkynge delectable.

But Mischeff is unabashed by this stately rebuff, and soon he is reinforced by the arrival of his three friends, New Gyse, Now-a-days, and Nought. Mercy is subjected to a rattling fire of chaff; but finally the four Vices retire and leave him to continue his moralizing, which he does not fail to do, with the added point that their lewd conversation has given him:

> The goode new gyse now-a-days I will not dysalow;
> I dyscomende the vycyouse gyse, I prey have me excusyde.

Mankynde appears, soliloquizing on the goodness of God; when, catching sight of Mercy, he greets him with reverence. They converse on spiritual topics; then Mercy gives Mankynde careful directions for the guidance of his life and leaves him. New Gyse, Now-a-days, and Nought come in, but Mankynde pretends not to see them, and delves busily in the earth with his spade "to eschew ydullnes." The three Vices tantalize him, make certain coarse suggestions as to the best methods of cultivating his land, and finally he loses his temper and beats them with his spade till they are glad to get out of his way. After a virtuous soliloquy, and a solemn promise to the audience "ryght sone" to "reverte," Mankynde leaves the stage.

Mischeff appears and is soon followed by New Gyse, Now-a-days, and Nought. They consult together, then call the devil, or Tityvullus, who enters roaring, "I com with my legges under me!" and tries to borrow a penny among the Vices. They have nothing to give him, however, so he sends them all out to steal and remains to formulate a plan for corrupting Mankynde.

The latter presently fulfills his promise to the audience and "revertes " to his labor with the spade ; but at last he grows tired, lies down, and goes to sleep. Tityvullus approaches the sleeper and whispers that Mercy has been hanged for stealing a mare, and that now he is to put his trust in New Gyse, Now-a-days, and Nought.

After Tityvullus retires, Mischeff and his three companions return from their foraging expedition. Mankynde awakes and approaches them in friendly and apologetic fashion. Then Mischeff presides at a council over Mankynde and makes him repeat a solemn promise to go out and perform murders and other wicked deeds. The whole company is departing when Mercy appears and tries to stop Mankynde, but he is put aside and left to mourn the desertion of his pupil.

After some time Mankynde returns, smitten with remorse for his sins, and calling for a rope to hang himself. The Vices have one ready for him, and New Gyse explains how one is hanged according to the new guise, almost hanging himself during the lesson. Then the Vices take to their heels and leave Mankynde grovelling in terror on the ground. Before he can destroy himself, however, Mercy returns and restores him to confidence and a state of grace.

The allegorical teaching is rendered more general and less effective by the elusive nature of the vicious characters. Mischeff is the chief Vice and stands for "all sins generally"; but his followers, New Gyse, Now-a-days, and Nought, do not stand for any specific vices, as we should expect them to do. They represent only, in a general way, the current vices of the day ; and this is explained to Mankynde when, after his regeneration, he tells Mercy how he has been deceived :

> Tityvilly, that goth invisibele, hynge hys nett be-fore my eye,
> And, by hys fantasticall visionys sedulously sowght,
> He Newgyse, Now-a-days, Nought causyd me to obey.

Mercy, in return, gives him a lecture upon the origin of temptation and evil, which are symbolized by his late companions:

> Ye haue iij adversarys, — he is master of them all, —
> That ys to sey, the dewell, the world, the flesh: & I the tell
> That Newgyse, Now-a-days & Nought, the world we may them call;
> And propyrlly Titiuilly syngnyfieth the fend of hell:
> The flesh, — that ys the vnclene concupisens of your body;
> These be your iij gostly enmys in whom ye have put your confidens:
> Thei browt yow to Myscheffe to conclude your temperull glory.
> As yt hath be schewyd this worschypfyll audiens.[1]

That is, New Gyse, Now-a-days, and Nought stand in a general way for the temptations of the world and the flesh, which assail the heart of Man and lure him away from virtue. The third of the trio of "gostly enmys" is represented less vaguely. The devil, or Tityvullus, here occupies an unusually important rôle, and does a great deal of the work usually assigned to the chief Vice, — one of the two cases where this happens in the Moralities.[2] His regular rôle is to look on and approve when Man falls into sin, or to give directions to the Vices, who are his servants; but here he appears as the actual tempter of Man.

Mercy is the only representative of goodness in the play, but he is a figure of sufficient importance to carry the day against the combined forces of evil without occasioning any suspicion of inconsistency in the outcome. The most potent of the Four Daughters of God, who were introduced repeatedly in mediaeval allegory, was Mercy. The Four Daughters symbolized the four attributes of God; that is, righteousness, peace, mercy, and truth, which hitherto it had been the convention to represent as women. In the present play, however, there are obvious reasons why the divine quality of mercy, if it was to be represented here at all, should be personified as a man rather than as a woman. But with this slight discrepancy Mercy is here the

---

[1] Lines 869–872, 876–884.

[2] The other case is in the Morality *Wisdom, Who is Christ.*

figure that had become familiar to mediaeval readers in many a debate concerning the fate of man. That he has this precise significance he himself indicates. in his conversation with Mankynde toward the close of the play.

> *Mank.* The egall Iustyse of God wyll not permytte sych a synfull wrech
> To be reuyuyd & restoryd a-geyn; yt were impossibyll.
> *Mercy.* The Iustice of God wyll as I wyll, as hym-sylfe doth pre-cyse:
> Nolo mortem peccatoris, inquit, yff he wyll be reducyble.
> *Mank.* Than, mercy, good Mercy! What ys a man wythowt Mercy?
> Lytyll ys our parte of paradyse where Mercy ne were.
> Good Mercy, excuse the inevetabyll obieccion of my gostly enmy:
> The prowerbe seyth, the trewth tryith the sylfe. Alas, I have mech care.
> *Mercy.* God wyll not make ʒou preuy on-to his last iugement:
> Iustyce & Equite xall be fortyfyid, I wyll not denye;
> Trowthe may not so cruelly procede in hys streyt argument
> But that Mercy schall rewle the mater with-owte controuersaye.[1]

The significance of the play, then, is this: Man, trying to lead a clean and virtuous life, is constantly tempted by the fashionable vices of the day and is hampered, as well, by the original sin in his own nature. He succeeds for a time in overcoming temptation, but when the devil puts false and evil thoughts in his heart he becomes confused and unable to discriminate between right and wrong. Then he falls into vicious ways and persists therein, refusing to avail himself of God's mercy, which is extended to all men. But eventually he comes to himself. Remorse for his sins takes hold on him, and in despair he meditates suicide. He is preserved, however, from this fate by a realization that God's mercy is infinite, and is extended even to the sinner who, in strict justice, should be sentenced to eternal punishment. With a grateful knowledge of his indebtedness to God he now resolves on a life of piety for the future, and definitely renounces the sins in which he has wasted so many years of his life.

[1] Lines 824–836.

Nature,[1] "a goodly interlude" by Henry Medwall, is like *The Castle of Perseverance* in that it presents a picture of life as a whole rather than of one period. It is not, however, so careful on this point as is the latter play. *The Castle of Perseverance* presents Man immediately after his birth, conducts him through life, and after his death accompanies him to the judgment seat of God. It is a complete biography within a limited scope. *Nature* presents Man first as an infant, or so we are led to suppose by the fact that he is naked and is accompanied by Innocence; there is no specific mention of infancy. At the close of the play Man has reached old age, but not the end of his days. This point is connected with another marked difference between the two plays. *Nature* is noticeable for an almost complete lack of religious instruction, while in *The Castle of Perseverance* a high religious tone is sustained throughout. The teaching in *Nature* is directed entirely toward the guidance of life in this world; and to end the play with the death of Man — which would necessitate a great deal of moralizing on the next life — would be noticeably inconsistent. The Moralities are not always remarkable for dramatic consistency, and when one encounters a real exhibition of this quality one is tempted to make the most of it.

The play might seem, at first, to belong more properly to the following subclass, where the conflict is for the mind of Man. But in spite of an almost complete lack of religious teaching there can be no question that the allegorical struggle is waged over the soul of the hero. This aspect is decided by the very nature of the abstractions taking part in the conflict. The temptations assailing Man are from the Seven Deadly Sins and other Vices of the same general character, and the attempt

[1] Between 1486–1500. In "*Lost*" *Tudor Plays*, ed. by J. S. Farmer. On the probable source of this play in Lydgate's *Reason and Sensuality*, see a forthcoming article by the present author.

is to lead him from a life of uprightness and virtue, not from a life of study. The representative of goodness, to be sure, is Reason, who in other plays figures as a guardian of the mind, not of the soul. But Reason pitted against Ignorance and Tediousness has a prize in view which, allegorically, is very different from the prize to be won when Reason is pitted against the Seven Deadly Sins. Obviously, in the former case the prize is the mind, in the latter the soul.

Lady Nature, at the beginning of the play, makes a long speech to Man, and ends by sending him on his way with Reason and Sensuality to guide him, and Innocency, his nurse, to wean him from the appetite for vice. Sensuality urges Nature not to send Reason with Man, and to allow him to be the only guide, but Nature insists on her original scheme and leaves them to get along as best they can. Reason and Sensuality then fall to disputing, and Reason stoutly maintains his superiority, though he has more lately come to Man's service. " Lo," he says,

> this is it that doth him (Man) dignify,
> And causeth him to be reputed so excellent.
> And of all this the chief doer am I,
> Which from Heaven into earth by God am sent,
> Only for that cause and final intent
> That I should this, his creature, demean and guide
> For the season that he doth in this world abide.
> Now compare thy virtues and mine together,
> And say which is the worthier of them two.

But Sensuality is impervious to any sharply drawn distinctions between virtue and vice, and exclaims,

> Which is the worthier? forsooth! I trow neither:
> We be good fellows.

Man, with an indulgent eye to the needs of thick skulls among the audience, cries

> O, blessed Lord! what manner strife is this
> Atwixt my reason and sensuality!

He finally puts an end to the argument by bidding Sensuality be tongue-tied till Reason has done speaking. Then they all proceed on their journey and come at last to the World, who gives them a hearty welcome and offers Man some clothing. Man, who is naked, says that the garment of innocence is enough for him, and in this Innocency supports him. But the World insists, and Man finally accepts the clothing and puts it on. The World then brings forward Worldly Affection, whom he recommends to Man as a good person to have in his service, along with Sensuality. On the advice of all these friends Man dismisses Innocency,[1] and places himself chiefly under the guidance of Sensuality.

Worldly Affection goes out to look after Man's affairs, leaving his master with Sensuality. Soon they are joined by Pride, who confides to Sensuality that he is very anxious to enter Man's service; then, when Man comes forward, he flatters him adroitly, says that his name is Worship, and is accepted as a servant. He shows his anxiety for his master's welfare by warning him earnestly against Reason — the same device that was used in *Mankind* to lure Man away from virtue :

> Marry, fie on him, knave!
> It were better the hangman were in his grave
> Than ever the lewd fool should have
> The governance of you.

Sensuality then takes Man out to a tavern to enjoy himself, and presently returns joyfully to announce to Pride and Worldly Affection that his master has taken up with Margery, a harlot, and has employed the six kinsmen of Pride, who have all changed their names " for to blear his eye." Covetise has

---

[1] The sex of Innocency remains a matter of some doubt. She is spoken of at first as a woman (p. 59), and later, when Man at the World's request decides to dismiss her, as a man (p. 63) ; and, to round out this information, Sensuality adds, " He is but a boy " (p. 64).

become Worldly Policy; Wrath, Manhood; Envy, Disdain; Gluttony, Good Fellowship; Sloth, Ease; and Lechery, Lust.

> Lo! these be fair names, parde!
> Both good and honest, as seemeth me:
> As for their conditions, what they be,
> Ye know well.

" Very just," answers Worldly Affection,

> I know their conditions on the best wise
> If they still keep their old guise.

" Yes," answers Sensuality, " that they do, on warrantise." Worldly Affection marvels that Covetousness should be accepted, and Sensuality explains that, though Man has no inclination to Covetousness now, he will follow him " when his head waxeth hoar." [1]

On Man's return from the tavern he is seized with misgivings as to what Reason will think when he sees him in this condition. Finally he concludes that he has followed Sensuality and Worldly Affection too long, and decides to seek Shamefacedness.[2] The latter at once puts in an appearance and promises to come to Man whenever he wants him. At this point Reason re-appears, Man confesses how much he needs his help, and Reason advises him to call on God for grace.

This ends the first part of the play. The second part, while a direct continuation of the foregoing, is so arranged that it could be produced as a sequel. This part of the play has not very much point. It consists largely of meetings and conversations between different pairs of Vices, while the hero himself plays only a small part. The tame presentation of the return to sin and final conversion should be compared with the stirring depiction of these stages in *The Castle of Perseverance*.

[1] See p. 64, above.
[2] This play is exceptional in that the human hero decides to change his mode of life without the intervention of abstract advisers.

Reason and Man converse, then Reason goes out, promising to return whenever Man needs him.[1] Next, Sensuality comes in, complains of Man's neglect, and weeps. Man begins to feel now that he has been having rather a dull time of it with Reason, and is easily persuaded to call back his old servants. In the company of Worldly Affection and Bodily Lust he goes out to enjoy himself with Margery. On his return he retires with Pride to inspect the new apparel which the latter has procured for him. Coming in again he encounters Gluttony, who fails to recognize him, he is so fallen away from living on Reason's diet. To amend this condition he retires with Gluttony and Wrath.

Then comes a bit of by-play to show the impartiality of Envy in creating trouble. Pride enters and encounters Envy; the latter warns him that Man has tired of his services and is about to dismiss him. Pride, in alarm, takes to his heels, to the immense delight of Envy, who recounts the exploit to Sensuality, admitting that he had no cause to injure Pride. It is simply his nature to destroy anyone in power.

But Sensuality has sad news to give in return. Age, he says, has come, bringing Reason with him; and, seeing this, Gluttony and Bodily Lust have left the service of Man. The speakers, alarmed for their own positions, rush out to hold a council with their friends; then Man, in a very penitent state of mind, enters conversing with Reason. He has definitely resigned his evil courses, and is presently joined by Charity, Patience, Good

---

[1] Great pains are taken in this play to show that Man may be under the influence of a personified quality, even though not constantly attended by that abstraction. Reason, as he leaves, says to Man (p. 91):

> Now, fare ye well! for I must be absent
> As for a season: and for your comfort
> Whensoever ye call me I shall to you resort.

And, later on, when Man falls from grace Bodily Lust assures him (p. 94):

> Sir, ye know well that ye and I
> Be never much asunder
> Albeit I be from you among.

Occupation, Liberality, Abstinence, and Chastity. With this imposing bodyguard of Virtues he is left to complete his life on earth.

The allegory may be interpreted thus : Man from his birth is endowed with reason on the one hand, and on the other with the natural desires of sense, which are necessary, and are useful so long as they are subordinated to reason. He is at first perfectly innocent, but his innocence disappears as soon as he begins to wear clothes, in accordance with the fashions of the world. This is the first step. Having begun to conform to worldly usages, he finds it easy and natural to follow them up, and ends by giving full sway to all his lusts and his desires for pleasure, and ceasing to follow the dictates of his reason. But he has not become completely depraved, and in the midst of his carousing a sense of shame comes to him. He decides to abandon his evil habits and to act as reason dictates. For some time he perseveres in his good resolves, but his bad habits have such a hold upon him that he finds a life of virtue decidedly dull and pines for his old pleasures. This is the beginning of his second downfall. He slides again into his vicious habits, and is not reclaimed until, with advancing years, he loses his desire for worldly pleasure. He then decides, finally, to spend his last years in virtue and uprightness. The allurements of the world and the flesh have ceased to attract him, and the impulse to avarice is quelled by the constant practice of charity and liberality.

In *Magnyfycence*,[1] by John Skelton, we have, as the human hero to be striven for by Virtues and Vices, not Mankind in general, but a special type of man, — the prince characterized by munificence. The hero goes by the abstract name of Magnyfycence, but from the beginning of the play he is shown to

---

[1] Ramsay (*Skelton's " Magnyfycence,"* pp. xxi–xxv) shows that this play was probably written between Sept. 14, 1515 and Aug. 13, 1516, or certainly between the former date and October, 1518.

be a great king of the earth,[1] not an abstraction; and, but for
the presence of some Vices whom I shall specify further on,
he would be the regular highly universalized type figure representing mankind.

The fact that the play is supposed to have been written as a
political satire would seem at first to indicate that it should be
placed among the Political Moralities of Class IV. But this
political element is the underlying current of the play, not its
avowed purpose. In technical structure it attaches itself to the
plays of the present class, and the political meaning which the
author probably intended must be supplied by the readers or
spectators. The same is true of the *Satyre of the Thrie Estaites*,
Part I, which also falls in this division.

The play opens with a monologue by Felicite, or Welthfull
Felicite, as he calls himself, that is, happiness resulting from
wealth. He tells what care must be practised in order to obtain
happiness from wealth. Liberte joins him, and the two fall into
a formal debate as to whether they can co-exist. Felicite thinks
that Liberte should be restrained by the "chayne of Continence,"
but Liberte himself is of the opinion that he should be without
restraint. Measure comes in, and is chosen by both as arbiter.
His view of the question is that

> Welthe without Measure wolde bere himselfe to bolde:
> Lyberte without Measure prove a thynge of nought;

[1] It has never been questioned that Skelton intended the play as a political satire, but opinion has varied as to the direct object of the satire. Ten
Brink (*Gesch. des engl. Lit.*, II, 480) simply asserts that Magnyfycence, the
hero, is an allegorical portrait of Henry VIII in his early years of lavish
expenditure. Hooper ("Skelton's Magnyfycence and Cardinal Wolsey,"
Modern Language Notes, XVI, 213) identifies Magnyfycence with Wolsey.
Koelbing (*Zur Characteristik John Skeltons*, Stuttgart, 1904, pp. 32, 151)
thinks that the play had a mildly satirical bearing on Henry, but he admits
nothing more than a very general application. Ramsay (*Skelton's "Magnyfycence,"* pp. cvii-cxxviii) goes into details to show that Magnyfycence is Henry,
and to identify the Vices who plot the ruin of Henry with Wolsey and his
followers.

ergo, Measure is the one that should rule. Felicite assents to this, but Lyberte has decided objections and is brought to a very reluctant assent only by the superior arguments of Measure.

Magnyfycence now appears. Measure offers himself as chief counsellor to Magnyfycence, and his two companions for subordinate positions under him. Magnyfycence places himself under the control of Measure, who now considers his future assured, and makes plans to guide his master with the assistance of Felicite and Lyberte. Lyberte makes a last insistent plea for a free hand, and finally Magnyfycence becomes angry and sends him away to be placed in the school of Measure.

Fansy breaks in rudely, introducing himself as Largesse. He is so impudent that Magnyfycence becomes angry with him; but he escapes dismissal by producing a letter, purporting to be from Sad Cyrcumspeccyon. Magnyfycence is at once mollified, reads the letter, then falls into friendly conversation with Fansy, and concludes by taking him into his service. Before they depart from the palace, Fansy drops a sly hint that, though Measure may do very well for merchants, he is not the sort of companion for a king.

Counterfet Countenaunce comes in to wait for his friend Fansy, and in the meantime explains his place in the scheme of things :

> For Counterfet Countenaunce knowen am I;
> This world is full of my Foly.
> I set not by him a fly
> That can not counterfet a lye,
> Swere, and stare, and byde therby,
> And countenaunce it clenly,
> And defend it manerly.

His long explanation is brought to an end by the reappearance of Fansy with Crafty Conveyaunce, who, having given out his name as Sure Surveyaunce, has been received by the king. Fansy tells of his luck at court, where he is known as Largesse,

and has been made a knight. In the course of the conversation
he lets drop the fact that the letter by which he has won his
way to court was forged by Counterfet Countenaunce. The three
rogues then attempt to hatch some good plan by which to overthrow Measure at court, and are almost in despair until Counterfet Countenaunce remembers his friend Cloked Colusyon,
who will be able to help them. The wished-for friend at this
moment puts in a convenient appearance, disguised as a priest;
and a plan is quickly made for all four to get into the king's
favor, ruin Measure, and set Lyberte free. In order to be well
received it is, of course, necessary that they shall all assume attractive names; so Counterfet Countenaunce and Cloked Colusyon, who have not yet taken that precaution, change their
names respectively to Good Demeynaunce and Sober Sadnesse.

Cloked Colusyon is left to wait while the other three go to
secure a position for him at court, and this interval he employs
in giving a not uncalled-for explanation of his character and
habits :

> Double Delynge and I be one;
> Craftynge and haftynge contryued is by me;
> I can dyssemble, I can bothe laughe and grone;
> Playne Delynge and I can never agre;
> But Dyvysyon, Dyssencyon, Dyrysyon, — these thre
> And I am counterfet of one mynde and thought.
> By the menys of Myschyef to bryng all thynges to nought.

These frank confessions are rudely interrupted by Courtly
Abusyon, a merry rascal who comes in singing, and attired
" after the cowrtly maner." He has all the latest styles in
clothing and manners; and, when Fansy returns to announce
complete success at court, and the freedom of Lyberte, he tells
Courtly Abusyon that there is a place for him also, if he will
change his name to Lusty Pleasure. To complete the list of
office-seekers, Foly, Fansy's brother, appears, leading a mangy
cur, which he presently trades off for a fine hawk that Fansy is

carrying on his wrist, and at the same time exchanges his purse
with an old buckle in it for his brother's purse containing twenty
marks. Foly, in fact, is no fool, as he is quite ready to admit :

> Nay, it is I that foles can make;
> For be he cayser or be he kynge,
> To felowshyp with Foly I can hym brynge.

He arranges for a position at court, and, because he " hathe a
full dry soule," insists on getting charge of the cellar.

Finally Magnyfycence himself appears with Felicite and
Lyberte, who renew their old argument about personal superiority. This time the king settles the dispute differently by
handing Felicite over to Fansy and Lyberte to be controlled.
He has now reached the height of his power, and loudly proclaims that Alexander, Caesar, Charlemagne, and all the other
great rulers were as nothing compared to him.

This is the turning point in his career. He has dismissed
Measure with insults, and has elevated to power all the advisers
who are opposed to Measure. Now, as he amuses himself by
listening to the senseless jargon of Foly, suddenly Fansy bursts
in with a scared face to report that the king's favorites have
made away with Felicite and have brought Adversity to court.
He has hardly delivered his news when Adversity comes in.
Fansy and Foly take to their heels ; and Adversity, after re-
proaching the king bitterly, beats him down, strips him, and
hands him over to Poverte, a diseased wretch, who rebukes him
further, then lays him on a couch and hobbles away to beg.
Lyberte, Crafty Conveyaunce, and Cloked Colusyon come and
exult over the prostrate Magnyfycence, tell him of the wealth
they have gained by despoiling him, then depart.

At last Dyspare approaches the king and recommends suicide.
Myschefe follows with a knife and halter, and seconds Dyspare.
But when the king is about to slay himself they run off, and
Good Hope comes in just in time to snatch away the knife.

He comforts the king, and is joined by Redresse, who sends for Circumspeccyon, in the meantime putting fresh garments on the naked monarch. When Circumspeccyon appears he is anxious to know the cause of the late misfortune, and is told by Magnyfycence that it was a letter from him that caused all the trouble. Then the truth comes out about Fansy's forgery at the beginning of his career. Magnyfycence is now well lectured on the foolishness of trusting himself in the hands of dishonest advisers; and, finally, Perseverance comes in and completes his change of heart.

The Vices accomplishing the downfall of the hero are here more varied than usual. They represent not only the impulses toward evil in man's nature, but also malignant forces from without; that is, the machinations of selfish and scheming companions. This is demanded, of course, for the political application of the lesson. We may divide the Vices, then, into two classes: Lyberte, Fansy, Foly, and Myschefe, representing destructive forces within the mind of the hero; and Counterfet Countenaunce, Crafty Conveyance, Cloked Colusyon, and Courtly Abusyon as malignant forces from without. The Virtues, also, are of two kinds: Measure, Good Hope, Circumspeccyon, and Perseverance, representing forces for good in man's nature; and Felicite (wealth wisely used) and Redresse representing beneficent forces from without. Adversyte, Dyspare, and Poverte are neither Vices nor Virtues, but represent trials sent by God for the schooling of man. They may be called Agents of Retribution.

The allegory, then, must be interpreted thus: A king begins his reign in prosperity. He has abundance of wealth, which he determines to use wisely and in moderation, restraining the extravagant impulses of his nature. But his imagination dwells on the pleasures that his wealth can obtain for him, and soon he persuades himself that these fancies are the dictates of reason, and that restraint in expenditure is to be practised by tradesmen and not by kings. In this he is encouraged by his flattering courtiers,[1] who count on the generous and confiding nature of their king to assist them in pocketing most of his wealth. They deceive him systematically, and lead him from one foolish extravagance to another, until they have obtained all his wealth. Then they desert him suddenly, and the king is left alone in abject poverty. He is in despair and meditates suicide. But hope is not quite dead in his heart. He gets new courage and decides to make a fresh start, profiting by his recent lesson.[2] Discovering that the flatterers of his court have deceived him and have been the cause of much of his extravagance, he is confirmed in the determination to guide his affairs moderately and carefully in the future.

The special satirical application of this Morality to an earthly king suffering from dishonest courtiers is made by the presence of the Vices Counterfet Countenaunce, Crafty Conveyaunce, Cloked Colusyon, and Courtly Abusyon. If these were removed, Magnyfycence would become simply the representative of mankind, striven for by the remaining personifications of the play. But it should be noted that, as in the later Morality by Lyndsay, these special Vices are the ones chiefly responsible for the downfall of the hero, while the regular Vices merely pave the way for their operations.

[1] In the case of such characters as Counterfet Countenaunce and his companions, representing human forces from without acting upon the hero, it is hard to avoid the confusion of personified abstraction and type figure. These figures stand here at first for flattery, dishonest practices, etc., at court; but toward the end of the play, when they abscond after robbing the king, they are nothing but type figures, representing self-seeking and dishonest courtiers. The same sort of characters figures prominently in Lyndsay's *Satyre of the Thrie Estaites*.

[2] In this picture of downfall and despair, followed by redress, the author reverts from his specialized treatment of a king to the common type of Morality where Man is the subject.

Mundus et Infans[1] belongs to the group of biographical plays which conduct the hero from childhood to old age. Like *Nature*, it refrains from specifying that the hero has just been born at the beginning of the play, and concludes before his death. The play has only five characters and is exceedingly simple in construction, — so simple that the audience is called upon to imagine the hero as passing through fourteen years of his life while he makes two short speeches explaining his growth and character. The lesson is of the most elementary and general kind. It instructs mankind to shun the seven deadly sins, follow the dictates of conscience, and persevere in a life of piety.

The play opens with the World seated on his throne, addressing the audience. He explains himself:

> For all the Worlde wyde, I wote well, is my name;
> All rychesse, redely, it renneth in me,
> All pleasure worldely, both myrthe and game.
> My-selfe semely in sale I send with you to be,

and commands them all to follow him. The Chylde[2] enters,

---

[1] Printed 1522. In Manly, Vol. I. See the *Publications of the Modern Language Association of America*, Sept. 1908 (Vol. XXIII, No. 3; New Series, Vol. XVI, No. 3) for an article by H. N. MacCracken, showing by a presentation of direct parallels the relation between *Mundus et Infans* and the earlier poem, *The Mirror of the Periods of Man's Life, or Bids of the Virtues and Vices for the Soul of Man* (placed by Dr. Furnivall at 1430, and by others at a later date).

[2] There is some confusion as to the age of the Chylde at his first appearance. From his opening speech one would surmise that he had just been born:

> Fourty wekes I was frely fedde
> Within my moders wombe;
> Full oft of dethe she was adred
> Whan that I sholde parte her from.
>
> Now into the Worlde she hathe me sent,
> Poore and naked as ye may se;
> I am not worthely wrapped nor went,
> But powerly prycked in poverte (p. 355).

But a minute later when he joins the Worlde and is asked his name, he answers:

> I wote not, syr, withouten blame;
> But ofte tyme my moder, in her game,
> Called me Dalyaunce (p. 355),

" poore and naked." He prays to Christ for grace and laments that he was conceived and born in sin. Then he approaches the Worlde, who performs the characteristic act of clothing him, to rob him of innocence, gives him a suitable name, or rather list of names — Love, Lust, and Lykynge — and sends him off to enjoy himself for seven years. When he returns to the Worlde, the latter changes his name to Manhode, dubs him knight, and charges him to worship above all things the seven kings, Pryde, Envy, Wrathe, Couvetous, Slouthe, Glotony, and Lechery.

The World now retires, leaving Manhode to make short work of the next seven years. The newly dubbed knight rants about the stage and actually succeeds in out-Heroding Herod :

> Every man is a-ferde whan I do on hym stare,
> For all mery medell-erthe maketh mencyon of me ;
>
> Yet all is my hande-werke, both by downe and by dale.
> Bothe the see and the lande and foules that fly ;
> And I were ones moved, I tell you in tale,
> There durst no sterre stere, that stondeth in the sky.

which indicates that he has been born some time before. Later the Worlde gives him a new name, and tells him :

> And also I gyve to the a name
> And clepe the Wanton, in every game,
> Tyl *xiij yere* be come and gone, —
> And then come agayne to me (p. 356).

When the Chylde is next approaching the Worlde he explains to the audience :

> But, syrs, whan I was seven yere of age,
> I was sent to the Worlde to take wage,
> And this *seven yere* I have ben his page
> And kept his commaundment (p. 357).

Then as he approaches the Worlde :

> Hayle, lorde of grete honour !
> This vii yere I have served you in hall and boure
> With all my trewe entent (p. 357).

The obvious conclusion, then, is that the Chylde is seven years old at the beginning of the play. The first seven years of his life are evidently regarded as a negligible period of infancy, or as the commonly specified period of innocence.

These powers, and many others, he has attained by the friendship of the seven kings, the Seven Deadly Sins.

To this mighty personage appears Conscyence, ruminating on
his unpopularity with mankind. The doughty Manhode is at
first inclined to take a high hand with Conscyence, but the
latter's mysterious utterances arouse his curiosity. When he is
accused of not knowing Conscyence he exclaims, " Conscyence!
what the devyll, man, is he ? "

" A techer of the spyrytualete," answers Conscyence.

" Spyrytualyte ! " shouts the astounded Manhode. " What
the devyll may that be ? "

Conscyence proceeds, gently but firmly, to argue Manhode
from his allegiance to the seven kings. Manhode is stubborn,
but he is slowly forced to resign one king after another, till they
come to the seventh, Covetous. Here Manhode puts his foot
down for good and all. He has, under compulsion, resigned six
of his kings, but when it comes to forcing him from Covetous
his teacher is going a bit too far. Conscyence, however, proves
equal to any emergency. He permits Manhode to retain Covetous, and then outlines the duties which yet remain :

> Coveyte ye to sle no man ;
> Ne do no lechery with no woman ;
> Your neyboures good take not be no waye ;
> And all false-wytnesse ye must denaye ;
>
> Neyther ye must not covete no mannes wyfe,
> Nor no good that hym be-lythe, —
> This covetys shall kepe you out of stryfe :
> These ben the commaundments ten.

Conscyence gives him special and repeated warnings against
" folye," which, he says, includes the seven deadly sins. Then,
having brought his pupil to a chastened and submissive frame
of mind, he leaves him to his growth in grace.

Manhode has barely time to give utterance to the virtuous

resolution to hold Conscyence for his king in future when Folye joins him in a jocund frame of mind. Manhode challenges him in rather arrogant style, and Folye insinuates that, among his other accomplishments, he is a "coryous buckler-player." "Wyll thou assaye?" he adds. Manhode reflects that Conscyence would not approve of a brawl, but Folye's taunt that he has a "false herte" overcomes his virtue, and they go at each other. After a stiff bout, in which Manhode seems to have the upper hand, the two sit down to friendly conversation.[1] When Manhode learns Folye's name he suddenly realizes that this must be the person that Conscyence warned him against. But Folye is a plausible rogue and has many tempting schemes on hand, so that Manhode is soon induced to accept him for a servant. He still has some lingering fear of Conscyence; so Folye removes the last traces of this by dubbing him Shame. After the addition of this name Manhode is ready to accompany Folye to his haunts, and the two march off, while Folye explains the significance of this act to the audience:

> *Manh.* Folye, go before and teche me the waye.
> *Folye.* Come after, Shame, I the praye,
> And Conscyence clere ye cast awaye.
> (*Aside*) Lo, syrs, this Folye techeth aye,
> For where Conscyence cometh with his cunnynge,
> Yet Folye full fetely shall make hym blynde:
> Folye before and Shame behynde, —
> Lo, syrs, thus fareth the worlde alwaye.

As they are leaving they encounter Conscyence, but the newly christened Shame brushes him aside impatiently and proceeds on his way. Conscyence laments, and goes to seek Perseveraunce.

---

[1] This victory has no allegorical significance, since Manhode, after getting the better of Folye, immediately becomes reconciled to him. Contrast with this the allegorical duel between Just and Lust in the *Trial of Treasure* (see p. 122, below). Here Just defeats Lust and drives him out; then the allegorical significance of the fight is commented on.

At last Manhode appears, old and broken by vicious living, and going by the name of Age. He bitterly repents his follies, and longs for Death to take him away from his sickness and despair. But Perseveraunce comes to his relief, hails him by his former name of Manhode, and brings him to a state of true contrition for his sins. Then he gives him the last of a long and varied list of names, and as Repentance our human hero concludes the play in hopeful conversation with Perseveraunce.

The characters are all easily placed in relation to Infans, who represents mankind. Mundus, as has already been explained, is one of the three great inimical forces seeking to lure mankind to eternal punishment. Folye is the embodiment of tendencies toward sin in the heart of man. He represents, for the sake of economy in the play, the seven deadly sins.[1] Conscyence and Perseveraunce are internal forces for good.

The interpretation follows easily: Man is born in sin. In early childhood he comes in contact with the world, and practises all the follies regularly indulged in by worldlings. During his youth he sins chiefly by yielding to his lusts and desires for light pleasures; but when he comes to manhood his vices are of a sterner quality and comprise the seven deadly sins. His conscience, however, begins to trouble him. He fights persistently against these misgivings and tries hard to persuade himself that he may retain some of his pet vices and still lead a godly life. But his conscience is inexorable, and he feels impelled to resign all his vices, one by one. He has not yet cultivated the strength of will, however, to persevere in a good life; and when temptation comes to him he yields to it, stills the voice of conscience, and returns to his old sins. After many years, when he is old and broken, he is able again to withdraw from his life of wickedness, and this time with the strength to persevere in virtue to the end.

---

[1] On p. 358, Manhode (Infans grown up) asks Conscyence what he means by "folye." Conscyence, in reply, enumerates the seven deadly sins, and concludes "These seven synnes I call folye."

Of all the Moralities which we shall have to consider Sir David Lyndsay's *Satyre of the Thrie Estaites* [1] is the most intricate and the most difficult to interpret allegorically. This is due to the wide political and national significance of the play. Lyndsay was not content merely to present an allegory to instruct kings in private virtues. The King, or Rex Humanitas, is the hero; but the play, as it goes on, broadens out to a merciless satire on the vices, religious and political, of Scotland, and finally presents a detailed and constructive scheme of reform. Leaving out of account the interludes, which have scarcely any allegorical action, we must consider the two parts of the play as two separate allegories, the first falling in the present class, the second to be considered with the plays of political and religious controversy under Class IV.

Diligence speaks the prologue, giving a general account of the play to follow. Then the hero, Rex Humanitas, appears and humbly announces his good intentions regarding the realm. He is joined presently by the three brothers, Wantonness, Placebo, and Solace, or Sandy Solace, who is drunk. These three good-natured rascals, whom the King addresses familiarly as his servants, are imbued with a common desire to see the King provide himself with a " lustie concubein," according to the approved fashion of the " Romane Kirk." This strikes the King as not being quite in accord with his virtuous resolutions of a moment before, but the three servants argue convincingly that lechery is no sin. A stronger argument is now presented in the appearance of the beautiful Dame Sensualitie, who enters with her two attendants, Hamelines (Familiarity) and Danger (Assumed Coyness). The King sees them, and on the advice of his servants

---

[1] *Ane Pleasant Satyre of the Thrie Estaites in Commendation of Vertew and Vituperatioun of Vyce*, in *The Poetical Works of Sir David Lyndsay*, ed. David Laing, Edinburgh, 1879. The date of the play is uncertain. It was performed before James V at Linlithgow in 1540, and it may have been performed elsewhere at an earlier date.

summons them to his presence. Wantonness leads Sensualitie before the King, who at once falls in love with her beauty and leads her to a private chamber, while his servants retire with Hamelines and Danger.

While they are gone Gude Counsall enters and laments the King's fall from grace. He realizes that disgrace and confusion are in store for anyone who rejects him.

> Finallie, for conclusioun
> Quha haldis me at delusioun
> Sall be brocht to confusioun
>   And this I understand
> For I have made my residence
> With Princes of greit puissance,
> In Ingland, Italie, and France,
>   And monie uther land.
> But, out of Scotland, wa, alace!
> I haf bene fleimit láng tyme space
> That garris our gyders all want grace,
>   And die befoir thair day.

Gude Counsall steps back, and Flatterie enters, " new landit out of France." After an appropriate address to the audience he calls for Falset, who enters and greets him as a brother. They lie down to wait for Dissait, "counsallour to the Merchandmen," and presently he joins them.[1]

Now that their number is complete the three rogues lay their plans to deceive the King and enrich themselves at his expense. The first step necessary for this scheme is that they should change their names, as the King would never receive them with their real titles disclosed. Flatterie dubs himself Devotioun, Falset becomes Sapience, and Dissait takes the name Discretioun. Thus disguised they have no doubts of their ability

---

[1] This trio, Flatterie, Falset, and Dissait are the real Vices of the play. Through Wantonness, Placebo, and Solace the King commits some indiscretions; but they merely wish the King to enjoy himself, and have no desire to compass his destruction, as is the case with the second trio.

to hoodwink the King. Their only fear is that they may be discovered by Correctioun, who can penetrate all disguises.

At this point the King returns from his conference with Sensualitie, summons his servants, who have been disporting themselves with Hamelines and Danger, and they all compare lewd notes on their recent experiences. The three Vices now approach and introduce themselves under their assumed names. The King welcomes them and takes them into his service. Gude Counsall appears, but is driven out by the newly appointed courtiers. The three ladies sing a song, and the King lies down among them.

Dame Veritie now comes in with a New Testament in her hand. The three Vices, not liking her appearance, hurry to inform Spiritualitie.[1] Then Chastitie enters, looking for a lodging, and complains that everywhere in the land she has been denied a home, and even a night's entertainment. She has applied at the nunneries, but the Ladies of Religioun would have nothing to do with her. Now she makes her plea to the three Lords of Spiritualitie, Spiritualitie, Abbot, and Persone, but they advise her to pass on. In despair she applies to Temporalitie,[2] but is again repulsed.

The play is now suspended for the performance of the first interlude, which is a burlesque continuance of the play. Chastitie, still seeking for lodgings, encounters the Sowtar and the Taylour, by whom she is welcomed. They all sit down to drink; but Jennie, the tailor's daughter, spies them and runs to tell her mother. Then the two wives come together, complain bitterly of the matrimonial abstinence of their husbands, and finally drive Chastitie away. After this victory they beat their husbands, start off to prepare a feast for themselves, and then the play is resumed.

---

[1] Spiritualitie represents the spiritual lords.
[2] Temporalitie represents the temporal lords.

Diligence befriends Chastitie by sending Solace to tell the King that a " Ladie fair of face " is seeking entertainment. Solace delivers his message, but the King is at once advised by Sensualitie to banish Chastitie. The King, ready to agree to anything that his mistress shall propose, issues the order for banishment, and poor Chastitie resigns her fruitless quest and suffers herself to be placed in the stocks beside her sister Veritie. The latter comforts her with the news that Divyne Correctioun has just landed in the country and is hastening to relieve their distress.

Correctioun's varlet enters and proclaims the approach of his master ; and at the news Flatterie, Falset, and Dissait are filled with alarm and make plans for escape. Falset steals the King's money box, but gets into a quarrel with Dissait, who beats him and then gets away from his companions with the treasure.

The long-expected advent now takes place. Divyne Correctioun enters and makes a speech on his relations with kings and realms. He is eagerly welcomed by Gude Counsall, who has been lying idle waiting for him ever since the King's fall from grace. They remove Chastitie and Veritie from the stocks, and the four go to the King, who is still sleeping among his minions. Correctioun awakes him, rebukes him sharply, and orders Sensualitie away. But Sensualitie still has friends to shelter her in time of need. She takes Hamelines and Danger with her and repairs to the Lords of the Spirituall Stait, where they are all lovingly received.

The King is now ordered by Correctioun to receive Gude Counsall, Veritie, and Chastitie, and to make " ane perpetuall band " with them, which command he very humbly obeys. He is then instructed to proclaim a parliament, and sends Diligence out on this errand. The stern reformer now censures Wantonness, Placebo, and Solace, but they humbly sue for pardon and crave permission to remain with the King in order to furnish him with innocent amusements, such as music, reading, and dancing. Correctioun admits that "Princes may sumtyme seik solace," and permits the three attendants to remain, with a solemn warning to "do na uther cryme."

The King inquires for his three friends Sapience, Discretioun, and Devotioun ; but Veritie and Chastitie tell him that these are only assumed names, that the real names are Falset, Dissait, and Flatterie, and that their owners have robbed him and fled from the country. The action of this first part of the play ends now with a summons to Parliament by Diligence.

The "Interlude of the Puir Man and the Pardoner" is played in the interval between the first and the second parts of the play. Pauper comes in, meets Diligence, and tells him of his troubles. These consist mainly of robberies on the part of churchmen, who have taken everything he had. Diligence listens to the tale, but goes out without evincing much interest, and Pauper lies down and goes to sleep. The Pardoner — otherwise known as Robert Rome-Raker — enters, followed by the Sowtar and his wife, who are actively engaged in a quarrel. They are anxious for a separation, which the Pardoner grants them on condition that they salute each other in the somewhat undignified fashion specified by him. Then Pauper awakes and breaks into fresh laments over the loss of his cow. The Pardoner offers to repair this loss on receipt of what ready money Pauper may have about him. Pauper pays over his last groat, but when the Pardoner's incantations fail to produce a cow, he grows angry with his deceiver, fights with him, and throws his relics in the water.

This first part, with Rex Humanitas as the human hero to be striven for, presents the normal scheme of the Morality : State of Goodness — Fall from Grace — Life in Sin — Repentance and Pardon. The abstractions are not easy to classify, since many of them are related, not only to the King, but to the land at large.[1] According to the internal evidence of the play, however, they must be divided as follows.

Wantonness, Placebo, and Solace represent desires for pleasure in the heart of the King. They are not essentially Vices, though they at first appear to be so. Toward the close of the action Divyne Correctioun censures them, but they plead for pardon, which is granted them:

> *Solace.* Sir, wee sall mend our conditioun,
> Sa ye give us remissioun,
> Bot, give us leave to sing;
> To dance, to play at chesse, and tabills,
> To reid stories, and mirrie fabils,
> For pleasure of our King.
> *Correctioun.* Sa that ye do na uther cryme,
> Ye sall be pardonit, at this tyme,
> For quhy? as I suppois,
> Princes may sumtyme seik solace,
> With mirth, and lawfull mirrines
> Thair spirits to rejoyis.

These three personifications, then, like Frewyll and Imagynacyon in *Hyckescorner*, represent human qualities neither good nor evil essentially, but good or evil according as they are directed. Sensualitie, on the other hand, is an uncompromising Vice. In the play she is introduced to the King by Wantonness, and represents a vicious quality in human nature (or, more specifically, in the nature of the King) which grows out of a comparatively innocent but unguided desire for pleasure. Hamelines and Danger occupy positions nowhere paralleled in the whole range of English Moralities. They are not to be considered as relating directly to the hero, but only indirectly, as being the attendants of Sensualitie, who *has* direct relations with the hero. They are the personifications of familiarity and

---

[1] In this respect the play differs materially from *Magnyfycence*, where all the personifications, whether representing human qualities or outer forces, are related directly, and only, to the hero.

of assumed diffidence or coyness, the two accompaniments of sensuality.[1] Allegorically, they are quite superfluous here.

The Vices who work the most harm are Flatterie, Falset, and Dissait. They correspond to the Vices, Counterfet Countenaunce, Crafty Conveyaunce, Cloked Colusyon, and Courtly Abusyon in Skelton's *Magnyfycence*, and represent evil forces directed from without upon the hero — the counsels of wicked advisers.

Of the Virtues none can be regarded exclusively as a force operating within the heart of the hero. Gude Counsall, Veritie, and Chastitie may be so regarded in one aspect of their characters. When the Vices, Sensualitie, Hamelines, and Danger, are driven away, Correctioun orders the King to make " ane perpetuall band" with them, and the King humbly complies. But in the main they are presented as forces for good operating in society at large.[2]

Veritie and Chastitie not only apply for the favor of the King, but come into direct relations with other type figures. The Lords of the Spirituall Stait order Veritie to be put in the stocks; and Chastitie, after applying for lodgings all over the country, suffers the same fate.

The other characters are easily disposed of. Divyne Correctioun belongs to the side of the Virtues. He represents the power of God directed upon human affairs. The Spiritual Lords, or Spiritualitie, Abbot, and Persone, are type figures, representing the rulers of the Catholic church, and Temporalitie, is a type figure representing the lords of the realm. (These type figures are of very little importance in the first part of the play.) Diligence is simply the prologue and messenger.

---

[1] Even these three characters are not confined, in their operations, to the hero. Toward the close of the action, when the King repents, they are ordered away, and go to the Lords of the Spirituall Stait, where they are received lovingly.

[2] See quotation on p. 88, above.

After this elaborate division of the characters it will be necessary to give only a very general interpretation of the allegory
(and here, of course, the special application to Scotland must
be ignored). A king of the earth begins his reign with the
honest desire to rule wisely, but his love of enjoyment leads
him to partake unwisely of pleasures which soon degenerate
into habitual sensual indulgence. Then he loses his ambition
to rule wisely, and refuses to listen to good counsel. This gives
an opportunity to flattering and dishonest courtiers to enter into
his service for their own gain ; and, having once been received
at court, they find it easy to persuade the king to turn a deaf
ear to honest advice. This example of dishonesty and sensuality
at court is followed by the influential people of the country, both
temporal and spiritual, and truth and chastity are nowhere practised. But God will not permit this state of things to last long.
He makes himself felt in the heart of the king, who comes to
himself, realizes the wickedness of his life, and determines to
abandon his vices and turn to a life of truth and chastity, retaining only those pleasures which are not sinful. He learns,
finally, that the flatterers in whom he has placed so much confidence are a set of rascals who have robbed him, and, at signs
of his reformation, have fled from the court.[1]

It will be seen that my interpretation of Rex Humanitas as a
king of the earth is, at most points, an unnecessary narrowing
of the character. Except in a few situations he could be regarded
as the typical human hero, like Everyman or Humanum Genus;
but these situations — where, for instance, Rex Humanitas is
the model of viciousness for the rest of the nation to copy from
— make it necessary, for a consistent interpretation of the whole
action, to regard him as a king. In thus departing from the traditional form Lyndsay, like Skelton, simply modified the orthodox
Morality in order to present a daring satire on Court conditions.

[1] Cf. p. 81, note 1, of this work.

Lusty Juventus,[1] like the half-play just discussed, is a Reformation Morality, without being primarily a controversial play.[2] Here the resemblance ceases abruptly. Lyndsay's *Satyre*, in spite of its plainly avowed and strictly maintained moral purpose, is an interesting play, full of eloquent passages and abounding in action ; *Lusty Juventus* is remarkable chiefly for its astonishingly dull exposition of Scripture and its heaping up of Scriptural quotations, with careful reference to book and chapter.

The Prologue announces that the play has been written to show the necessity of controlling the child with a firm hand :

> Give him no liberty in youth, nor his folly excuse,
> Bow down his neck, and help him in good awe,
> Lest he be stubborn : no labor refuse
> To train him in wisdom and teach him God's law,
> For youth is frail and easy to draw
> By grace to goodness, by nature to ill :
> That nature hath engrafted, is hard to kill.

Then Lusty Juventus, or Youth, enters and almost redeems a very tiresome play by singing the beautiful lyric, " In youth is pleasure." He is in high spirits, and is much disappointed at not finding a merry company. In his joyous frame of mind it does not suit him to be alone, and he is just starting off to look up some jovial companions when Good Counsel comes upon him. Youth inquires if he has seen any minstrels. " Sir," says Good Counsel, " I will ask you a question by your favor : what would you with a minstrel do ? " Youth innocently rises to the fly with

> Nothing but have a dance or two,
> To pass the time away in pleasure.

Whereat Good Counsel, having hooked his victim, proceeds to play him with the rod of the Holy Scriptures until the exhausted

[1] Written between 1547 and 1553. The text used is that in Dodsley, Vol. II.
[2] Cf. p. 43, above.

Youth at length comes to the surface with, " Now, in faith, I cry you mercy." Good Counsel instructs him how to live " christianly," and Youth kneels and receives his blessing. Knowledge, or as he prefers to be called, True Knowledge of God's Verity, joins Good Counsel in putting Youth through a complete course of Scriptural erudition, and they retire at last with Youth uttering a solemn promise never to leave his teachers while he lives in the world.

The Devil comes in howling his grief for the loss of Youth, and lamenting that the young people are no longer content to live " in old traditions." [1] He is not prepared, however, to resign Youth without a struggle, and calls in his son Hypocrisy as being the most likely person to help him in this crisis.

Hypocrisy joins his father, proclaiming loudly that he is by occupation a butcher. The Devil greets him almost tearfully. He is in a very downcast frame of mind, and his pessimism contrasts strongly with the sturdiness and cheerful self-reliance of Hypocrisy, who is full of plans to seduce Youth again by means of his old weapons, " holy cardinals, holy popes," and all the other " holy " appliances of his own pet institution. The Devil's cheerfulness is restored. He gives his son a more attractive name, Friendship, and leaves him to carry out his plans.

The disguised Hypocrisy discloses his scheme of seduction in a soliloquy. He will introduce his wicked friend Fellowship to Youth, and present to him, in due course of time, the harlot Abominable Living, whom he will first take the precaution of renaming Unknowen Honesty. By these means he is confident of his power to plunge Youth into a course of carnal living, and thus to bind him securely to his father the Devil.

Youth reappears, and Hypocrisy introduces himself as Friendship. The gullible Youth is glad to see him, but shies at his

---

[1] A fling at the Catholic Church.

companion's first inducements to the life of pleasure. "My intention," he asserts modestly, "is to go hear a preaching." But the wily Hypocrisy beats down his objections one by one, and soon brings him to the point of admitting that he would fain enjoy himself but for the fear of being detected by his teachers. Hypocrisy now throws in his most telling inducement. They will go out, he says, to a feast, and have a pudding. "By the mass," cries the delighted Youth,

> that meat I love above all thing;
> You may draw me about the town with a pudding.

They are joined by Fellowship, a merry rascal who falls in enthusiastically with all their plans. There is just one thing lacking to Youth's felicity, so his companions assure him. He must have a mistress. This appears reasonable enough to Youth; and when they are presently joined by Abominable Living, who is introduced as Unknowen Honesty, he greets her with transports of joy. His affection is returned to such an extent that Hypocrisy and Fellowship become a bit jealous. However, after a little bickering, the whole party sallies forth singing a merry song.[1]

They are no sooner gone than Good Counsel returns in great tribulation, and grieving for the downfall of Youth. While he voices his sorrow Youth reappears, looking for some one to play at dice with him. Good Counsel heaps reproaches upon him, and is at first answered with blustering and defiance. But by a judicious combination of Scriptural quotations Good Counsel finally convicts his erring pupil of sin. Youth lies down

---

[1] If the songs here are original, the author had, at least, a decided lyrical talent. The song at the beginning of the play has been already referred to. The one at this point is only inferior to it in beauty:

> Do not the flowers spring fresh and gay,
> Pleasant and sweet in the month of May?
> And when their time cometh they fade away.
> Report me to you, report me to you.

in utter despair for his sins, but now Good Counsel takes a
different tack, and assures him kindly, "God's mercy doth
exceed thy sin." Youth refuses to be comforted until God's
Merciful Promises comes in and assures him that God will
pardon him, not through his own deserts, but purely through
divine mercy. Youth is overcome with gratitude, renounces his
evil courses forever, and plans to complete his life in humble
service to God.

The least that one could ask in compensation for the dullness
of the play is that the allegory should be unequivocal, but the
author has made no concessions. Hypocrisy and Fellowship, the
two hardest characters to analyze, may stand for evil forces
either within or without the nature of Youth, and Fellowship
may be either an abstraction or a type figure representing boon
companions. I do not feel inclined, on the whole, to regard them
as forces within the hero's nature. Hypocrisy, for instance, is
summoned by the Devil and sent to corrupt Juventus, and he
accomplishes his mission by introducing Juventus to a harlot,
Abominable Living. Thus far it would be easy enough to explain the action by saying that the young man, after his conversion, becomes hypocritical and lives a vile life in secret.
But Hypocrisy introduces Abominable Living to Juventus under
the assumed name of Unknown Honesty, and it would be obviously ridiculous to say that a young man, becoming imbued
with hypocrisy, falls into vile habits in the mistaken belief that
they are honorable. Hypocrisy, then, is best interpreted as
representing a vice practised *by other people*, through which the
young man is deceived and led into a life of sin. Fellowship
can be brought down to two possibilities: he is either the
friendliness in youth's nature, or the representative of youth's
boon companions. Since he is the companion of Hypocrisy,
and aids in the deception by which Juventus is led to take up
with Abominable Living, he is best regarded as representing

boon companions. These two Vices, then, I take to represent the hypocritical and roystering companions of Juventus.[1]

Good Counsel, on the side of the Virtues, is the same sort of character as Hypocrisy the Vice; that is, he represents either religious advice, or the people giving religious advice to Juventus. Knowledge, who blesses Juventus after Good Counsel has given his advice, represents a virtue within the mind of the hero. The other characters are sufficiently obvious to pass without explanation.

The interpretation is as follows: The young man, living a happy and thoughtless life, comes under the influence of religious teaching. He listens to this, acquires a knowledge of God's truth, and begins to lead a better life. But through the false representations of his hypocritical friends and boon companions he is soon decoyed back into a life of sin. After a period he once more encounters the teaching of God's word, but he has now become so hardened that at first he refuses to listen. In the end, however, he is convicted of sin and is plunged in remorse until there comes to him a realization of God's promises of mercy toward repentant sinners, when he is imbued with a fresh determination to persist in a life of virtue.

The Interlude of Youth[2] is one of the few Moralities leaning toward Catholicism. It contains no avowed controversy, but its

[1] Here again it will be seen that, as soon as we interpret characters with abstract names as forces working from without upon the hero, we are compelled to regard them sometimes as type figures. See p. 81, note 1, above.

[2] Dated usually between 1553 and 1558. The text used here is that in Dodsley, Vol. II. The term "Interlude," which is applied to this and many other Moralities, has caused a great deal of discussion; but I am convinced that, in its application to Moralities, it has no special significance whatever, except in such cases as the interludes in the intervals of Lyndsay's *Satyre of the Thrie Estaites*. The New English Dictionary defines the Interlude as "a dramatic or mimic representation, usually of a light or humourous character, such as was commonly introduced between the acts of the long mystery plays or moralities, or exhibited as part of an elaborate entertainment." Ward, I, 108, says: "It [*i.e.*, the term "Interlude"] seems to have been applied to plays performed by

attitude and sympathies are on the Catholic side. It is, on the whole, remarkably well constructed for a Morality. The speeches are short and vivid, and no time is wasted on long-winded moralizings. Youth himself is far in advance of the ordinary puppet hero. He has a real sense of humor, and this combines with his breezy vigor and self-assertion to make him a very attractive and really human figure. In situation this play has a good deal in common with *Lusty Juventus*. The hero — the typical young man — is the same in both, and in both cases he comes on the stage exulting in the gaiety and freedom of youth.

There is no prologue to this play. Charity appears first and simply gives an explanation of his character, laying heavy stress on his importance to Man. Then Youth enters with a rush, rejoicing in his strength and happiness:

> Aback, fellows, and give me room,
> Or I shall make you to avoid soon!
> I am goodly of person;
> I am peerless wherever I come.
> My name is Youth, I tell thee,
> I flourish as the vine tree:
> Who may be likened unto me,
> In my youth and jollity?

professional actors from the time of Edward IV onwards. Its origin is doubtless to be found in the fact that such plays were occasionally performed in the intervals of banquets and entertainments, which of course would have been out of the question in the case of religious plays proper." Chambers, II, 181 ff., recognizing the wide application of the term to almost every species of play from the fourteenth century on, is not satisfied with the existing definitions. He says (p. 183): "I am inclined myself to think that the force of *inter* in the combination has been misunderstood, and that an *interludium* is not a *ludus* in the intervals of something else, but a *ludus* carried on between (*inter*) two or more performers; in fact, a *ludus* in dialogue. The term would then apply primarily to any kind of dramatic performance whatever."

This last definition has the appearance of being rather far-fetched. It seems to me more reasonable to suppose that the term was first used in the ordinary signification of entertainment in the intervals of something else, but came to be applied loosely and indiscriminately to any kind of dramatic performance.

My hair is royal and brushed thick;
My body pliant as a hazel-stick;
Mine arms be both big and strong,
My fingers be both fair and long;
My chest big as a tun,
My legs be full light for to run,
To hop and dance, and make merry.
By the mass, I reck not a cherry,
    Whatsoever I do!
I am the heir of all my father's land,
And it is come into my hand:
    I care for no more.

Charity at once realizes that here is a fitting object for his arguments, and approaches Youth with the suggestion that he would be better occupied asking God's mercy than praising his body. Youth flies into a rage at this interference with his natural rights, and requests Charity in unequivocal terms to attend to his own affairs. But Charity is not an easy person to get rid of. He appeals to Youth with every argument at his command, reminds him of the approach of old age and the loss of his strength, holds forth the hope of heavenly bliss, and quotes Scripture, but all in vain. Youth repels every advance with insults and threats, and at last Charity is brought to realize that he can never gain his point without the aid of his brother Humility. So he starts off to seek his brother, and is sped on his way by the incorrigible Youth with:

Yea, marry, sir, I pray you of that;
Methink it were a good sight of your back;
I would see your heels hither,
And your brother and you together
    Fettered fine fast!
I-wis, and I had the key,
Ye should sing well-away
Ere I let you loose!

Riot now appears and is accorded a very different reception. He and Youth are evidently on terms of intimate friendship, and their conversation is that of a pair of boon companions, not at all like the usual contact of Vice with human figure, where the latter is the innocent and confiding dupe of his clever tempter. Youth here is quite a match for Riot in repartee and needs no urging toward the life of sin; so, instead of the usual temptation scene, we get a recital of Riot's madcap adventures in the city, with expressions of curiosity mingled with chaffing on the part of Youth. Riot tells how he was put in Newgate for pocketing a man's purse, and then how the Mayor of London sent for him "for to preach at Tyburn." "By our Lady!" says Youth,

> he did promote thee,
> To make thee preach at the gallow-tree!
> But, sir, how didst thou 'scape?
>   *Riot.* Verily, sir, the rope brake,
> And so I fell to the ground,
> And ran away, safe and sound:
> By the way I met with a courtier's lad,
> And twenty nobles of gold in his purse he had:
> I took the lad on the ear,
> Beside his horse I felled him there:
> I took his purse in my hand,
> And twenty nobles therein I fand.
>   Lord, how I was merry!

And so the conversation goes on, as if a pair of Vices had come together to compare notes; for it is almost unnecessary to add that when two Vices meet they nearly always assume the tone of a couple of dishonest rascals fresh from the performance of crime.

Riot at last suggests that they go along to the tavern for a surfeit of wine and a kiss from a pretty wench; but there is some business to be settled first. Youth, full of importance from the acquisition of his father's estate, wishes a servant to be in constant attendance upon him, and Riot assures him that he can procure "a servant of price," Master Pride. Pride, accordingly, is brought in and welcomed by Youth, whom he at once proceeds to instruct in the proper manner of deportment. He is to consider himself better than anyone else, be arrogant to the poor, and wear gay clothes. Youth, for the first time, adopts a tone of grateful humility :

> Sir, I thank thee, by the rood,
> For thy counsel that is so good;
> And I commit me even now
> Under the teaching of Riot and you.

Pride, thus encouraged, advises Youth to get a wife, but here Riot breaks in with violent objections. Let Youth have a mistress by all means, he says, but under no condition a wife :

> The devil said he had liever burn all his life
> Than once for to take a wife.

But Pride has a sister, Lechery, and Riot suggests that she would be a suitable leman for Youth. Pride is agreed and departs for his sister, with whom he presently returns. Youth is delighted with his new acquisition, and is now impatient to depart for the tavern for fear Charity may return and make things unpleasant for them. Just as the company is leaving, Youth's fears are realized. Charity does appear and requests a word with Youth, but the others turn upon him violently in spite of Youth's indecisive

> Yet, sirs, let this cease,
> And let us talk of goodness.[1]

Riot hurries out, returns with an appliance which is referred to once as " a pair of rings " and again as " a good chain," and they tie Charity up[2] and sally forth on their long-deferred trip to the tavern.

---

[1] This apparent wavering on the part of Youth is very curious. It is only momentary, no notice is taken of it, and the next time Youth speaks he is in full sympathy with Charity's tormentors.

[2] Compare the scene in *Hyckescorner*, where the Vices put Pity in the stocks. See page 41, above.

Charity, considering the provocation, shows great self-restraint in the short speech in which he laments the foolishness of Man to turn from good to evil. Humility soon appears and frees him from his bonds. The two brothers have barely time to exchange assurances of loyalty in the fight for Youth when the object of their solicitude returns, more arrogant than ever, and still accompanied by Riot and Pride. The teachings of the latter have fallen upon fertile soil, for Youth now loudly asserts:

> By right I am king eternal;
> Neither duke ne lord, baron ne knight,
> That may be likened unto me.
> They be subdued to me by right,
> As servants to their masters should be.

Charity and Humility, nothing daunted, settle down to the apparently hopeless task of converting him. Youth at first answers them with high disdain, and reiterates his determination to continue with Riot and Pride, who back him up stoutly, abuse their opponents, and hold out to Youth the prospect of some day becoming emperor if he retains them in his service. At last Charity happens on an argument that interests Youth. He tells him that God set him free when he was "bond." Youth is at once curious to know how that may be, since he "was never bond unto none in England." Then Charity explains the Redemption, and Youth immediately offers to change his ways and be ruled by Charity and Humility if they will tell him how to save his soul. They tell him that he must ask God's mercy and forsake Pride and Riot. These directions Youth proceeds to follow, and his old attendants leave him in sorrow and anger. He is instructed in his new way of life, and, after a short prayer by Humility, the play ends.

The scheme here is the simplest to be found in the whole range of English Moralities. It presents only two stages, State of Wickedness and Final Conversion. The plot is much less complicated than that of *Lusty Juventus*. All the characters, both virtuous and vicious, are to be interpreted solely as forces struggling for supremacy in the heart of the hero. On the one side are pride, lust, and all the riotous feelings of youth; on the other, the leanings of youth — at first almost imperceptible, but steadily growing in intensity — toward meekness and charity. The interpretation may be thus outlined : The young man exults in his health and strength, and scorns the idea of practising virtue. To enjoy the pleasures of the world and to satisfy the lusts of his flesh are for him the great objects of life. His soul will have to be chastened by humility before he can leave off his riotous pleasures and practise Christian charity. At times, in the midst of his pleasures, he feels the faint stirring of virtue in his heart, but refuses to give it expression. When he becomes older, however, and more thoughtful, his heart is humbled. He turns away from his worldly pleasures and devotes himself to a life of charity.

Impatient Poverty,[1] the next play on the list, differs from any play hitherto discussed in having a subplot. Impatient Poverty himself is the hero of the main action, and Abundance is the chief figure in the subplot. The experiment — if it were one — cannot be regarded as successful. In this particular class of Moralities the success depends largely on having the attention fastened from beginning to end upon one central figure who is steadily and earnestly striven for by two opposing factions, the good and the evil.

Peace does the work of a prologue, explaining that Man, to be prosperous and happy, must befriend him and avoid that false wretch, Envy. He is suddenly joined by Envy, who has caught the drift of his remarks, and who now challenges him fiercely to prove that peace is better than war. What would the armorers

---

[1] Printed in 1560. The text used is that in "*Lost*" *Tudor Plays*, edited by John S. Farmer.

and soldiers do without war ? he demands. And the surgeons, who make their living by mending broken pates ?

> And what sayest thou by men of law?
> Their living were not worth a straw
> And every man should live in peace!

Peace, having a complacent realization that he is right any-how, does not trouble himself much with refuting Envy's argu-ments, but contents himself with assuring him that he is wrong, and a lewd fellow into the bargain. However, he is capable of defending his position when real need comes, as he proves when Envy complicates the argument with the question,

> If your wife made you cuckold, you being present,
> What would you do?

Peace seems to fall readily into the trap. " Give her such pun-ishment," he replies calmly, " as longeth thereto."

> *Envy.* A false, flattering whoreson, lo!
> Now thou sayest against thine own declaration:
> If thou fight where is then peace become?
> *Peace.* I break not peace with doing due correction;
> For correction should be done charitably —
> Irascemini et nolite peccare.

The couple then take leave of each other, breathing threatenings and slaughter.

Peace remains and is soon joined by Impatient Poverty, who enters in a great fume because " a knave would have rested " him. "I owe him but forty pence," he adds irascibly. "He shall abide, by God's dear blest!" Peace rebukes him for his dis-honest attitude, and is answered with curses and ridicule; but his arguments in favor of peace and charity of conduct gradually awaken the interest of Impatient Poverty, who ends by placing himself under the instruction of Peace, with a solemn promise to live a sober Christian life. Thereupon Peace gives him new

vesture to symbolize his change of heart, changes his name to
Prosperity, and gives him a final warning against the temptations
that will come to him, bidding him in particular beware of Envy.
Then the two go out together.

Abundance and Conscience come in conversing. Abundance
boasts loudly of his wealth and explains his methods of gaining
it, which are dishonest in the extreme. Conscience rebukes him
severely for his dishonesty, to his great surprise. He is inclined
at first to regard Conscience as a fool for bringing up such far-
fetched objections to what he regards as regular methods of
business, but at length is brought to see the error of his ways.
" What remedy ? " he inquires.

> *Cons.* To make restitution.
> *Abun.* What call ye restitution?
> *Cons.* Restore such goods as ye have gotten
> Wrongfully, by oppression.
> *Abun.* Then shall I have little in my possession :
> I will make God amends another way.
> I will fast and I will pray,
> And I will give alms every day.
> That I have done amiss, I am sorry, therefore.

But this will not satisfy Conscience ; and Abundance, after receiving a solemn warning to profit by the example of King
Ahab, leaves unconverted.

Envy comes running in laughing, and out of breath with
haste to deliver himself of a merry and ribald tale. He finds a
rather cold audience in Conscience, whose sole response to these
efforts to entertain him is,

> Good fellow, thou art to blame
> Such words to have: no good thou can.

Envy at once sees that he has made a mistake and skillfully
changes his tack. He only thought to make things pleasant for
Conscience, he explains. His name is Charity. He is much

neglected by both Spirituality and Temporality, and is in constant danger of becoming an outcast. "This is to me a strange case," says Conscience. "What hear ye by Conscience?" Then the pinchbeck Charity admits that things are looking very black for Conscience. The wisest course for him would be to flee from the country and thus avoid being burned at Tyburn. Then Conscience hurries out with great haste, and in much distress. Envy dances about in high glee at the success of his trick.

Prosperity enters with a prayer on his lips and is welcomed as Impatient Poverty by Envy, who is again thrown suddenly on his resources when he is piously assured that Impatient Poverty is a discarded name. He begs Prosperity's pardon, and explains that he used the old name merely for the convenience of the audience, who are used to it. But Prosperity is in a very self-sufficient mood now. He shakes Envy off in spite of the latter's protestations that his name is Charity, and starts to go out, when the resourceful Envy requests him, as a parting favor, to keep his bag containing "three hundred pound" of gold while he journeys to Jerusalem. Prosperity now recognizes him as his "cousin Charity," and begs his pardon. Envy follows up this advantage by telling Prosperity that he must have a greater retinue of servants, and go in more for pleasure. Prosperity agrees, and retires to act upon this advice.

Envy is in high feather at his success, and confides to the audience that his chief purpose is to bring Prosperity to evil condition. Then his friend Misrule joins him, fresh from the stews, and trolling out a macaronic song. The two rogues plan to combine against Prosperity.

Their dupe returns at this point, and Envy introduces Misrule, under the name of Mirth, as a fitting man for a servant to Prosperity. The latter accepts him gladly; and, thus encouraged, the two tempters advise him to provide himself with a wench

and other appurtenances of a jovial life. Prosperity remembers
that Peace has forbidden this, but when his two friends abuse
Peace he gives in. " By my troth ! " he admits,

> I may say to thee
> Sith I to him did assent
> Had I never merry day ;
> But lived in fear and dread alway,
> Nothing to mine intent.
> Another while I will me sport,
> Sing and dance, to my comfort.

The Vices then remove from him the vestures of Peace, and
they all prepare to go out and enjoy themselves. As they are
leaving, Peace encounters Prosperity and rebukes him, but the
latter orders him away, and the Vices finally drive him out.
Then they tell Prosperity of one Colhazard, a great dice-player,
and Prosperity boasts that he will play with him " as long as an
hundred pound will last."

In the next scene Misrule enters exulting in the ruin of
Prosperity. Envy joins him, and the two exchange congratulations. Then Colhazard follows with the money which he has
fleeced from Prosperity, but refuses to share it with his confederates. The upshot of this difference in point of view is that
the three leave the stage fighting savagely over the bag of coin.

Prosperity returns, poorly clad, and sorely lamenting his folly.
His name has been changed to Poverty to suit his new condition.
Envy and Misrule come in for a few minutes to exult over him ;
then retire, in spite of Poverty's earnest entreaties to them to
stay. Poverty urges the audience to learn a lesson by his
blunders ; then the Sumner comes in and arrests him for debt.

A short scene follows in which Abundance is boasting that
he keeps a wench in his chamber. The Sumner arrives to
arrest him for this offense, but is at once mollified by a bribe,
and instructs Abundance how to buy himself off from justice.

Finally, as Poverty is in the depths of misfortune and despair, and is doing "penance" for his debt, Peace again joins him and learns of his downfall. Poverty tells him how Abundance has sinned and yet has gone scot-free in consideration of a bribe, whereat the Sumner is rebuked and sent out by Peace. Poverty is deeply humbled and begs for comfort; and Peace, who considers him well punished, reclothes him in his own vesture, gives him careful instructions and warnings for his future life, and changes his name back to Prosperity. The two end the play with prayers for the Queen and her realm.

The hero of the main action, variously entitled Impatient Poverty, Prosperity, and Poverty, is, like Magnyfycence and several other Morality heroes, a type figure called by an abstract name. He does not typify a class, but mankind in general; and, as his names clearly indicate, he is treated entirely from the point of view of worldly prosperity. Peace on the one hand, and Envy and Misrule on the other, represent qualities within the heart of man, warring against each other. Colhazard is an unimportant character, and it is immaterial whether we regard him as a gambler or as the vice of gambling. On the whole I prefer to take the latter view. In the subplot Abundance is also a type figure—the unscrupulous man of wealth, who refuses to listen to the voice of Conscience.

As to the moral, Peace gives us a not uncalled-for explanation (p. 313):

> The devil, the world, and the flesh, these three in special,
> Which setteth division between the soul and the body;
> In like wise envy setteth debate between party and party.
> I speak for the cause; daily ye may see
> How that by envy and malice many be destroyed,
> Which if they had lived in peace with patient humility,
> Riches and prosperity with them had been employed.

So much for the moral animating the action. A step-by-step interpretation is still necessary. Man, living in a state of poverty, is much irritated at his condition until he learns that the surest way to prosperity is to lead a peaceful Christian life. This change in his nature is followed by worldly comfort and happiness. But he is not long satisfied with the good that he has, and becomes envious of the riches of other people. Thus he is led to enter into strife with his fellow-men and finally attempts to increase his wealth easily by gambling. He is properly rewarded for this by being fleeced of all his riches and is reduced to abject poverty, when he realizes that his prosperity is dependent on his living quietly and at peace with everybody. Acting upon this discovery he soon repairs his broken fortunes, and, profiting by his late experience, he determines to keep out of strife in the future.

The Life and Repentance of Marie Magdalene,[1] by Lewis Wager, is, strictly speaking, a Miracle-Morality. The Miracle element, to be sure, is kept pretty consistently in the background; but, even so, the play, from the allegorical point of view, is considerably hampered by its presence. In the first place, the human hero (or, in this case, heroine) to be striven for is a specific character derived from Scripture and saint's legend,[2] and in the present play there is no attempt to broaden her significance; whereas in the earlier play on the same subject it is explicitly stated that " she xall byn abyll to dystroye helle "[3] unless she is corrupted to a life of sin. In the second place, since the conversion of Marie is accomplished mainly by a miracle on the part of Christ, there is a complete absence of Virtues from the main action of the play. This in itself would hardly constitute a fault in the eyes of a carnal-minded audience; but the author, if compelled by the exigencies of his subject to banish Virtues from the main action, was not minded to let

---

[1] Edited by Frederic Ives Carpenter, Chicago, 1904. Carpenter conjectures (Introduction, p. xv) that the play was probably printed about 1550, though not entered in the Stationers' Register till 1556.

[2] See p. 37, note 2, above.

[3] See p. 35, note 3, above.

his audience suffer for any lack of virtuous admonishment. The Vices grow almost virtuous in their anxiety to have the audience see through their perfidy. Infidelitie, the chief Vice, on his first appearance issues an earnest warning to the audience:

> Beware of me, Infidelity!
> Like as Faith is the root of all goodnesse,
> So am I the head of all iniquitie,
> The well and spryng of all wickednesse![1]

This serious tone is so often adopted by Infidelitie that he almost seems, at times, to occupy the paradoxical position of a personified vice striving to overthrow wickedness; whereas the fact is that the author is constitutionally unable to refrain from moral didacticism, and if there is no personified virtue on the stage to be made the vehicle of this moralizing he will use any character that does happen to be there, even if that character is the chief Vice of the play.

The prologue takes at first the form of a sermon on the text,

> Nulla tam modesta felicitas est
> Quae malignantis dentes vitare possit,

then announces the subject to be treated in the play, and concludes with this curious apology for employing the allegorical method:

> We desire no man in this poynt to be offended,
> In that vertues with vice we shall here introduce;
> For in men and women they have depended:
> And therefore figuratively to speak, it is the use.
> I trust that all wise men will accept our excuse.

Next Infidelitie, the chief Vice, appears and gives a prolonged account of himself to the audience. He announces his determination to overthrow the plans of Christ, who, he hears, has

[1] P. 7 (ll. 31–35). See the whole of this speech; also, for further examples of this virtuous tone on the part of a Vice, see p. 10 (ll. 120, etc.) and p. 12 (ll. 174, etc.).

lately come to the land. He hopes to accomplish his work easily
by the aid of his seven helpers, the Seven Deadly Sins :

> Mary, syr, yet I convey my matters cleane !
> Like as I have a visour of vertue,
> So my impes, whiche vnto my person do leane,
> The visour of honestie doth endue ;
> As these : Pride I vsed to call cleanlynesse ;
> Enuie I colour with the face of prudence ;
> Wrathe putteth on the coate of manlynesse ;
> Couetise is profite in every man's sentence ;
> Slouthe or idlenesse I painte out with quiete ;
> Gluttonie or excesse I name honest chere ;
> Lechery, vsed for many men's diete,
> I set on with the face of love, both farre and nere.[1]

As Infidelitie ceases speaking Marie Magdalene enters,
"triflyng with her garmentes" and beshrewing the tailors for
the "bungarly" work they have done on her new clothes.
Infidelity is all sympathy at once, but his condolences are
received with scorn :

> What haue you to do? Holde your bablyng tong.
> Haue you any thyng to doe with the same?

But when Infidelitie makes up his mind to be sympathetic he
is not lightly to be turned from his purpose. He returns bravely
to the charge, flatters Mary in unmeasured terms, and soon
worms himself into her confidence to such an extent that she
requests him to be her chief adviser in all matters pertaining to
the guidance of her life.

He tells her that, since she has inherited riches from her
parents, and has the castle of Magdalene at her command,[2] she

---

[1] These changes of name indicate, when interpreted, that man does not
embrace sins as sins, but under the delusion that they are virtues or legitimate
pleasures.

[2] The author, for the most part, confines himself strictly to the biblical
story, and it is only in one or two references to Marie's parental training and
riches, at the beginning of the play, that we find any influence from the saint's
legend. See Carpenter, Introduction, p. xxxii.

must "make good chere." This advice accords with Mary's desires, and she goes out to array herself in finer garments.

Infidelitie is now joined by Pride of Lyfe, Cupiditie, and Carnall Concupiscence. After the greetings Infidelitie tells them of his success with Mary. They all remember her, and boast of the desires they have already kindled in her heart. Her fall has not yet been accomplished, but her feelings are already tending downward. As usual the Vices decide to change their names in order to be admitted to the friendship of their intended victim. Pride is to be called Nobilitie or Honour, Cupiditie is given the name Utilitie, and Carnall Concupiscence becomes Pleasure. Infidelitie has several names available for use at different times, but he selects Prudence as the one most likely to appeal to Mary and accomplish her downfall.

Mary returns complaining about the inattention of her servants. Infidelitie, alias Prudence, tells her his name, which he has omitted to mention before, and introduces his friends. Mary is greatly attracted to them all, and shows her pleasure at the meeting by kissing the company all round several times. This friendly intercourse Infidelitie is willing to prolong indefinitely, but Pride breaks in impatiently, "Leve kissyng, and treate we of matters more ernest." So they settle down to business, and Mary is carefully instructed by her friends in the best methods of setting off her personal beauty in order to win the love of men. Finally, after a song, the three minor Vices depart, and Mary with Infidelitie sets off for Jerusalem, where a banquet is to be prepared for her.

Simon the Pharisee comes in with Malicious Judgement. The two are making plans to compass the ruin of Christ, and finally Simon agrees to invite their intended victim to a feast at his house, where he hopes to entrap him into saying something contrary to the laws. He sets out to look for Christ, and Infidelitie enters with the joyous news that Mary's downfall has

been accomplished. But Malicious Judgement has other interests at stake, and cannot take much interest in this matter for the
present. After inviting Infidelitie to join them at Simon's feast
he goes about his business, " seekyng for the same Christ both
farre and nere."

Mary reappears and talks in a matter-of-fact way to Infidelitie
about her amours. Suddenly they espy some one coming toward
them with tables of stone in his hand. They stand aside to
listen, and the newcomer approaches and proclaims himself to
be the Lawe of God. He explains how the curse of God must
follow sin ; and Mary, listening, is seized with remorse. She
cries out, lamenting her past sin, but the Lawe has little consolation to offer. " Thy heart," he tells her,

> hath great occasion to blede,
> For many lustes and dedes hath defiled thy conscience.

Then, to crown Mary's remorse, Knowledge of Sinne follows
to assure her :

> I am evermore before the conscience sight,
> Shewyng before hym his condemnation,
> So that by the dedes of the law, or by his own might,
> He cannot attaine vnto saluation.

Infidelitie makes frantic efforts to draw Mary away, but she
is so filled with horror at her abasement that she can take no
notice of him. The two worthies, however, are so unyielding in
their condemnation that Mary cries out against the severity
of God's justice ; and Infidelitie, commending her heartily for
this view of the situation, again bids her to follow him and make
merry while she may, since she sees " no remedy but utter damnation." Mary would like to follow this advice, but she realizes
that she can never forget the horrible appearance of Knowledge
of Sinne. At this Lawe relents somewhat and tells her that if
she can believe in Christ he will forgive her.

Mary is again left alone with Infidelitie, who urges her to forget her late experience and enjoy life again. But she has entirely lost her zest for pleasure, and is in a very irresolute state of mind, when Christ enters announcing that his mission is not to judge the world but to preach forgiveness and pardon. Infidelitie starts to heap abuse on him, but is sternly ordered to " avoide out of this woman . . . with the vii divels which have her possessed." As Infidelitie disappears Mary falls to the earth, there is a loud roaring of devils behind the scenes, and then Christ bids her arise. Faith and Repentance enter, and Christ presents them to Mary. She is given directions for her new life, and then departs with Faith and Repentance, whom Christ sends to bear her company.

The play, to all intents and purposes, ends here ; but there are several scenes coming after, which continue the Scriptural narrative. Simon the Pharisee and Malicious Judgement come and bid Christ to dinner. Malicious Judgement takes Infidelitie along to help in their plans. Then the dinner takes place, Mary comes in, washes the feet of Christ, and is forgiven her sins. During the dinner a long conversation is carried on, in which Simon, Malicious Judgement, and Infidelitie attempt to entrap Christ into a statement that will lay him open to the law. And, finally, in a brief closing scene Justification and Love bestow their comfort and advice upon the repentant Mary.

The action presents the usual scheme of State of Innocence — Fall from Grace — Life in Sin — Repentance and Conversion. At first glance it seems that Mary is a sinful person at the beginning of the play ; but this is not so. She merely exhibits possibilities ; and though the Vices ultimately find her an easy victim, they have as yet entered into no friendly relations with her.

There is no difficulty in assigning the characters to their places. Mary, the person to be striven for, is, of course, an individual, and there is no attempt to enlarge her into a type of the human race. The play, therefore, is not a pure Morality, but a compound of Miracle and Morality, and the reason for discussing it here is that it is not a play with allegorical features, but primarily a Morality, though added to, and hampered by, the slight thread of Scriptural narrative. The Vices, Infidelitie, Pride of Life, Cupiditie, and Carnall Concupiscence, when successful have their abode within the heart of the heroine, as we are carefully informed when Pride of Life outlines to Infidelitie the campaign of vice :

> If thou be once rooted within the hart,
> Then maist thou make an entrance by thy craft and art,
> So that we may come into hir at pleasure,
> Filling hir with wickednesse beyond all measure ! [1]

Malicious Judgement, also belonging to the Vice faction, is an outside force, operating in society at large. Among the Virtues, Faith, Repentance, and Love are forces operating within the heart, and Justification is a power from without. They have scarcely any part in the action, merely coming to the relief of Mary after she has been pardoned by Christ. The Lawe and Knowledge of Sinne are, strictly speaking, neither Virtues nor Vices, but Agents of Retribution, though the Lawe comes near taking the part of a Virtue. The latter represents a power acting from without, while Knowledge represents a force springing up in the heart. Christ and Simon are, of course, individuals.

In the interpretation I shall leave the Bible story out of account and confine myself to the allegorical aspect of the play. Infidelity, having sprung up in the heart, soon gives rise to the most wicked feelings and desires, — pride, greed, and lust.

---

[1] P. 16 (ll. 287–291). Such language as this, referring to a literal occupation of the heart by vice, is, of course, a serious flaw in the allegory. There is, however, an excuse for it here in the fact that later Christ literally casts the seven devils out of Mary. It is another example of the way in which the allegory is hampered by the Miracle element.

The sinner continues his life of wickedness until he hears or reads the commandments of God, when a full knowledge comes to him of the hideousness of his past sin. He is in despair until he turns to Christ, who alone has power to relieve and forgive him. Then, with his repentance, his heart is imbued with faith and love, and he is justified in the sight of God.

In the Morality of *Albion, Knight*[1] we are forced to make conjectures as to a great deal of the action, since the beginning and the end of the manuscript have disappeared. Fortunately, the remaining fragment gives enough to warrant us in making pretty confident generalizations on the play as a whole. That a rigid economy of actors was practised the following list of *dramatis personae* will show :

Albion, Knight			Principality	
Justice	} actually		Peace	
Injury	} appear		Maintenance	} are mentioned
Division			Rest	} in text
			Old Debate	
			Double Device	
			Dame Plenty	

That is, the author could not introduce all the figures that his scheme called for, but was compelled to limit his list of *dramatis personae* to the powers of a small company of four actors.

When our fragment takes up the play, Injury and Justice are engaged in an argument. Injury is exerting himself to make Justice and Albion believe that he is Manhood, and Justice is rather suspicious of his honesty. But Albion, who is apparently of a trustful disposition, shows great anxiety that they should all be friends ; so Justice, still a little doubtful, consents at last to join hands with the supposed Manhood. After the reconciliation Albion and Justice go out, and Injury then explains his true character to the audience.

[1] *Six Anonymous Plays*, edited by John Farmer. The play was acted between 1560 and 1565.

Division appears and greets his friend and co-worker Injury. They exchange a few passes of coarse wit, in the usual manner of Vices, then fall to making plans for corrupting Albion.

> *Injury.* This Justice is a fellow of a far cast,
> And driveth such drifts to rule at the last:
> And Peace is his brother, of one degree,
> Which hath a fair daughter that is called Plenty:
> And Albion as long as Rest him treats,
> He loveth fair flesh of all meats:
> And it is a common saying that Justice, Peace and he
> Will conclude a marriage with fair Dame Plenty.
> And then will Albion, that old sot,
> With Rest and Peace, so on her dote
> That then she, by her and her friends,
> Shall sail in storms at all winds.

It is the object of Injury and Division to prevent this union from taking place, and Injury makes the last speech of the fragment:

> Thou shalt teach him a wrong cross row:
> And tell him best it is, after thine advice,
> With mirth and prodigality him to exercise:
> And take of his own good while he may,
> Lest all at last be bribed away.

Thus, though but a small part of the play is left, we can form fairly safe conjectures as to what the completed action is likely to have been, from the careful and elaborate plans laid down by the Vices for their campaign. We can feel quite certain that Albion was deceived and corrupted by the Vices, and almost equally sure that he was finally brought to his senses by Justice and led to a triumphant and permanent union with the " fair Dame Plenty."

It may easily be seen that the play has strong political tendencies.[1] For this reason it is usually referred to as a controversial

---

[1] It [*i.e.*, *Albion, Knight*] turns chiefly on the want of concord between the lords spiritual and the lords temporal, and must date, I think, soon after Elizabeth's accession. — Fleay, p. 66.

Morality; but the real basis for classification — technical structure — decides its place as being in the present class.

The only characters that can safely be discussed are the four that appear in person as actors. Albion, Knight, in the controversial aspect of the play, probably represents England,[1] but this is reading a secondary signification between the lines. As the play stands he is the regular highly universalized type of hero, the representative of mankind to be striven for. He has evidently begun in a state of goodness, since at the beginning of the fragment (which is manifestly almost the beginning of the action) he is on friendly terms with Justice, the Virtue or representative of goodness in the play. Justice is to be regarded here solely as an internal force, — the sense of justice in the heart of man. Injury, the chief Vice, also represents a power within the heart. When he is striving to win the favor of Albion he poses as Manhood, which is the regular device of the Deadly Sin, Wrath; so Injury is simply another name for Wrath. Division is practically the same sort of character, but he may be slightly differentiated as representing a tendency in the heart of Man to create division or discord.

The fragment, then, being interpreted, presents to us Man at peace, with a desire to act justly toward his fellow-men.[2] His sense of justice, however, becomes subordinated to the violent elements in his nature. In the mistaken belief that he is merely

[1] In this and the other plays with controversial tendencies outside of Class IV, the controversial element is merely incidental to the play. It may be expressed in the dialogue or, as in the present case, it may be a mere underlying element. But never except in the plays grouped in Class IV is it made the basis of the play; and, except in the latter plays, it might be removed without seriously affecting the action.

[2] The fact that the human hero in these plays is universalized into a type of the whole human race does not preclude the idea of fellow-mortals, though this idea is usually kept in the background. In the *Castle of Perseverance*, Humanum Genus is instructed how to act toward his fellow-men, and the same idea is introduced in several of the Moralities.

asserting his manhood he allows himself to inflict injuries upon his neighbors. The fragment carries us no further, but we can readily forecast the degradation of man into a creature of discords and strife, and his final awakening to a real sense of justice, with a determination to live forever in peace. Though this last is pure conjecture, we have abundant warrant for it from our knowledge of other plays of the same type.

The Trial of Treasure [1] differs in one important respect from any other play of its class. The human hero, Just (*i.e.*, the just man), leads an upright life from beginning to end. Though he is repeatedly assailed by Vices, he never once swerves from the paths of righteousness. This may add to our respect for the good Just, but it certainly contributes nothing to the interest of the play. The life in sin is what gives the touch of human interest to the Moralities. The author of the present play, wishing to picture a man consistently just or good, seeks a substitute for this by taking one of his personified vices, Lust, and depicting him from time to time as a vicious human character, surrounded by a set of merry and wide-awake Vices.

The play thus presents two motives, rather confusingly mingled, — the allegorical soul-struggle, with a human hero, which forms the regular plot of the class under consideration, and an additional motive of the contrast of two lives, one good and the other evil, with poetic justice meted out at the end. This second motive occurs again in a Morality to be considered later, *Like Will to Like, Quoth the Devil to the Collier*, and also in the moral tragedy, *The Nice Wanton*. It is almost certainly due to French influence. [2]

[1] Printed in 1567. The text used is in Dodsley, Vol. III.

[2] The earliest French Morality remaining is *Bien Avisé, Mal Avisé*, which was performed at Rennes in 1439. This play represents side by side the careers of Bien Avisé and Mal Avisé, two highly universalized type figures. Bien Avisé is under the influence of Virtues through his whole life, he dies in the arms of Bonne Fin, and his soul is taken to heaven. Mal Avisé consorts

The first, or English, motive is the more important and is the one that, on the whole, dominates the play. But the two motives are so closely connected that sometimes a single scene will jump rapidly from one to the other. In order to explain this effectively I shall have to present part of a scene between Just and Lust, which begins with an argument between two widely different types of mankind and ends with the successful attempt of the just man to throw off the lusts of the flesh:

> *Enter Lust, like a gallant, singing this song*
>> Heigho, care away, let the world pass,
>> For I am as lusty as ever I was;
>> In flowers I flourish as blossoms in May,
>> Heigho, care away; heigho, care away!
>
> *Lust.* What the devil ailed me to sing thus?
>> I cry you mercy, by my faith, for ent'ring:
>> Most like I have ridden on the flying Pegasus,
>> Or in Cock Lorel's barge I have been a vent'ring.
>> Sing? why, I would sing if I were to do again.
>> With Orpheus and Amphion I went to school:
>> What! lads must be lively attending on the train
>> Of Lady Delectation, which is no small fool.
>> Hey rouse, fill all the pots in the house;
>> Tush, man, in good fellowship let us be merry.
>> Look up like a man, or it is not worth a louse;
>> Heigho, troly; hey, dery, dery,
>> Ha, pleasant youth and lusty juventus,
>> In faith it is good to be merry this May:

throughout with Vices, and he is finally strangled and handed over to the Devil. Another play, *L'Homme Juste et l'Homme Mondain* (presented in 1476) has the same motive. In this play the good man is called Juste, or le Juste, so the evidence for direct influence here is very strong. The French play represents scenes in Hell, in Purgatory, and in Heaven after the death of the two heroes; but *The Trial of Treasure*, like the rest of the later English Moralities, is interested only in representing the present life. Cf. Petit de Julleville, *Histoire du Théâtre en France*, IV, 39, 69, and Creizenach, I, 470. Creizenach states here that the motive of *Bien Avisé, Mal Avisé* is not represented in the English Moralities.

For of man's living here there is no point endentus,
Therefore a little mirth is worth much sorrow some say.[1]

Enter Just

Just. But remember ye not the wise man's sentence?
It is better in the house of mourning to be
Than in the house of laughter, where folly hath residence.
For lightness with wisdom cannot agree;
Though many have pleasure in foolish fantasy,
Ensuing their inclination and lust,
Yet much better is the life of one who is just.

Lust. Sir, in this you seem against me to inveigh.

Just. Nothing but reason, I think, I do say.

Lust. Marry, you shall have a nightcap for making the reason.
Friend, have you not a piece of stock-fish to sell?
I would you had a dish of buttered peason.
By my faith, your communication likes me well,
But, I beseech you, tell me, is not your name Just?

Just. Yes, forsooth.

Lust. And my name, thou shalt understand is Lust,
And according thereto I am lusty indeed;
But I think thou hast drunk of Morpheus seed.
Thou goest like a dromedary, dreamy and drowsy;
I hold twenty pound the knave is lousy!

Just. Mine apparel is not like unto thine,
Disguised and jagged, of sundry fashion;
Howbeit, it is not gold always that doth shine,
But corrupting copper of small valuation;
Too horrible besides is thy operation,
Nothing more odious unto the just
Than the beastly desires of inordinate lust.[2]

Lust. It is a shameful thing, as Cicero doth say,
That a man his own acts should praise and commend;
Hypocrites accustom the like, day by day,
Checking other men, when they do offend.

[1] Compare this entrance with that of the young man in *Youth* and in *Lusty Juventus*.

[2] It is possible to suppose — though I do not take this view — from the last three lines that Just for the moment regards his adversary as the quality of lust; but, if so, Lust swings back to his previous character in his next speech.

Just. Yea, but it is an hard thing, saith the philosopher,
For a foolish man to have his manners reprehended;
And even at this day it is come so far,
God grant, for his mercy, it may be amended!
For tell a man now friendly of his fault,
Being blasphemy, pride, or vile fornication,
He will be as presumptuous as Haman the halt,
And repay with revenge or else defamation:
Thus few men a friendly monition will bear,
But stoutly persist and maintain their ill;
And in noblemen's houses truly I do fear,
There are too many have such forward will.

Lust. Wounds and hearts, who can abide this?
Nay, ye vile villain, I will dress you therefore;
Your lazy bones I pretend[1] so to bless,
That you shall have small lust to prate any more.

Just. Behold the image of incipient fools!
There ['re] not a few even now of thy property;
Until you be put into poverty's schools
Ye will not forsake this foolish insolency.

Lust. Nay, soft, with thee I have not made an end.

(Draw out his sword)

Just. The just against lust must always contend,[2]
Therefore I propose to wrestle with thee. *(put it up)*
Who shall have the victory, straightway we shall see.

Lust. When thou wilt, by his flesh, I shall hold the wag.

(Wrestle, and let Lust seem to have the better at the first)

Just. I know that Lust useth not little to brag.

Lust. Thou shalt find me as mighty as Samson the strong.

Just. Yea, the battle of lust endureth long.

Lust. Wounds and flesh! I was almost down on my back;
But yet I will wrestle till my bones crack.   *(Stay, and then speak)*

Just. The end of thy presumption now doth appear.

Lust. Yet do what thou canst, I will not lie here;
No, by his wounds, you old doting knave!

(Cast him, and let him arise again)

[1] Intend.

[2] Up to this point the scene has presented Lust in the main, if not entirely,
as the man actuated by lust, opposed to the just man. But from this speech
on through the action following, the combat is that of the just man against the
lusts of his flesh.

Thinkest thou that Lust will be made a slave?
I shall meet you in Smithfield or else other-where,
By his flesh and blood, I will thee not forbear!
 Just. Not of my power I do thee expel,
But by the might of his spirit that dwelleth in me:
Inordinate lust with the just may not dwell,
And therefore may not I accompany thee.
 Lust. Well, goodman Just, it is no matter,
But, in faith, I pretend not with thee to flatter;
Though from thy company depart I must
I shall live as much in wealthiness, I trust.
                                     (*Go out. He must drive him out*)

So ends the first struggle of the just, or good, man to conquer his base appetites. The proof that the fight just depicted has this allegorical significance is clinched by the soliloquy of Just after his victory:

Where most wealth is, and most delectation,
There Lust is commonly of most estimation;
For whereas wealth wanteth, idleness doth slake,
For where idleness is, Lust parteth the stake. (*Pause*)
Thus have you seen the conflict of the just,
Which all good men ought to use and frequent;
For horrible are the fruits of inordinate lust,
Which in some case resembleth Hydra the serpent,
Whose head being cut off, another riseth incontinent.
So, one of Lust's cogitations being cut away,
There riseth up another, yea, many, we may say.[1]
It is requisite therefore that every degree
Against this his lust both strive and contend;
And though, at the first, he seem sturdy to be,
The Lord will convince [2] him for you in the end.
Your cause unto him therefore wholly commend,
Labouring to avoid all inordinate lust,
And to practice in life to live after the Just.

In the next scene Lust appears with a group of Vices, and not as a patron of the Vices, but as one of their number. And so the

---

[1] This is, of course, to explain Lust's repeated returns to the fight just concluded, after repeated repulses from Just.   [2] Conquer.

play goes on presenting him in one aspect, then in another, until at last he is condemned by God's Visitation in these words :

> Thou incipient fool, thou hast followed thy lust,
> Disdaining the doctrine declared by Sapience.

So it is in the character of "l'homme mondain" that Lust disappears from sight.

This lengthy presentation of the two chief characters has been absolutely necessary for a clear understanding of the play ; but now, having cleared away the only real obstacles, we can proceed with an outline of the action.

The prologue is delivered on the appropriate text, — which might be widened to a general text for all Moralities, — " Do all things to edify the congregation." Then enters Lust, attired like a gallant and singing a song suggestive of his entire freedom from the cares of this world. After a rousing soliloquy, to which the foregoing song furnishes the keynote, he is interrupted by the stately Just, who puts an entirely new face on the situation. Just feels more drawn to the " house of mourning " than to the " house of laughter," and he naturally enough concludes that any wise man would agree with him. Ergo, Lust, who has given indubitable proofs of his residence in the " house of laughter," must be a fool. Lust is not prepared to accept this conclusion tamely, and he attacks his censor vigorously, first with his tongue, and then with his sword. At the beginning of the latter encounter he seems to get the better of his opponent, but the upshot of the encounter is that Just conquers Lust and drives him off the stage. After commenting on the significance of his victory Just retires and Inclination comes in.

Inclination has had a long and triumphant career, the importance of which is not minimized in his narrative. When presently he is joined by Lust and Sturdiness he shows a disposition to take a high hand with them ; but, after a bit of swordplay, they convince him that, although he may be competent to subdue "the mighty on the earth," yet he is not supreme in the realm of vice. But Lust generously reassures him, and the three friends are soon joined by Elation and Greedy-gut, who have come to swell the ranks of Lust. These companions of Lust swear to serve him in all his desires and sing a song expressive of their relations to him :

> Lust shall be led by me Inclination
>   To Carnal Cogitation;
> Where Lust is wholly led by me,
>   He must fall to cupidity;
> For carnal cares shall him assail,
>   And speedily they shall prevail;
> I, Sturdiness, will face it out
> In his cause, sturdy, stiff, and stout,
> Then Greedy-gut shall make him eat
> Both house and land like bread and meat;
>   Elation shall puff him high
>   For to aspire above the sky;
> Then natural and lordly Lust
> Shall with his power despise the Just.[1]

[1] This whole scene is another good example of the combination of two motives, centering in the double character of Lust as, first, the Vice and, second, the man actuated by lust. At the beginning of the scene he is the Vice, surrounded by personifications of kindred vices; at the close he is the lustful or worldly-minded man, accompanied by figures representing his inclinations and desires. The speech of Sturdiness, which closes the scene, corroborates this latter part of the interpretation (p. 275):

> This Lust is the image of all wicked men,
> Which in seeking the world have all delectation;
> They regard not God, nor his commandments ten,
> But are wholly led by their own inclination.
> First to inculcate with Carnal Cogitation
> And after to the desire of all worldly treasure,
> Which alone they esteem the fulness of pleasure.
> With Elation or Pride he is also associate,
> Which puffeth up his senses with presumption pestilent;
> Then Greedy-gut maketh them continually to grate
> On the mock of this world, which he thinketh permanent.
> I, Sturdiness, to hear out all things am bent:
> Thus see you how men that are led by their lust,
> Dissent from the virtuous, goodly, and just.

As this ungodly crew retires Just and Sapience enter. Sapience exhorts Just to be circumspect in the guidance of his life, and Just in his virtuous and learned answers shows that he has no intention of doing anything else. They are interrupted by Inclination, who comes in to announce gleefully that Lust and Carnal Cogitation " in one bed doth lie," and then starts to retire hastily when he sees Just, whom he knows to be proof against his influence. But he is too late. Just and Sapience catch sight of him and intercept him. He attempts to conceal his identity by talking French, and the astute Sapience remarks,

> To deceive us now himself he doth prepare.

Then he tries German, and finally makes a despairing appeal in his own person. But the inexorable pair seize him, put the bridle " called Restraint" on him, and go out leaving him securely tied.

Soon Greedy-gut comes tumbling in, and mistakes Inclination for a colt. After receiving a few vigorous kicks, however, his eyesight becomes bright enough to discern his old friend under the disguise. Inclination persuades him to hurry out for Lust, who alone is able to remove the bridle, and in a few moments Lust comes running in and sets him free. Lust then confides to his friend that his heart is on fire with love for the lady Treasure, and Inclination readily consents to lead him to the object of his desires.

When they retire, Just, Trust, and Contentation appear. Just is in a very self-congratulatory mood, and is encouraged by his companions. Then they all cite examples from classical history and from the Bible to prove that worldly-minded men, who bend their energies toward the procuring of wealth and pleasure on earth, come to grief at the last, while

> God doth so guide the hearts of the just,
> That they respect chiefly the celestial treasure.

Finally they pledge themselves to a continuance of friendship,[1] and go out singing, "The man is blest that feareth God."

Then Inclination comes back with the happy news of a match between Lust and Lady Treasure. Suddenly he breaks off with

> Hark, I hear Lust and my Lady Treasure.
> They are given to solace, singing, and pleasure.

The happy lovers appear, assuring each other of ardent affection and fidelity, while Inclination, by his asides, shows that he is quite conscious of the ephemeral nature of such a union. Lust reminds his lady that she has mentioned a brother of hers, named Pleasure, with whom he is very anxious to become acquainted. Treasure assures him that her brother will join them shortly, and in a few moments Pleasure appears singing. He greets Lust in friendly fashion and assures him that he will remain true to him as long as Lust retains Treasure. Lust is now in a state of ecstatic happiness and breaks into song in honor of his lady, when suddenly he is interrupted by the ominous entrance of God's Visitation.

A stern rebuke is now imposed on the unfortunate Lust; and, as God's Visitation talks on, Lust becomes more and more tortured in mind and in body. Then Pleasure is taken away to wait on Just, and Visitation, as he goes out, warns Lust that this is a foretaste of worse things in store for him. Lust has

---

[1] There is a good example here of what is fairly common in the Moralities, — the mingling of allegorical with literal speech. Just makes a statement of the allegorical relationship between himself and his companions (p. 286):

> As I, being properly nominate Just,
> Am here associate with Contentation,
> So have I my whole felicity in Trust,
> Who illumineth my eyes to see salvation,

and Trust replies:

> Fear ye not, shortly you shall have consolation,
> *If I were once grown in you to perfection.*
> Even thus goeth it always with the children of election.

begun to take heart again, however, when Time enters and
summons him away with Treasure:

> Both Lust and Treasure come forth with speed
> Into the shop of the most mighty God.
> There shall you be beaten to powder indeed,
> And for your abusion feel his scourge and rod.

Then Just leads forward Inclination, who is once more securely
bridled. He is joined by Trust and Consolation; and Trust,
who is very fond of interpreting allegorical action, remarks:

> Most blessed and happy, I say, are the just,
> Even because they restrain their own inclination.

Consolation is presented to Just, who receives him lovingly,
then goes out to put Inclination in prison. Time enters to report that Lust " is converted into dust," " and Treasure in like
case is turned to rust." Then the triumphant Just reappears
and complacently receives the congratulations and commenda-
tions of Time, and the play ends with an apology to the audience
by Consolation, " sith somewhat tedious to you we have been."

Just and Lust, the two chief characters in the play, have
already been explained. Of the other characters little need
be said. They all represent abstractions, and all, excepting
God's Visitation, Time, and Treasure, represent forces within
the nature of Man.

The action contains so much allegorical by-play that it would
be hopeless to attempt to go into all the details of the interpretation. The main outline is this: The just man determines to
lead a virtuous life. He has at first a hard struggle to subdue
the desires of his flesh, but having gained one victory he finds
it easier afterwards to persist in virtue. He attains wisdom by
his sober and studious life, and rigorously practises self-restraint
to stifle his inclinations. By this life he acquires a contented
mind and a firm trust in the mercy of God with assurance of

his future salvation. On the other hand, the man who yields himself to his lusts obtains worldly pleasures and riches for a short time; but soon his wealth is destroyed and he himself is sentenced by God to an eternity of punishment.

The Longer Thou Livest the More Foole Thou Art[1] is the thought-compelling title of the next Morality on the list. From the fortunate circumstance of its being next to *The Trial of Treasure*, through the chronological arrangement of the list, it can be compared directly with that play in plot. In *The Trial of Treasure* the hero remained virtuous throughout the action. In the present play the hero, Moros ("a foole by interpretacion") is depraved from start to finish, in spite of the frequent and violent efforts of the Virtues to convert him. In every other Morality of this class we find the fluctuation between virtue and sin.

The Prologue, in a long speech, indicates the purpose of the play, — to illustrate the evil results of bad rearing of children, and of youthful idleness.

> Holsom lessons now and than we shall enterlace,
> Good for the ignorant, not hurtfull to the wise;
> Honest mirth shall com in, and appeare in place,
> Not to thaduancement, but to the shame of vice;
> To extoll Vertue, without faile, is our devise.

Thus the author, who, on the whole, has produced a very bright and readable play, takes care to notify the audience that, in spite of the apparently contradictory evidence of some details, his constant purpose is to be edifying. A good deal of "mirth" does come in, and nowadays we are too prudish to consider it all as strictly "honest." But these aspects of the Morality, even though we need not regard them as reformatory in the strict sense of the word, undoubtedly widened the appeal of the play

[1] Written by W. Wager. Edited by Brandl in the *Jahrbuch der deutschen Shakespeare-Gesellschaft*, Vol. XXXVI. Brandl dates the play 1559–1560, and Gayley, p. 310, agreeing with Fleay, 1571–1576.

in those days, and enabled the author to present his general
commendation of virtue to many people who were human enough
to wish to have their laugh out first; and it is easy to imagine
that the morality-loving English audience, after being comfortably
assured that the coming " mirth " would be " not to thaduance-
ment, but to the shame of vice," settled down to enjoy the mad
pranks and questionable jokes without troubling much to enquire
into their individual " honesty."

After the prologue Moros enters, singing a foolish parody
beginning,

> Brome, Brome on hill,
> The gentle Brome on hill hill.

For this wanton waste of time he is sternly rebuked by Discipline,
who quotes Latin proverbs to show him the foolishness of his
conduct. Discipline is soon reinforced by Pietie and Exercitation, and the three labor hard to convert Moros to a useful and
religious life, but without result. Moros is willing to listen to
what they have to say, and is even cheerful over the situation.
" I may tell you," he confides to them,

> my father did like me well,
> I am the wisest child that ever he had.
> Often times I haue herd him say or tell,
> My boy Moros will proue a wise Lad,

and Exercitation responds despairingly :

> If you can remember your father's saying,
> Why can you not remember good lessons as well?

Finally the would-be instructors recite a lesson for Moros to
repeat after them; but the buoyant spirits of Moros get the
better of him, and he wilfully confuses the lesson. At this the
teachers lose their last shred of patience and fall to beating him,
whereat he howls dolefully and promises to do better. Then he
is committed to Pietie for schooling in religion and is given a
Testament to study. Discipline throws out dark hints that a

thrashing is the natural result of carelessness or backsliding,
then Moros retires with Pietie. Exercitation and Discipline discuss the possibility of a conversion. Discipline states hopefully :

> Vnto labour, vertue, and veritie
> I will hope him easely to winne;

but Exercitation is pessimistic. His conclusion is :

> For if he to any vertue be bente,
> I am much deceaued, truly, in my minde.

The only remedy Discipline can suggest is to watch Moros and
give him a sound thrashing if he falters by the way ; so the two
worthies go out to spy on his actions.

Idlenesse, "the parent of all vice," comes in to fulfill an
engagement with Moros, and is joined by Incontinence and
Wrath. They have all heard of the attempt to make a wise and
good man of Moros, and are determined to offset this by their
influence. Wrath is inclined to regard him as a confirmed fool
already, but Idlenesse, who is shrewder, realizes that Moros has
a small amount of wit which may be nourished into growth if
he really comes under the influence of Discipline and his friends.

> But he shalbe a more foole yet
> When all we three be vnto him annexed.

Therefore Idlenesse holds it advisable that all their names shall
be changed. He is already known to Moros as Pastime, and he
suggests that Incontinence be called Pleasure, whereat Incontinence in turn reminds Wrath of his usual disguise behind the
name Manhode. " In good faith," bursts out the irate Wrath,

> little needeth this devise,
> To be called by our names is as good :
> Doth he know what Idlenesse doth meane?
> Knoweth he Incontinencie to be leacherie?
> He discerneth not cleane from uncleane.
> His minde is all set on foolerie.

But Idlenesse carries the day.

At this juncture Moros comes in, pretending to read a book, but in reality translating its contents into an unintelligible jargon, and at the same time keeping a shrewd weather-eye open for Discipline. He gladly joins the three Vices, who introduce themselves to him by their assumed names, and give him thorough instruction in various forms of sin. Idlenesse persuades him to throw his book away, and gives him a pack of cards instead. Wrath presents him with a sword, with instructions on the proper way to avenge an insult with it, and Moros is brandishing his new weapon with a lively appearance of manliness when Discipline suddenly appears. Then his new-found courage quickly deserts him, and he throws away the sword and hides. His friends urge him to attack Discipline, but he is in a pitiful state of terror, and they finally go out, taking him with them, and leaving Discipline to comment on the evident results of lax training on the part of parents.

After Discipline has made his mournful exit Fortune appears, proclaiming her power. Incontinencie joins her, and she tells him of her intention to raise Moros to a position of honor and wealth.

> Seeing that vulgares will me not prayse
> For exalting good men and sapient,
> I will get me a name an other wayes,
> That is, by erecting fooles insipient.

When Moros next appears he is a man in the prime of life, a greater fool than ever, and enjoying the wealth which Fortune has sent him. His chief confidant and friend now is Ignorance, a very sage person, of the same general type as Folly in *Magnyfycence* (who explains that he is no fool himself though he makes fools of others). With Ignorance, who introduces himself as Antiquitie, are associated Impietie, alias Philosophie, and Crueltie, alias Prudence. Moros receives them unquestioningly and follows all their precepts.

But the Virtues have not yet given over the struggle. While Moros is conversing with his friend Ignorance he is interrupted by Discipline, who enters with the oft-repeated denunciation, "The longer thou livest the more fool thou art." The much befooled Moros goes up to his censor with a great show of bravery, and answers his rebukes with railing and curses; but he has not yet imbibed sufficient courage to draw his sword, as Ignorance urges him to do. The two friends make their escape from the merciless tongue of Discipline, who takes care to impress his moral upon the audience before he retires.

There is now a lull in the action. During this time Moros is supposed to be advancing toward old age, and to abridge the period People comes in with the naïve explanation:

> My name is People, for I represent
> All the people where Moros doth dwell,

then proceeds to explain the wicked and useless life that Moros is spending among his villainous friends.

At last Moros appears again, an old man, and looking furiously for someone to punish. While he is raging about searching for a victim, suddenly God's Judgement approaches and strikes him down. Then Confusion comes in and is ordered by God's Judgement to complete the punishment.

> Confusion, spoil him of his aray,
> Geue him his fooles coate for him due:
> His chayne and his staffe take thou away,
> In sorow and care for euer let him rue.

Moros, still unrepentant, is led away by Confusion, and God's Judgement advises the audience to take warning by the example of this foolish man. He becomes warmed up to his subject, and then generously concludes that his audience may have had enough moralizing for one day.

> Many thinges moe of fooles we could talke,
> But we have detained long our audience.

Exercitation, Pietie, and the inexorable Discipline are of another mind. They feel that the audience can stand, or should be made to stand, a good deal more of virtuous teaching; and in consequence they occupy the final scene with much good advice on the text of Moros's downfall, and conclude with prayers for the Queen.

The play, in the absence of the usual stages of wickedness, conversion, and so on, divides itself according to another scheme, into the three stages of youth, manhood, and old age. The allegory is unusually clear and easy to follow, and there is no difficulty in explaining the nature and office of every character. Fortune and God's Judgement are external powers brought to bear upon the hero, and all the other figures — except People, who appears but once in the office of chorus — represent abstract qualities struggling for the soul of Moros. The Prologue, as usual, makes plain the moral (II, 52–58):

> By him [1] we shall declare the unthrifty abuse
> Of such as had lever to Folly and Idlenes fall,
> Then to hearken to Sapience when he doth call:
> Their processe, how their whole life they do spende,
> And what shame they come to at the last ende.
> Wherefore this our matter we entitle and name:
> The longer thou livest the more Foole thou arte.

So much for the text. Now for the sermon. The boy who is foolishly brought up by his parents is likely to remain foolish and vicious to the end. When he becomes old enough to understand the danger of idleness he still remains true to the teachings of his childhood, smothers all the better impulses toward an active life of piety and self-restraint that spring up in his heart, and steadily adds to his vicious habits. He is ignorant, because he refuses to study; and, as he advances in life, the irresponsible idleness of boyhood gives place to cruelty, lust,

[1] *I.e.*, Moros.

and impiety. The accession of wealth only gives him better opportunities to gratify his evil desires. But in his dishonest old age he is stricken down by the judgment of God. His wealth disappears, and he spends his last days in sorrow and poverty, though unrepentant to the end.

The play, though belonging to the present class, has also affiliations with Class II, as illustrating the special text indicated in the title.

The Conflict of Conscience[1] is the last Morality of this particular type. It is bitterly anti-Catholic in sentiment, without being avowedly controversial; and this bitterness is expressed mainly by placing all the Vices of the play in the common service of the Devil and the Pope.

As I have explained in a previous chapter,[2] the Morality is based upon a tale of the apostasy of Francis Spira, or Spiera, an Italian lawyer; but this tale is used by the author merely as a starting point, — a suggestion for the motive of the play, — and it can be practically neglected here. The hero, Philologus, is no longer the Italian lawyer, but a type — to all intents and purposes a highly universalized type. The author, however, still somewhat restrained by the consciousness of the actual case of apostasy that he started from, explains his hero as a type of the men who are always ready to talk about the word of God, but are prone to lapses in conduct — after all, a sufficiently common type. The same restraint — speaking always from the point of view of the Morality — is felt in the introduction of friends and family for the hero; but these persons are so much subordinated as to be almost negligible, and the Morality atmosphere predominates throughout.

[1] Dodsley, Vol. VI. The play is by Nathaniell Woodes, and was printed in 1581, though Collier, in a preface to the present edition, conjectures that it was written about 1570. For a preliminary discussion of the play and its sources see pp. 11–13, above.

[2] See p. 11, above.

The Prologue explains, at some length, the motives of "our Author" in writing the play, and in planning it just as he did. The plot, as the audience is informed, has been drawn from an historical event, but the play is universalized in its treatment because comedy is not permitted to discuss the vices of one private man, and because, if the play were written about one individual, the audience might fail to apply the moral to themselves. Some "honest mirth" is to be mixed in, but not of a kind to exceed the bounds of decorum. Having thus paved the way for an intelligent enjoyment of the play, the Prologue retires.

He is followed by Satan, who in a long speech tells the audience of his power in the world and of his methods of corrupting men. He is loud in praise of the Pope, who is his "darling dear," his "eldest boy," and who is upheld by two stout champions, Avarice and Tyranny. But as people of late have been plotting to overthrow the Pope, Satan decides to send Hypocrisy to his aid.

When Satan retires, the two friends, Mathetes and Philologus, come forward discussing the relations between God and his people. Mathetes is much puzzled by the afflictions which are constantly undergone by the sincere followers of God. History, he says, is full of instances of suffering and martyrdom in the cause of Christianity, and these seem naturally to indicate that God is angry with his people. What he chiefly wishes to obtain is some method of discerning the difference between God's wrath and his love.

Philologus, who is laboring under no such doubts, readily undertakes to explain away the mystery for his friend,

> for because it is most chiefly pertinent
> Unto mine office to instruct and teach each christian wight
> True godliness, and show to them the path that leadeth right
> Unto God's kingdom, where we shall inherit our salvation,
> Given unto us from God by Christ our true propitiation.

He not only admits what Mathetes says about the sufferings of God's elect, but goes farther and piles up instances from Scripture and history to show that Christians in all ages of the world endured bitter trials for the faith. But the explanation is quite easy to omniscient Philologus, and from the mass of his learned argument Mathetes extracts the following correct conclusion :

> This is the sum of all your talk, if that I guess aright,
> > That God doth punish his elect to keep their faith in ure,
> Or lest that, if continual ease and rest enjoy they might,
> > God to forget through haughtiness frail nature should procure:
> Or else by feeling punishment our sins for to abjure ;
> > Or else to prove our constancy ; or lastly, that we may
> Be instruments, in whom his might God may abroad display.

Having gleaned the desired instruction on this point, Mathetes becomes conscious of a more practical yearning. " It is now high dinner-time," he suggests. "My stomach meat doth crave." So the two depart amicably on this new quest.

Hypocrisy now arrives on the scene and treats the audience to a disquisition on his nature and properties. Avarice and Tyranny soon join him. The three Vices are all in the service of the Devil, but each is ambitious to be leader, and they fall into a long and tiresome wrangle on the question of supremacy. But they are unable to come to any conclusion, for the simple reason that no one of the three will admit himself to be in any way inferior to either of the others, so they finally give the problem up and join forces in the common service of the Pope. The duty that now lies nearest them is to furnish all possible assistance to the Pope's Legate, who has just come to the country. Hypocrisy sees that his friends' names will mar all if they are openly proclaimed, so, for the nonce, he dubs Tyranny Zeal, and calls Avarice Careful Provision.

Philologus again appears for a short scene, during which he soliloquizes on the danger that he and his family are likely to

incur from the arrival of the Pope's Legate. Realizing that if
he once comes into the power of the Legate he must either
give up his faith or suffer ruin and torture, he takes his leave
in considerable trepidation of spirit.

The Vices return in high feather to announce their favorable
reception by the Pope's Legate. They have all been placed in
high positions and are making their power felt throughout the
country. While they are exulting in their good fortune, Cacon,
a priest with a broad Scotch accent, joins them. He is in
thorough sympathy with the work they are doing; and after a
friendly conversation over the affairs of the church, he informs
them that one Philologus, a learned man, has been making himself unduly busy in his zeal against the Pope and the time-
honored customs of the Catholic Church. Tyranny and Avarice
are at once anxious to get their clutches on the offender; so
Cacon undertakes to lead them to his house, while Hypocrisy
goes out to fulfill an engagement with his friend the Legate.

In the next scene the Legate, who is accompanied by
Hypocrisy and Avarice, issues an order to bring forth the
heretic whom they have captured, and Tyranny appears,
leading Philologus. The Cardinal orders Philologus to abjure
his faith, and a long debate follows, in which Philologus holds
stoutly to his religion. The united efforts of the Cardinal and
his three followers are not enough to shake him, and at last
Hypocrisy sends Tyranny for Sensual Suggestion to add the
weight of his arguments. Sensual Suggestion, on his arrival,
tries to appeal to Philologus by telling him of his weeping wife
and children. Philologus is visibly moved, and his tempter
goes on heaping one argument upon another, finally making
him an offer of worldly joys and riches, and giving him a
mirror in which to behold the pleasures that are in store for
him if he will but give up his stubborn adherence to his
religion. Upon looking into the mirror Philologus breaks into

transports of joy at the bliss there revealed. His virtue is overcome, and he willingly resigns his faith for the promised delights of the mirror. Then he departs, with Sensual Suggestion for a companion, to enjoy his new life.

The next scene shows the hero still in the company of his new-found friend. But Spirit appears and gives him a solemn warning of the danger he is in.

> Let not suggestion of thy flesh thy conscience thee betray,
> Who doth conduct thee in the path that leadeth to all woe.
> Weigh well this warning given from God, before thou further go,
> And sell not everlasting joy for pleasures temporal,
> From which thou soon shalt go, or they from thee bereaved shall.

Philologus is troubled, but Sensual Suggestion at once presents his glass, and Philologus, seeing " nought else but pleasure, pomp, and wealth " within, is reassured. Then appears a more serious troubler, Conscience, who denounces him roundly and seeks in every way to draw him from his worldly life. At this attack Philologus is deeply moved, and for a time almost gives way to despair; but Sensual Suggestion is still able to prevail, though it takes his most artful reasonings to induce his companion to leave Conscience.

But a more powerful influence is soon to appear and wreck this life of sensual delights. Philologus is enjoying himself with his two sons when Horror makes his entrance and pronounces his curse upon him :

My name is called Confusion and Horror of the mind,
And to correct impenitents of God I am assigned,
And for thou dost despise God's mercy and his grace,
And wouldst no admonition take by them that did thee warn,
Neither when Conscience counselled thee thou wouldst his words embrace,
Who would have had thee unto God obedience true to learn ;
Nor couldst between Suggestion's craft and Conscience' truth discern :
Behold, therefore, thou shalt of me another lesson hear,
Which (will thou, nill thou) with torment of Conscience thou shalt bear.

Then the mirror furnished by Sensual Suggestion is transformed into the "glass of deadly desperation."

From now on Philologus is plunged in gloom. Theologus and Eusebius visit him and try to re-convert him, but in vain. Philologus pronounces a prayer dictated by them, but even while he repeats the forms of devotion, his heart is filled with hatred and blasphemy, and at last he retires in the blackest despair.

In a final scene Nuntius appears and explains to the audience that Philologus, after suffering for thirty weeks, during which time he has refused all food and has attempted to hang himself, "is now converted unto God with many bitter tears."

The nature of the hero, Philologus, has already been discussed. Of the other characters only seven are strictly necessary, or even desirable, for the play as a Morality ; that is, — Conscience, Spirit, Hypocrisy, Tyranny, Avarice, Suggestion, and Horror. The others (with the exception of Satan, who appears only once, at the beginning of the play) are introduced in memory of the story behind the play. From the point of view of the unbiased student of the drama, *The Conflict of Conscience* presents a decided advance from the old-fashioned Morality toward the drama of real life ; but from the biased point of view of the student of Moralities, who through long familiarity has learned by successive stages to endure, to pity, and to embrace, the present play is a good Morality sadly encumbered by the too solid flesh of many individuals.

Of the strictly Morality characters, Hypocrisy, Tyranny, and Avarice are the most active. They are, needless to say, Vices ; and since after a prolonged argument they themselves are unable to settle the question of preëminence, it would be a difficult matter for us to decide it for them. But as Hypocrisy is the first to appear and address the audience the presumption is in favor of Hypocrisy as chief Vice. These three cannot be regarded as representing vices in the heart of the hero. They do not sue for his favor, which is the allegorical method of representing qualities, vicious or virtuous, as springing up in the heart. They are instrumental in persuading and coercing Philologus to renounce his faith, and thus represent forces abroad in the land.[1] Suggestion, or Sensual Suggestion, on the other hand, represents a vice of the heart, and he becomes the follower and confidant of the apostate Philologus.

Spirit and Conscience are the two Virtues, and they, of course, represent internal forces for good.[2] Horror is an Agent of Retribution.

The interpretation of the allegory — ignoring the elements that make for the drama of real life — is this : The religion of man is too likely to take the form of zeal for discussion of the word of God, and to lack the element of constancy which upholds the possessor in the face of worldly persecution and the temptations of worldly prosperity. These may be resisted for a time, but as a result of repeated attacks and repeated temptations the unstable Christian becomes wickedly desirous of temporal ease and pleasures, and at last resigns his piety to obtain them. His conscience and his inner knowledge of what is right cause him considerable disquiet at times, but he is now so enamored of the pleasures of sense that he persists in them in spite of his inner promptings. Retribution comes at last, however, when his eyes are opened to the real wickedness of his life. He is overcome by horror of his sin, and can derive no comfort from earthly assurances of God's mercy. His only chance now for salvation is in the direct intervention of God.

[1] The fact that they are in the service of the Pope is of no significance here.

[2] It is interesting to notice the consistency with which the author makes Sensual Suggestion the only one of the Vices to come into contact with Spirit and Conscience.

2. CONFLICT FOR THE POSSESSION OF MAN INTELLECTUAL

The *Interlude of the Four Elements* [1] is the only surviving example of a class of plays which one might easily suppose to have been popular in that age of didacticism. As the case stands now, this is the only existing English Morality where Virtues strive to win man over to a life of study in the face of constant opposition on the part of Vices. It must not be forgotten, however, that it is a technical distinction that makes this play stand alone. The three " Wit " plays of the following subdivision exhibit exactly the same attitude, that is, a desire to induce study rather than virtue in the strict sense of the term, the difference being that in the " Wit " plays the personified intelligence of Man is the hero instead of the type figure Man.

To the twentieth-century mind the *Four Elements* sounds the base string of dullness ; but we must attempt to realize that an elementary lesson in physical geography may have been no less replete with interest to the early sixteenth-century listener than the long-deferred account of the North Pole is to us.

The play is introduced in a long speech by the Messenger, who complains of the ignorance and frivolity of the times. The Greeks and Romans, as well as learned clerks of other nations, he declares, wrote many works useful for edification. But in England there are many persons, of noble as well as of mean birth, who can understand no language but English ; therefore the useful works of other nations should be translated into English so that all can have the benefit of them. As to the subject of this play, continues the Messenger, there are many men nowadays who can barely read and write, and yet they think it no shame to spend their time in composing ballads, or books on love, " or other matter not worth a mite," and

---

[1] Printed 1519. Reprinted in Dodsley, Vol. I.

> Why should not then the author of this interlude
> Utter his own fantasy and conceit also,
> As well as divers other nowadays do?

The "fantasy" of the author, as his Messenger explains, is to instruct the audience in some plain matters of God's creation, so that those who presume to discuss the mysteries of God may not remain ignorant of "these visible things inferial." Having thus eased his mind, the melancholy Messenger departs.

Then Nature, Studious Desire, and Humanity appear, and Nature delivers a speech upon his own functions [1] and on the character of the four elements. Humanity's curiosity is much stimulated, and he begs to be taken under Nature's guidance. Thus encouraged, Nature proceeds with a lesson on physical geography, which so delights Humanity that he thinks he can never have enough of this pleasant learning; so Nature presents him with Studious Desire for an attendant, and departs with a promise to return and instruct Humanity in more "high points of cunning." Studious Desire continues the physical geography lesson for the delectation of the eager Humanity. But when the teacher insists on the roundness of the earth he is forcing a pill on Humanity which the latter will hardly swallow. Studious Desire is unable to convince him, and has to fall back at last on the authority of "a man called Experience," who is able to prove the matter beyond a doubt. Humanity is at once aflame with desire to meet Experience, but at this point they are interrupted by the entrance of Sensual Appetite.

---

[1] As Nature defines himself here he is not quite the same as Nature in the Morality of that name. The latter figure really represents human nature; the former, the active principle of external nature. This is the explanation:

> So, He by His goodness hath ordained and created
> Me here his minister, called Nature Naturate
> Wherefore I am the very naturate nature,
> The immediate minister for the preservation
> Of everything in his kind to endure,
> And cause of generation, and corruption
> Of that thing that is brought to destruction (p. 10).

This merry Vice at once falls to reviling Studious Desire, and warns Humanity that he is in very bad company, —

> For if ye knew him as well as I,
> Ye would not use his company
> Nor love him in no wise.

Studious Desire remonstrates indignantly, but he is no match in wits for his tormentor. Humanity is soon persuaded that his health and happiness demand that he should take an outing with Sensual Appetite, and he dismisses his teacher with an apologetic promise to return to him.

> Sir, I pray you be content,
> It is not utterly mine intent
> Your company to exile;
> But only to have communication,
> And a pastime of recreation
> With this man for a while.

Studious Desire goes out very meekly, and Sensual Appetite calls loudly for the Taverner. This worthy appears and is ordered to prepare a feast; but as he is in too jocular a mood to regard the order seriously, a war of wits follows, mainly between him and Sensual Appetite. Finally, however, the jovial Taverner is induced to recognize the real need for viands, and he hurries out to prepare his feast, with Humanity and Sensual Appetite following at a more leisurely pace. Then, lest the audience should become demoralized along with Humanity, Experience comes in with Studious Desire and gives him a long lesson on geography, from the map.

While the good pair are thus engaged, Humanity, with his friend, happens upon them. Sensual Appetite begins, as usual, to ridicule and revile his opponents. But Humanity is glad to make the acquaintance of Experience; and, when the latter says that he cannot remain while Sensual Appetite is there, Humanity requests the Vice to retire for a season. Then

Experience begins the long-promised exposition on the roundness of the earth.

But before Humanity is convinced, we come, unfortunately, to
a gap of eight leaves in the manuscript of the play. Crossing
this gap, we reach a conversation between Sensual Appetite
and Ignorance. Ignorance is proclaiming that he is "a lord of
greater puissance than the king of England or France," and
Sensual Appetite breaks in with a bragging tale of the number
of people he has killed in a "shrewd fray." Then they begin
to wonder what has become of Humanity, and finally discover
him sleeping in a corner, presumably wearied with study.
Ignorance is for cutting off his head at once, but Sensual
Appetite thinks it would not be worth while to take such
violent action;

> For he is but an innocent, lo!
>   In manner of a fool.
> For as soon as I speak to him again,
>   I shall turn his mind clean,
>   And make him follow my school.[1]

They awake Humanity, and he arises in a state of great will-
ingness to enjoy their society. Sensual Appetite goes out and
fetches a company of dancers. After the song and dance
Ignorance takes the floor and sings a foolish, incoherent song
about Robin Hood.

In the midst of this revelry Nature comes back and sternly
rebukes Humanity. But at this point the manuscript is again
mutilated, and ends imperfectly; so we miss the conclusion of
what was probably the Final Conversion scene.

The motive, it will be seen, is very simple. It represents
the battle of conflicting feelings in the mind of man. The

---

[1] This open contempt of the Vices for their human quarry is very unusual.
They usually preserve the outward appearance, at least, of great respect towards
Man, and show a constant desire, both before him and behind his back, to
prove attractive in his eyes.

characters are easily assigned their places, since all the Virtues and Vices, when reduced to literal terms, have their dwelling exclusively within the mind. The Messenger, of course, may be neglected, as acting merely the part of Prologue, and the Taverner, as being the representative of a class, who is here introduced for the sake of his humor, but without significance in the plot. Humanity is the *genus homo*, the human hero who is the object of strife. Nature Naturata is simply what his name indicates.[1] Studious Desire and Experience, the representatives of goodness, are pitted against Sensual Appetite and Ignorance, the representatives of evil, from the intellectual point of view. All four stand for internal forces.

The lesson that the audience would gather from this play can now be read into the following interpretation with probably about the same amount of ease with which the audience of the time read it into the allegorical representation. Man gets his first knowledge of the world by simple observation of nature. By this he is stimulated to go deeper into useful studies, and all would be well but for his lack of experience, which makes him rather unstable and inclined to scepticism. While in this state he weakly resigns his studies, obeys the dictates of his sensual appetites, and for a time leads an ignorant and vicious life. But his former taste of study has not been in vain, and in the midst of his idleness and dissipation he decides to return to the work which was formerly so interesting to him. With the added advantage of experience Man seems now to be devoted to a life of study; but he is still prone to the follies of the world, and in a period of weariness resulting from overstudy he again gives rein to his passions and lapses into a state of vice and ignorance.[2]

[1] See p. 145, note 1, above.

[2] The final regeneration of man, which any student of the Moralities would feel confident is to follow here, can only be conjectured, since the manuscript is imperfect.

3. CONFLICT FOR THE POSSESSION OF MAN REPRESENTED MERELY BY ONE OR MORE PERSONIFIED ATTRIBUTES

In the final subdivision of this most important class of Moralities the human hero ceases to appear, and his place is taken by abstract representations of the mind or soul of man, or both. In the " Wit " plays, which constitute three fifths of this group, the effect is almost the same as if Man himself were introduced as the object of strife, but in the Morality of *Wisdom, who is Christ*[1] the effect is very different.

Instead of the simple human hero, we have in this play Anima, or the Soul, with her attendant train of the Five Wyttes, arrayed as " five vergynes," and " the 3 Powers of every Christian Soul," Mynde, Wylle, and Understondyng. This formidable array of human attributes seems, at first, to threaten complications in the plot; but the action is kept fairly simple by the fact that there is only one active representative of evil, Lucyfer, pitted against only one representative of goodness, Wysdom, or Christ. There is, therefore, strictly speaking, no Vice in the play, this being one of the rare occasions when the devil himself plays the part of chief tempter.[2] There are whole herds of Vices in the service of the corrupted Mynde, Wylle, and Understondyng, but these, appearing only as silent retainers, are not to be regarded as real actors. The only representative of goodness, also, is the real figure of Christ thinly veiled as the personified abstraction of wisdom.[3]

Wysdom first appears and gives an account of himself. His name, he explains, is " everlastynge Wysdom," which name applies to each of the three persons of the Trinity, but more

[1] *The Macro Plays*, edited by Furnivall and Pollard. Probably produced between 1480 and 1490.

[2] The only other occasion is in the Morality *Mankind*.

[3] Christ is also referred to as " Wysdam " in the *Salutation and Conception* scene of the Coventry cycle.

especially to the Son, who is both God and Man. Then the Soul comes in, kneels before Wysdom, and confesses her love for him. A long conversation follows, on the nature of wisdom and of love. Wysdom expounds the relation of the soul to God, and the origin and nature of the seven sacraments. He asks the Soul for her heart and obedience, which she joyfully grants. The five wits, arrayed as five virgins, enter and receive their instructions from Wysdom, who then reminds the Soul that

> Thre myghtis every cresten sowll has,
> Wyche bethe applyede to þe trinyte.[1]

[1] P. 41. This play has an unusual amount of literal, in place of allegorical, discussion, and thus is a very imperfect allegory. In the above scene Mynde, Wylle, and Understondyng speak of themselves, and are spoken of, as human faculties rather than as allegorical figures. When, for instance, Wylle says (p. 42)

> And I of þe soull am þe wyll;
> Off þe godhede lyknes & fygure.
> Wyth goode wyll no man may spyll
> Nor without goode wyll of blys be sure,

he is using literal, and not allegorical, language. The only point of connection with allegory is that the man on the stage speaks in the first person. In order to be consistently allegorical Wylle would have to speak of himself as a companion or a blood relation of the Soul.

This inconsistency appears from time to time through the whole play. When Lucyfer is planning to corrupt Mynde, Wylle, and Understondyng, he says (p. 47):

> To þe mynde of þe soule I xall mak suggestyun,
> Ande brynge hys wndyrstondynge to delectacion,
> So þat hys wyll make confyrmacion.

It is only when Lucyfer (arrayed as "a galaunt") tempts them that we get really allegorical speech. He incites Wylle to a life of enjoyment (p. 51):

> Therfor, Wyll, I rede yow inclyne;
> Lewe yowur stodyes, þow [þey] ben dywyn;
> Yowur prayers, yowur penance, of Ipocryitis þe syne,
> Ande lede a comun lyff.

But a few lines further on, when Lucyfer produces serious arguments in favor of his advice, he assures Wylle:

> The Wyll of þe soule hathe fre dominacion.

In answer to this suggestion Mynde, Wylle, and Understondyng present themselves humbly to Wysdom for guidance, and he requests each to give a full account of his character. When these explanations are concluded Wysdom gives them a solemn warning against the World, the Flesh, and the Devil, their three deadly enemies, and exhorts them to remain loyal to himself. Then, after more eulogy of Wysdom by the Soul, the whole company retires.

Lucyfer now appears, and proclaims that he was once an angel, but is now lowest in Hell. He plans to corrupt the

Then, after Lucyfer has accomplished his work, and the Soul appears, disfigured by sin, Wysdom points to her and says to Mynde (p. 65):

> Se howe ye have dysvyguryde yowur soule!
> Be-holde yowur selff; loke veryly in mynde!

Here, instead of Mynde's being one of the "thre myghtis" of the Soul, he is for the moment elevated into the position of a man, with a mind and a soul; and the Soul, who has previously been spoken of in literal language as being a part of man, and including mind, is now referred to as *the soul of the man Mynde, whose mind and soul are degraded by vice.* Wysdom continues his censure of the degraded Mynde (p. 65):

> As many dedly synnys as ye have vsyde,
> So many deullys in yowur soule be.
> Be-holde wat ys þer-in reclusyde!
> Alas, man! of þi soule have pyte!

Shortly after this, the Soul, convicted of sin, speaks of herself as *a person having a soul, of which the mind, will, and understanding are parts* (p. 68):

> To owur modyr, holy chyrche, I wyll resort,
> My lyff pleyn schewenge to here syght,
> With mynde, vndyrstondynge, & wyll ryght,
> Wyche of my sowll þe partyes be.

This discussion might be carried further, but these are the main points of confusion in the allegory. The only consistent allegorical scenes in the play are those depicting Mynde, Wylle, and Understondyng leading a life of sin. This same sort of allegorical confusion appears, to some extent, in a great many of the Moralities, but never in anything like the abundance that we find here; and, in this play, the special confusion is largely the result of personifying four related attributes of Man and presenting them as common objects of strife.

Soul by tempting Mynd, Wylle, and Understondyng to sin, and for this purpose retires to array himself as a "goodly galont." When he returns he is joined by Mynde, Wylle, and Understondyng, who are busily engaged in proclaiming their loyalty to God, and their intention to live in contemplation of His goodness. A discussion follows on the relative merits of the active and the contemplative life. Lucyfer urges that there is a time for prayer and a time for worldly labor and enjoyment. Did Christ live in contemplation? he asks, and Mynde is obliged to answer, "I suppos not, by my relacion." The three companions are completely confused by Lucyfer's subtle arguments, and are soon brought to admit that "man may be in the worlde, and be ryght goode."

After this it is all smooth sailing for Lucyfer. He persuades them to leave their studies and penance and go out into the world, where they can dress well, live well, and be happy with their fellow-men. Then, with final instructions to beware of preachers, who are wolves in sheep's clothing, and a repeated exhortation to get all the pleasures that the world affords, he sends them out, and remains to exult over his mastery of the Soul.[1]

The next scene shows how completely and unreservedly Lucyfer's instructions have been followed out by Mynde, Wylle, and Understondyng. These three friends, who a short time ago took all their pleasure in communion with God, now talk of nothing but fine clothes, money, and wenches. Mynde calls in his train of followers, consisting of Indignation, Sturdynes, Males (Malice), Hastynes, Wreche, and Dyscorde. He himself,

---

[1] The Devil and the world are thus made to figure in the downfall of Man, though the world is not allegorically represented. But Wysdom has warned the Soul and her "thre myghtis" against the three enemies of Man, i.e., the World, the Flesh, and the Devil, so the flesh is referred to by Lucyfer as participating in the work, though indirectly (p. 47):

> And the flesche of man that ys so changeable,
> That wyll I tempte, as I gees.

he says, is called Mayntennance. The six followers of Mynde go through a dance, then give way to the attendants of Understondyng, who are called Wronge, Sleyght, Dobullnes, Falsnes, Raveyn, and Dyscheyit (Deceit), and who make up the Holborn Quest. Understondyng then explains that he, the leader and "fownder" of the Quest, is called Perjury. After these merry lads go through their dance, Wylle calls in his company, comprising Rekleshede, Idyllnes, Surfet, Gredynes, Spouse-breche (Adultery), and Fornycacion. But Mynde is insulted by their appearance in the "gyse of France," and demands that they be sent out.

The attendants all leave, and the three friends proceed to lay plans for the future. Mynde is to continue imposing on people, Understondyng will indict citizens falsely, and Wylle's ambitions extend only as far as the stews. He mentions a certain Janet, whom he desires, but cannot enjoy because her husband is always in the way. But Understondyng tells him how they can easily get rid of the husband, and here one gets a curious bit of insight into the legal methods of the time. They are on the point of going out when Wysdom appears and rebukes them sternly for their sins. Mynde begins to relent, but Understondyng is defiant, and Wylle is not yet prepared to resign his pleasant vices. He reminds his friends that they are still but young. "We may a-mende wen we be sage," he adds comfortably. But before they can escape from Wysdom, the Soul "apperythe in the most horrybull wyse, fowlere than a fende," and six devils come running out from under her robe. The three culprits are overcome with fear at the sight, and hastily confess their sins, while the Soul cries aloud to God for mercy. Wysdom tells them that, to obtain forgiveness, they must become filled with sorrow and contrition, and they go out singing dolefully.

Wysdom now edifies the audience with a long speech, enumerating the nine points most pleasing to God. At the conclusion of his harangue the reformed sinners, who in the meantime have been assuming their former robes, return in symbolical procession. The Soul is the central figure. She is preceded by the Fyve Wyttes, and is accompanied by Mynde on one side, and Understondyng on the other, while Wylle brings up the rear. Wysdom receives them lovingly, and assures the Soul that since her conversion she is dearer to him than ever before. The repentant sinners all emphasize the sincerity of their conversion, and the Soul ends the play with a last appeal to the audience to " eschew vycys, ande so to ende with perfeccion."

The nature of each character is sufficiently evident, and no explanation is needed except that, in the play, Wysdom is regarded as the personification of the attribute rather than as the individual Christ. It must also be borne in mind that, while Anima, or the Soul, is the real object of strife, her downfall and subsequent regeneration are accomplished through the triple medium of Mynde, Wylle, and Understondyng, literally and awkwardly designated throughout the play as three attributes of the soul, instead of being given some allegorical relationship.

The interpretation runs thus : The soul instinctively worships and loves true wisdom, of which Christ is the exemplar. But the Devil is ever on the watch to draw the soul away from wisdom and into his own power. This he accomplishes by inventing worldly temptations which appeal to the mind, the will, and the understanding. Through indulgence in these sins the soul is debased, since the soul cannot be dissociated from these other human attributes. But the mind, having once loved the good, becomes uneasy at the consciousness of present degradation, and upon direct contact with the wisdom of Christ is convicted of sin. This is accompanied by horror at the debasement of the soul, which, in the light of wisdom, now becomes apparent. Deep contrition follows, the will is subdued and brought into accordance with the will of God, the lapses from sin are pardoned, and the soul is reinstated in a condition of purity.

In discussing the *Interlude of the Four Elements* I mentioned the "Wit" plays, which, while not to be classed technically with the *Four Elements*, were written with the same purpose, that is, to popularize learning, or science.[1] These plays, three in number, belong to the present class.

The Play of Wyt and Science,[2] though coinciding with the *Four Elements* in purpose, falls at the opposite extreme when regarded from the point of view of literary merit. The latter play is one of the most prosaic and didactic (in the worst sense of the word) of the Moralities ; the former is not only among the finest of the Moralities, but is one of the most perfect allegories in existence.

The play is incomplete at the beginning, though it is evident that not very much is missing. As the existing portion begins, Reason is offering "a glas of Reason" to someone, either to Wyt himself, or to Instruccion, the attendant of Wyt. As we are informed later in the play, Wyt has been suing for the hand of Science, the daughter of Reason, and in this mutilated scene at the beginning he has either approached Reason himself with his request, or has sent his friend Instruccion to ask for him. The latter is probably the case, since, at the end of his speech, while Reason is presenting the glass, he bids farewell to Instruccion, and no one else is mentioned. The purpose and use of the glass Reason explains :

> Namely when ye
> Cum neere my dowghter, Science, then see
> That all thynges be cleane and trycke abowte ye,
> Least of sum sloogyshnes she myght dowte ye,
> Thys glas of Reason shall showe ye all.

[1] "Science," in all these plays, has the broad meaning of learning, or knowledge.

[2] Manly, Vol. I. The Morality was written by John Redford, about 1545.

Reason, left alone, soliloquizes on the proposed match between' his daughter and Wyt. Some people, he says, may marvel that he bestows his daughter thus basely, but he is of opinion that, when two young people are so well fitted for each other, and so much disposed toward mutual love, they ought to be joined in marriage. If Wyt be in want Science will have enough for them both; and, for his part, Reason has no desire to bestow his daughter from worldly considerations, since love and harmony are of greater importance.[1] He reflects that Wyt will need some cheering and refreshing influence, and determines to hire Honest Recreacion, a good woman who dwells hard by, to wait upon him. "If Wyt were halfe deade," he muses, with a forecast of what afterwards happens, "she cowld revyve hym." With this generous thought in mind he hurries out to seek Honest Recreacion; and then Confydence goes by with a picture of his master Wyt, which he is taking to present to Science.

Wyt now appears with his two attendants, Study and Dylygence, and asks their advice as to which road he shall travel. Dylygence, who is of an impetuous turn of mind, urges him at once to take the most travelled road, but the cautious Study wishes to wait and get the advice of Instruccion. In a few moments Instruccion joins them and rebukes Wyt for running aimlessly about without applying to him for guidance. The road that Dylygence has pointed out, he argues, would be a very dangerous one for Wyt to attempt without having some further token of Science's favor, and especially without the sword called Comfort, which Science will soon bestow upon him if he will contain himself in patience for a while longer. Without this weapon he will certainly be attacked by the giant Tedyousnes,

---

[1] The speech here referred to is typical of the play, and indicates the superiority of *Wyt and Science* to most of the other Moralities. Usually a situation like that above would be made the occasion for much literal and didactic speech on the benefits of science to men. Here the language is consistently allegorical.

who lives on this road. But Wyt is impatient to be off, and Dylygence assures him of his fidelity in case of an attack. Study is by no means so eager for the journey. His head is beginning to ache, and he would gladly turn back ; but Wyt and Dylygence compel him to accompany them, and the three start off, leaving Instruccion to mourn his master's foolhardiness.

In the next scene the giant Tedyousnes comes out in a towering rage. He has heard that Wyt is on his way to the lady Science, and he vows to "bete hym to dust" before he can reach his lady-love. Then Wyt comes along, accompanied by Dylygence, who is still urging his master to the fray, and by Study, whose head is now in a very bad condition. The giant rushes out, attacks them savagely, and strikes Wyt dead, while the two attendants run for their lives. Tedyousnes bestows " another kuffe" upon the prostrate Wyt to make sure of him, and then retires in triumph.

Honest Recreacion now comes to the rescue with her attendants, Comfort, Quycknes, and Strength. They kneel about the lifeless body and chant a song of comfort and hope which gradually brings Wyt back to life. At the last verse they raise him to his feet, fully restored.

Reason comes in at this juncture and tells Wyt that he has sent the life-giving company to him. But now that their work is done he exhorts Wyt to dismiss them and go forward on his journey. But Wyt has been through some trying experiences of late, and he does not feel like losing his pleasant company so soon. " I shall to your daughter all at leyser," he assures Reason evasively. Comfort, Quycknes, and Strength retire, but Wyt insists on retaining Honest Recreacion, and with a reproachful " Well, Wyt, I went (*i.e.*, thought) ye had bene no such man as now I see," Reason bids him farewell.

Wyt now proves an arrant traitor to his absent mistress, and makes violent love to Honest Recreacion, laying some emphasis on his desire for a kiss. His companion shows surprise that he should forget Lady Science thus easily, but he reassures her with the easy gallantry of a lover speaking to a new mistress about an old one :

> Shall I tell you trothe?
> I never lovde her.

To win Honest Recreacion, however, he must prove himself in certain ways. First, she challenges him to a dance ; and Wyt, in order to respond to the challenge, finds that he must remove the " cumbryng garment " which Science has given him. Then the minstrels play, the dance begins, and, unnoticed, Idellnes comes softly in and sits down.

Finally Wyt grows weary with the exertion of dancing and lies down, settling his head comfortably in the lap of Idellnes. Honest Recreacion becomes indignant. She recognizes Idellnes as a harlot, and loses no time in telling her so. Idellnes, on her part, is at no loss for a retort ; and Wyt, taking a judicial view of the situation, remarks, "While I take my ese, youre toonges now frame." A distinctly feminine quarrel ensues, and is followed by a debate on the respective merits of the two suitors for Wyt's favor. In the end Wyt goes to sleep, and then Honest Recreacion departs of her own accord, " syns Wyt lyethe as wone that neyther heerth nor seeth." Then Idellnes puts her mark on the sleeper, and whistles for Ingnorance.

The thick-skulled Ingnorance comes shambling on in response to the whistle, and Idellnes sets to work, with infinite pains, to teach him the almost impossible task of spelling his own name.[1] When this is finally accomplished Idellnes performs the almost equally difficult feat of making her pupil realize that he has learned his lesson ; then, as a reward, she gives him Wyt's coat, puts his coat on Wyt in exchange, and the pair, teacher

---

[1] Ingnorance should be contrasted with the Ignorance who figures in *The Longer Thou Livest*. The latter is a very wise person, though he makes fools of others ; the former is the most extreme type of fool.

and pupil, retire in high glee, — Ingnorance because he has earned a new coat, and Idellnes because she has " conjured " her victim " from Wyt into a starke foole."

While Wyt is slumbering quietly in a corner, Confidence comes in seeking him. But he fails to notice the prostrate figure, and goes out mourning the loss of his master. Then Woorshyppe, Favour, Riches, and Fame come in singing ; and when Science presently appears, with her mother Experyence, they offer their services to her, saying that they have been sent by the World. But Science answers mournfully that she has small cause to care for the World's favoring now that Wyt has deserted her, and the delegates of the World are sent away.

At this point Wyt awakens, and, seeing his former mistress before him, advances to excuse himself for his laxity in wooing. But Science, perceiving this strange figure in the motley coat of Ingnorance and with face blackened by the marks of Idellnes, repulses him indignantly. Wyt, blissfully unconscious of his foolish appearance, and laboring under the delusion that his lady is only coy, grows bolder and proffers his customary request for a kiss. Then Science, waiving all nicety of expression, denounces him roundly as an arrant fool, and finally goes out, with her mother, in a state of dignified annoyance.

Wyt at first leaps about in a towering rage at this ungentle treatment, and fumbles for his sword, which is gone. Then he remembers the mirror which Reason gave him, and produces it in order to satisfy himself that Science and Experyence were slandering his personal appearance. At the first glance he is convinced, though not in the way he had expected ; and then his rage takes a sudden turn against Idellnes, whom he rightly blames for the disfigurement. Now Shame enters, with a whip, accompanied by Reason, and administers a sound thrashing to the unhappy Wyt, who kneels and beseeches Reason to pardon him. Reason orders Shame to stay his hand, and cheers the

penitent Wyt by a promise to admit him again as a suitor for
the hand of Science. Then he calls in Study, Dylygence, and
Instruccion, and orders them to return to the service of Wyt.
The restored attendants retire with their master in order to put
new apparel on him, and Reason soliloquizes on the probability
of Wyt's proving worthy of his daughter's hand.

Wyt soon reappears, new-clothed, and carrying the " sword
of comfort," a gift from Science. Fortified now by the presence
of Study and Dylygence, and guided by the sage counsels of
Instruccion, he goes forward to a fresh combat with the giant
Tedyousnes. The giant comes out, as before, but soon falls
before the vigorous attacks of Wyt and his followers. Then
Confydence comes running in to announce to the victor that
Science has been watching the conflict from a mountain, and
is coming to reward him. This announcement is followed by
the entrance of Science with her parents, Reason and Experyence. A duet ensues between " Wyt and his Cumpanye " and
" Science and hir Cumpanye." Speeches are made all round,
and the union of Science and Wyt is sanctioned by Reason
and Experyence.

Wyt here occupies the place usually held by the representative of mankind. In fact, in the broadest sense he may be said
to represent mankind, since he is the personification of the
human mind or intelligence. It will be at once obvious to a
student of the Moralities that the substitution of one of the
attributes of Man in the place of Man himself greatly increases
the opportunities for consistent allegorical action. In the present play there is not a scene, with the exception of Ingnorance's
lesson in spelling,[1] that is not a distinct and significant step in
the progress of the allegory.

[1] Courthope, II, 339, referring to this mere episode, says of the play that
" its leading feature is a conversation in rustic dialogue between Idleness
and Ignorance."

It is apparent, also, that the personified abstractions here are not of the same general character as those we are accustomed to in the Moralities with a human hero. There we have, as a rule, representations of virtues or vices which, when practised by men, are said to be qualities of the mind or heart. There are four such qualities personified in the list here, Confydence and Dylygence on the side of Virtue, Ignorance and Idellnes on the side of Vice. But the other active figures here, Honest Recreation, Study, and Instruccion on the side of goodness, and Tediousnes on the side of evil, represent conditions or influences affecting the mind of man, but not qualities of the mind. Science represents knowledge or learning, the fitting object of the mind's desire. Reason, the father of Science, is of course the reasoning faculty of man, which originates science. Experyence does not figure in the play except as the mother of Science. Shame is merely an agent of retribution. The other characters, Comforte, Quycknes, and Strength in one group, and Fame, Ryches, Favour, and Woorshyppe in the other, are introduced only once in short allegorical scenes which are explained by the mere account of them in the outline of the play given above.

The allegory may be reduced to the following bald statement : The human mind desires learning, but learning is not to be acquired except by diligence and study properly guided, or instructed. The dictates of reason impel the mind in this direction ; but reason also suggests that the mind cannot be held to a continuous career of study, but must occasionally have recourse to innocent recreations which will brace and strengthen it for the sterner work of the search for knowledge. The mind, by a diligent application to study, is at first too eager to grasp knowledge, and, lacking proper guidance and confidence, is soon completely discouraged by the tediousness of work. The reasonable course at this juncture is to turn for the moment to the bracing influence of honest amusements, such as music; but the mind, having become excessively wearied by study, now goes to the opposite extreme, and from an indulgence in innocent pastimes relapses into complete idleness, which soon results in ignorance. This ignorance at first induces a feeling of contentment and complacence; but the mind, by the light of reason, soon comes to realize its debased condition, and is plunged in shame. The feeling of intense shame acts as a wholesome corrective; and the mind, submitting humbly to the dictates of reason, becomes again devoted to study. Confidence returns, and the mind, steadied now by proper methods of instruction, is no longer hindered by the tediousness of work. Under these new conditions, in fact, tediousness soon disappears, and the mind is at last ennobled by the acquisition of knowledge.

The even tenor of the "Wit" plays must be broken for a moment now by the intrusion of a Morality with an entirely different set of ideals, — *Wealth and Health*.[1] The object of the "Wit" plays is to urge men to make the most of their minds and of their opportunities for advancement in learning. *Wealth and Health* has a distinctly patriotic tone, and its object is to induce men — and especially Englishmen — to preserve wealth, health, and liberty within their borders. Though it is constructed primarily for the guidance of men in general, it has in another aspect a political and controversial leaning which allies it at some points with Group IV.

The play opens with the entry of Wealth and Health, who come on the stage singing, and then fall into a debate on their comparative merits. Wealth at first takes a high hand, refusing to admit that anyone else can compare with him in the estimation of men; but Health, speaking modestly, makes out so good

[1] In '*Lost*' *Tudor Plays*, edited by John S. Farmer. The play was entered in the Stationers' Register, 1557.

a case for himself that Wealth is finally brought to admit that
he was mistaken in his estimate of Health, and begs the latter's
pardon. This is readily accorded, and the two agree for the
future to remain in each other's company. Then Liberty enters,
also in a tuneful frame of mind, which is soon altered to dejection when he sees that Wealth and Health keep together but
fail to make up to him. Plucking up his spirits, however, he
advances and opens an argument with the two friends to prove
that he is better than either of them, and that neither of them
could get along without him. Wealth and Health are not prepared to adopt this point of view at once, but gradually all three
come to realize that their interests are common, after which
discovery they promise to stick together for the future.

This amicable resolve is no sooner taken than Ill Will
approaches and introduces himself to the trio as their very
humble servant Will. The three friends are inclined to be a
bit suspicious of their suddenly conferred mastership; but the
pretended Will glibly talks them round, and persuades Liberty
that he is related to him.

> Will and Liberty is of ancestry old:
> Without Liberty, Will dare not be bold:
> And where Will lacketh, Liberty is full cold:
> Therefore, Will and Liberty must needs be of kin.

The three companions, completely deceived, agree to take him
into their common service, and then withdraw, for no reason
except the dramatic one of allowing Ill Will to explain his
innate wickedness to the audience.

When Ill Will has finished this account of his personality,
he is joined by his friend Shrewd Wit, who recounts, in the
usual fashion of the Vice, his recent exploit of stealing a
purse. Their confidences are interrupted by the rude entry of
Hance, otherwise called War, a drunken Fleming, who is first
tuneful, then garrulous, in broken English. At the mention of

the name Wealth he asserts that Wealth is in Flanders and that he himself brought him there; to which Ill Will assents with a curse, agreeing by implication that wealth did come by war in Flanders. Then the merry Hance staggers out, the two villains lay a hurried plan for deceiving Wealth, Health, and Liberty, and drop suddenly to their knees and pretend to pray when they see their trio of masters coming in. Their piety is warmly commended, and Shrewd Wit, modestly giving his name simply as Wit, is employed as a servant along with his friend. Then the two servants retire, singing in the fullness of their hearts.

The three friends are now joined by Remedy, whom they greet with great respect, judging by his appearance that he is one having authority. Remedy returns their greetings in kindly fashion, and tells them :

> To maintain you is all my desire and faculty :
> Yet hard it is to do, the people be so variable :
> And many be so wilful they will not be reformable . . .
> My authority is given to me, most special,
> To maintain you three in this realm to be.

After they have come to a full understanding with each other, Remedy sends the trio out with a final warning against "ill and shrewd company." Then, while he lingers to impress his views on the audience, the two Vices return and stumble across him. He recognizes them and curses them heartily as Ill Will and Shrewd Wit, while they, for their defence, retort that he is a liar, and order him to call them by their proper names, Will and Wit. Remedy, however, not easily to be hoodwinked, declines to call them by any names of their own invention. He warns them that they will soon come to punishment for their crimes, and leaves them.

To combat this new enemy the Vices decide to tell lies about him to their masters, and thus to ruin his character with them. The aforesaid masters conveniently appearing when this plan is completed, the Vices proceed to carry out their program, then threaten to leave if they are not well used; whereat the three guileless employers entreat them earnestly to remain. The sensitive retainers give in graciously, and the whole company, employers and employed, retire in amicable discussion.

Remedy comes back and explains to the audience that his office is "to amend all faults." He has come to see how Wealth, Health, and Liberty are prospering. While he is talking, the bibulous Hance again puts in an unwelcome appearance, and is sternly rebuked by Remedy, not for being drunk, but for being a Fleming.

> Fie on thee, flattering knave! fie on all you aliants, I say!
> Ye can, with craft and subtle figure, Englishmen's wealth away.

When the much-berated Hance is properly disposed of, Remedy is joined by Health, who comes in sadly, with a kerchief around his head, and wailing that he is "infect, both body and soul." His friends Wealth and Liberty are in even worse case, as he tells Remedy.

> As for Wealth, he is fallen in decay and necessity
> By waste and war, through Ill Will and Shrewd Wit;
> And Liberty is kept in durance and captivity.

Remedy promises to help them, but is forced to admit that he cannot do much till he catches Ill Will and Shrewd Wit. They stand aside and wait, and presently the two Vices come in boldly, seeing no one around. Remedy leaps out upon them, and Ill Will attempts to disguise his identity by talking a kind of Spanish; but the inexorable Remedy binds them and hands them over to Health to be taken away to prison.

We are to imagine that, after the capture and imprisonment of the two Vices, Remedy at once proceeded to relieve the distresses of his three guileless wards, who, in the final scene, come in together and ask pardon very contritely of their benefactor.

Remedy graciously comforts them, warns them against a repetition of their fall from grace, and ends the play with a prayer for Queen Elizabeth and the country.

It may look at first like a plain case of hair-splitting to separate this Morality from such a play as *The Three Laws*,[1] where the three abstractions, Law of Christ, Law of Moses, and Law of Nature are striven against and for a time overthrown by a set of Vices. But technically there is a distinct difference. In the latter play the " three laws " are consciously *pitted against* the Vices. They are never deceived in the character of the Vices, who make no attempt to enter their service, but accomplish their temporary downfall by corrupting men. In the present play Wealth, Health, and Liberty occupy the place usually taken by the human hero, as Wit does in the " Wit " plays. They are for a time deceived by the Vices, admit them to their service, are debased in consequence, and are finally restored by turning to Remedy, the Virtue of the play.

There is one noticeable point of difference from the other plays of this special group. In this play there is no depiction of the Life in Sin. In the Morality of *Wisdom, Who is Christ*, Mind, Will, and Understanding are corrupted and for a time live in sin, just as the human hero does. The same is true of Wit in the " Wit " plays. But in the present play the abstract personifications over whom the war is waged cannot be shown as living in sin, since they are essentially good. They are weakened, however, in consequence of the machinations of the Vices, in whom they place an abused confidence, and in much the same manner in which the " three laws " are weakened. Health is " infect, both body and soul," Wealth lapses into " decay and necessity " through the contrivances of Ill Will and Shrewd Wit, and Liberty is imprisoned. In *The Three Laws*

---

[1] See pp. 43 ff., above.

the Law of Nature becomes leprous, the Law of Moses becomes
" stark blind," and the Law of Christ is bound and sentenced
to be burned.

All the chief characters in the present play represent forces
at work in the land at large. Wealth, Health, and Liberty are
national blessings which should be maintained. Ill Will and
Shrewd Wit are the forces which make for disturbance and war,
and Remedy is the salutary power of good law, the chief function of which is to keep down disturbing forces and to maintain
wealth, health, and liberty. Hance is a type figure, introduced
for a bit of patriotic by-play.

The interpretation is brief and simple : Wealth, health, and
liberty are all necessary to the welfare of a country. They are
of equal importance, and are always found together. When
desires for sharp practice and lust for war arise in a country,
these national blessings are quickly reduced, and would in time
disappear entirely but for the intervention of sound and patriotic
laws. The enforcing of these laws curbs war and dishonesty, and
restores wealth, health, and liberty in the land.

The popularity of *The Play of Wyt and Science* is attested
by the fact that it was reproduced a few years later, in slightly
altered form, with the title *The Marriage of Wit and Science*.[1]
In allegorical structure the two plays are almost identical, but
with one very important difference : Wit, in the second play, is
accompanied throughout by Will, a new figure, who represents
inclination. The second author, also, had it in mind that the
element of age must be regarded when one speaks of the acquisition of knowledge by the intellect, and he brings Wit on
the stage as a boy seven years old,[2] — though, to be sure, we
hear nothing more of the age of Wit (except that in the second

[1] Dodsley, Vol. III.
[2] Of course the same specification of age may have been given in the
beginning of the other play, which, as it stands, is incomplete at that end.

act Will thinks he is "seventeen or thereabout"), but must
imagine that he grows steadily older, if not steadily wiser, as
the play goes on.

This failure of the hero to wax steadily in wisdom as in
stature brings up a point which, though obvious enough, de-
serves a remark in passing. The Morality playwright did not
advocate the doctrine that a human being can grow, uninter-
ruptedly, better or wiser with the advancing years. Whether the
hero be good or evil in the beginning, he has his strongly contrasted periods of progress and of retrogression before the ideal
ending in peace;[1] and his final conversion, in nearly every case,
is accomplished through a powerful spiritual upheaval.

The play is not introduced by a Prologue. Nature comes on
leading her son Wit, a boy seven years old. The precocious Wit
announces to his mother that he is deeply in love;

> And though I wed not yet, yet am I old enou'
> To serve my lady to my power, and to begin to woo.

Nature enquires the name of the lady who has enflamed her
son's youthful heart, and Wit confesses that it is Science, the
daughter of Reason and Experience. He implores his mother
to aid him in his suit, but she tells him gravely that it is not
within her power to unite him with such a famous lady as
Science. There are but few that could prove themselves worthy
of so high an honor, and Wit must win his lady by patient
zeal through time and travail. To aid him in his toil she gives
him a boy to wait upon him, "A bird of mine, some kin to
thee; his name is Will." The new servant, when interrogated
by Wit as to his powers of service, proves evasive. He admits

---

[1] I have already called attention to two exceptions which will test this rule.
In *The Trial of Treasure* Just is good at the beginning and remains, without a
lapse, good to the end. In *The Longer Thou Livest the More Fool Thou Art*
Moros, foolish and vicious at the start, becomes steadily more foolish and
more vicious as the play proceeds.

that he can do all things when it pleases him, but refuses to say anything more definite than, " If ye bid me run, perhaps I will go." [1] Wit is inclined to grow impatient at this show of independence, but Nature desires them to be agreeable to each other. Then, with a final request to Will for obedience to his master, she leaves the two boys to their fate.

The beginning of the second act shows Wit already puzzled and annoyed by the independence and flightiness of his servant. He is urging Will to repair at once to Science with an offer of his master's hand, and Will, after teasing him for a while with incoherent replies, finally admits that he himself is not anxious to bring about the marriage. While Wit remains a bachelor (he has evidently grown beyond his seven years now) he may go about and enjoy life freely; but if he is " tied by the toe " in marriage he will speedily become " solemn and sour, and angry as a wasp," and all his care will be to hamper his poor servant Will. Wit hastens to assure his disconsolate follower that a marriage shall make no difference in their pleasant relations, and finally he persuades Will to act as messenger.

We are next introduced to the lady Science, who is in a state of profound dejection. Many suitors have presented themselves, and have spent their youth and wealth in the desire to obtain her hand; but none has succeeded, and she feels that, for the present at least, she ought not to encourage any more advances. But Reason, her father, wisely urges her to retain hope. Among the many thousands who are striving for her favor there must be a chosen one who will prove worthy, and when this one comes she must yield herself freely and willingly to him. Experience, the mother, seconds Reason's counsel, and Science, though unconvinced, gives in wearily :

> Fall out as it will : there is no help, I see.
> Some one or other in time must marry me.

[1] *Go* has here the usual Middle English sense of " walk."

While this conversation has been going on, Will has been in the background listening, and now he comes forth buoyantly with a matrimonial offer from his master, who will not stick, he says, to marry Science within the hour if she will but give the word. He proceeds to describe his master as a well-favored youth of " seventeen or thereabout," and, to back up his statements, produces a picture which Wit has sent so that Science may know the appearance of the man who is suing for her hand. After scanning the picture, Science admits that " nature in him hath done her part," and despatches Will back to his master with an invitation to come and talk matters over.

In the third act Will delivers his message to Wit, who is transported with delight, and presses on at once to the house of Science, taking Will along with him. Here an interview takes place between the lovers, in company with Reason and Experience, and with Will, who begins to take a very gloomy view of the projected union. The solemn faces of Science and her parents — especially the mother — are not to his taste, and he tells his master so in very vigorous asides. Wit is informed by his mistress that there is a formidable enemy whom he must vanquish before he can win her hand, and that this enemy is so powerful that he will have to overcome him not by force, but by sleight. To aid him in the perilous enterprise, Experience goes out to procure Instruction, a trusted friend and retainer of the family, who, with his two servants, Study and Diligence, will accompany Wit and give him the benefit of their counsels ; and Reason gives him a " glass of crystal clear," in which to study his defects. Presently the three counsellors arrive, and Wit, after greeting them cordially, takes them off to his own house, along with the disgruntled Will.

Act IV shows Wit becoming very restive under the counsels of Instruction, Study, and Diligence. He is a hot-headed and ardent young lover, and they persist in their policy of delay until he shall become worthy of the hand of Science. Will is now in open enmity with the three counsellors, and he urges his master to take the management of affairs into his own hands. In the midst of the argument Reason and Experience appear with their daughter, and Wit now appeals directly to his mistress, urging her to bestow herself upon him and put an end to his miserable period of probation. Science answers that her lover must undergo a stern trial of strength before he can claim her. In a neighboring wood dwells the giant Tediousness, who has sworn to slay all claimants for the hand of Science. Already he has slain tens of thousands of suitors, and unless Wit can overcome this monster and bring his head as a trophy to Science he will have to share the common fate. Wit is at once on fire for the combat, and Will urges him on. Diligence is willing to accompany them, but Instruction refuses to be a party to such an immature and rash adventure, and Study, complaining of an aching head, decides to remain behind with Instruction.

The rest of the play follows substantially the same lines as *The Play of Wyt and Science.*

This second version of the Wit and Science plot is not, in general, so well motivated as the first one. For example, one of the most important incidents — the slumbering of Wit in the lap of Idleness and his consequent disgrace and punishment — is thoroughly motivated in the first play, and is decidedly weak in the second. In the former case Wit, after his resuscitation, refuses to listen to the advice of Reason ; then he deliberately leaves Honest Recreation for Idleness, and when Reason finally brings Shame in to chastise him one feels that his punishment is richly merited. In the latter case Wit becomes wearied with his exertions, decides to rest before resuming his labors, and innocently places his head upon the convenient lap of Idleness. He has disdained no good counsels, and, upon awakening, he is prepared to return at once to his arduous task of winning

Science; but after a quiet scene, in which he modestly attempts to procure recognition from Reason and Science, Reason calls Shame in to administer a whipping to the unoffending Wit. These scenes are quite as well motivated as the average Morality incidents, but in comparison with the corresponding scenes in the first " Wit " play they fall quite flat.

The only new characters here—and consequently the only ones that now require explanation — are Nature and Will. Nature is here pictured as the great guiding force of children, their teacher during the early years before they must turn to the education of the world. Will, who is brought on the stage as a child coeval with Wit, is, I take it, the representative of human inclination or impulse, which is not essentially wicked, but which is likely to influence the mind in the direction of pleasure rather than of study. When Wit is in a state of degradation Reason says to him,

> Remember, how Instruction should have been followed still,
> And how thou wouldst be ruled by none but by Will,[1]

which points to this explanation of the character of Will. He is the same sort of figure as Frewyl or Imagynacyon in *Hyckescorner*,[2] neither essentially good nor essentially bad. How important a factor he is in the later version the following interpretation will show.

The human mind early in life ceases to follow merely the guidance of nature. The learning of the world begins to appeal to it, and soon becomes the chief object of its desire. But the natural inclinations, which would help in the quest for learning if rightly directed, often influence the mind in the direction of ease and pleasure. The mind addresses itself with diligence to the work of study, is wisely guided in its labors, and bids fair to become successful. The inclinations, however, soon begin to pull the other way, and end by imbuing the mind with a strong

---

[1] Act V, scene 2, p. 385.   [2] See note 1, p. 50, above.

distaste for study. The tediousness of study completes the work ; and the mind, turning at first to innocent pleasures, soon lapses into idleness and ignorance. But human reason will not permit the mind to fall irretrievably into the dull unconsciousness of the brute. By a sudden stirring of reason the mind realizes its degradation, is struck with intense shame, and returns with vigor to the pursuit of learning. The inclination joins in this pursuit, study loses all its tediousness, and the mind at last becomes enriched by knowledge.

The third and last of the "Wit" plays is *The Marriage of Wit and Wisdom*,[1] as bad a play as the other two are good. The first two are skillful allegories, dignified and pure in tone ; the third, though it employs the same motive, is disconnected, and is varied with low comedy scenes of a grossness uncommon even in a Morality.

The author here, to be sure, is adapting his work to the desires of an audience becoming enamored of scenes from actual life, and growing impatient of unmixed allegory, however skillful and consistent. The resulting play is allegorical in its main structure, and teaches a lesson for the guidance of life ; but even in the allegorical parts — to say nothing of the unmixed low comedy scenes — there is an evident desire to raise a laugh rather than to induce the reflective and repentant mood. This Morality, then, is one of those which come very near the bounds of the comedy of actual life, while remaining, by virtue of their technical structure, within the limits of the earlier species.

After a brief outline of the play by the Prologue, Severity and his wife Indulgence enter and hold a family conference with their easy-going son Wit. The uncompromising Severity tells Wit that he has it in mind to procure a wife for him, and that if Wit does not behave well in general he will never cost

[1] See *Five Anonymous Plays* (Early English Dramatic Series), edited by John S. Farmer. The play is usually dated about 1579.

his father another groat. Indulgence also expresses her desire to see their son well married, but uses much milder terms than the choleric father. Severity now comes to the point by proposing Dame Wisdom as a fitting and desirable mate for his son, and the proposal pleases Wit, as, indeed, all proposals do, whatever their nature or source. Finally, Severity warns his son to apply himself diligently to his book and avoid Idleness, also to beware of Irksomeness, a monster who has his lair near the house of Lady Wisdom. Then the parents retire, and Wit, dutifully resolving to follow their precepts, goes out to give a practical demonstration of his virtue.

Idleness, the chief Vice of the play, enters and in the usual manner lays his nature bare before the audience. He is determined to corrupt Wit, and to prevent the union between him and Wisdom; but, as Wit in his present virtuous condition of mind would not be likely to strike up a friendship with a person named Idleness, the wily schemer plans to alter his name to Honest Recreation, a name which, as he knows, will be attractive to Wit. Then Wantonness joins him, and he makes arrangements to employ her in his attack on the virtue of Wit.

The innocent subject of these plans now comes upon the scene, and extends a warm greeting to Idleness when the latter introduces himself under his assumed name. Then Wantonness is presented as Mistress Modest Mirth, a name which endears her at once to the chaste mind of Wit. After some friendly conversation they all sit down, and Wit is easily induced to take a short nap, with his head in the lap of Wantonness. She then sets a fool's bauble on his head and blackens his face, while Idleness steals his purse. The two conspirators retire in high good humor with their success, and Good Nurture enters, seeking for Wit. In searching about the stage he stumbles heavily on the sleeping dupe and wakes him up. Then Wit, on having his attention drawn to the obvious defects in his personal appearance, washes his face and removes the fool's bauble from his head. Good Nurture calls in the genuine Honest Recreation, presents him to Wit in the capacity of servant, and they all retire.

Idleness, whose constant function in this play is to amuse the audience, whether at his own expense or not, makes his second entrance rigged out as a doctor, and carrying the purse that he has filched from Wit. He lays down the purse in a corner, and presently two rogues named Snatch and Catch appear and combine against him. They steal the purse, then seize Idleness, tie a sheet over his head, beat him soundly, and go out with the purse. But soon Wit comes to the rescue, with Honest Recreation at his heels. He frees Idleness from his inconvenient headgear, and listens sympathetically and with a characteristic ignoring of his previous experiences when the latter emerges from the sheet and introduces himself as Due Disport.

On the advice of the so-called Due Disport the confiding Wit now dismisses Honest Recreation from his service and starts off to enjoy himself with his new friend, rejoicing that he has got rid of Honest Recreation, who was becoming tiresome. Idleness leads him straight to the lair of Irksomeness, then runs away, and Irksomeness leaps out, beats Wit down with his club, and leaves him for dead. But Lady Wisdom now makes her appearance. She approaches Wit and helps him to his feet, and he apparently comes to life at once, as he answers her the moment she addresses him. She urges him to attack Irksomeness again, and presents him with a sword. Fortified with this new weapon he challenges the monster to a second trial of strength, and this time the luck is on Wit's side. He pursues Irksomeness off the stage, returns with the head of his enemy, and rushes off to tell the news to his father.

The obliging Idleness returns, this time in the character of rat-catcher. Search, the constable, follows, seeking for Idleness, whom he wishes to arrest for cozening Wit. He fails to recognize the offender in his new garb, and offers to pay him if he will cry a proclamation offering a reward for the criminal. Idleness consents and mounts a chair. Then a series of dull witticisms follows, at the end of which Search runs away without paying what he has promised, and Idleness rushes off in pursuit. Dame Fancy now appears, planning to capture Wit for a husband; and Wit, who is always ready to coöperate heartily with anyone who wishes to make a fool of him, comes in to place himself at the disposal of Fancy. She tells him that she is a messenger from Lady Wisdom, and hands him a letter which bids him go with the messenger to a place where Wisdom will meet him. Fancy then leads him into her own house, and there makes him an offer of herself and her fortune. But Wit, for the first time in his career, asserts himself. He protests that he is in love with Wisdom; so Fancy, unable to prevail over his stubborn heart, goes out and leaves him in durance vile.

Then Idleness, still in the character of general entertainer, comes in, spies an empty house, steals the pottage-pot, and leaves. Presently the two servants, Doll and Lob, who have been engaged in a questionable amusement in the barn, come back and discover the loss of the pot; and when Mother Bee, their mistress, returns, she beats them soundly for their carelessness. Inquisition enters with Idleness, whom he has caught with the pot about his neck. The pot is given up, and Inquisition leads Idleness away to justice.

Good Nurture comes in, again looking for Wit, and hears the latter bewailing his fate in bitter terms from the prison of Fancy. He breaks the prison door, releases Wit, and leads him away. Then Idleness makes his last appearance in the play. He is attired like a priest, and invites all "who list not to work" to follow him.

In the final scene the father Severity enters with his chastened son Wit, who is now to be united with Wisdom. Good Nurture enters with the bride, and the young lovers sing by turns to each other, as in the first Wit play. Then the company sets forth to the wedding, and the Epilogue ends the play by impressing the moral upon the audience.

The only characters that need concern us seriously are those that figure in the allegory. Severity and Indulgence are the father and mother of Wit, but why they should be so one is at a loss to understand. The author fails to make this relationship allegorically reasonable, and we must conclude that this is simply one more point of approximation to the drama of actual life; that is, in the mind of the author and in the minds of his audience the scenes presenting Severity, Indulgence, and Wit are merely the family conferences of a severe father, an indulgent mother, and an easy-going and complaisant son. Any attempt to go beyond this in the interpretation of the first two characters would, I am sure, be only a display of allegoristic skill on the part of the interpreter, and would also be a work of supererogation, since Severity and Indulgence have no part in the play but to exhibit a strong parental anxiety that their son may be well married. Inquisition, another character with an allegorical name, is likewise of no importance. He is simply an officer of the law, who arrests Idleness toward the close of the play. Snatch, Catch, and Search are type figures with suggestive names. Mother Bee, Doll, and Lob are individuals introduced in a short scene of rough humor.

The characters, then, upon whom the allegory depends are Wit, Wisdom, Idleness, Irksomeness, Honest Recreation, Fancy, Wantonness, and Good Nurture; and most of these have been discussed before. Wisdom, of course, is the same character as Science in the two previous plays, and Irksomeness the same as Tediousness. Fancy here sets herself up in opposition to

Wisdom as the fitting object of Wit's desire, and represents empty imaginings as opposed to solid learning. Wantonness, like Idleness, represents a quality of the corrupted mind, and Good Nurture stands for good bringing-up, or good training, a force or condition affecting the mind, but not a quality of the mind.

The Epilogue skillfully avoids giving us the clew to the allegory :

> For though the style be rough, and phrases found unfit,
> Yet may you say, upon the head the very nail is hit!
> Wherefor, the moral mark! for Finis let it pass,
> And Wit may well and worthy then use it for a glass.
> Whereby for to essue his foes, that always do await him,
> And never hang upon the hook, wherewith they seek to bait him.[1]

Every reader of *The Marriage of Wit and Wisdom* will agree with the first line of this quotation, but will be inclined to balk at the second. Instead of hitting the very nail on the head the author has made an awkward attempt to hit several nails on the head at once, with the result that not one of them is driven home. In fact, one is almost tempted to throw up the whole business of arguing for the play as a Morality, and to let the interpretation go at something like this : Let Wit — or any other gullible young man — beware whom he trusts. But it is obvious that the main structure of the play is allegorical, that the chief characters are of the kind necessary to an allegory, and that, with this machinery, the play teaches one lesson for the guidance of life ; so one must make the best of an unfortunate situation.

Much of the action, in fact, has been planned without any strict sense of allegorical fitness. The author keeps the main situations of the other two " Wit " plays, but fails to lead up to them in a consistent fashion. For instance, in the other two plays Wit is beaten down by Tediousness, but this is because

[1] P. 298.

(to introduce literal with allegorical language) he is studying in a misguided or spiritless fashion. In the present play, after Wit has passed from the company of Honest Recreation to that of Idleness, he is tricked by Idleness into visiting the den of Irksomeness, where he is beaten into insensibility. That is, the mind, while wasting away in idleness, is rendered apathetic by the irksomeness of work, a paradoxical condition of things, surely. Then, as if this were not enough, Wit is jerked back to activity by Wisdom, the signification being that the mind, in a condition of ignorance and paralysis, is recalled by wisdom, the result of diligent study.

But, with such glaring inconsistencies in mind, we can present the interpretation in a general sort of way: The mind, while desiring the wisdom resulting from study, often ignorantly employs the wrong methods of acquiring this wisdom. Realizing that innocent pleasures are lawful, it relapses into idleness in the mistaken belief that this is rest and recreation. The result is that it grows besotted through wanton desires, and is redeemed only by the application to it of wise training, which permits for purposes of recreation only those pleasures which are really innocent. After a period of virtue the mind grows weary of that relaxation which employs only harmless amusements, and, influenced by its desires, again has recourse to idle delights; but these, by contrast, make studies seem intolerably irksome, and the mind soon falls into a state of apathy. From this condition it at length recovers, and, with a renewed desire for wisdom, overcomes the tediousness of study. There is, however, one more obstacle to be overcome. Empty fancies begin to appeal to the mind, and for a time render it unfit for serious work. But the influence of good training again brings salvation; and now the mind, after sundry lapses, goes on steadily in its search for wisdom, with which it is at length rewarded.

CHAPTER VI

MORALITIES ILLUSTRATING A SPECIAL TEXT

The second main division of the Moralities contains three plays, each one enforcing and illustrating a particular text which is announced in the title, is repeated from time to time in the dialogue, and in general is made the watchword of the play. In every case it is the text that binds the play together and gives it unity. There is no hero upon whose fortunes to concentrate our interest from first to last. Each play is a bundle of loosely connected scenes,— or of scenes that would be loosely connected if it were not for the one central thought that each new scene, as it comes, presents in some fresh aspect.

The first of these plays, then, to give it the full advantage of its sonorous title, is *Like Will to Like, Quoth the Devil to the Collier*.[1] The action consists, on the one hand, in the mating of several vicious human types by the Vice, Nichol Newfangle, in the service of their common master the Devil; and, on the other hand, in the mating of Virtuous Life with his allegorical companions, Good Fame and Honour. In the end poetical justice is meted out to all the characters. The vicious type figures, after being borne in hand by Nichol Newfangle, are ruined and then die shameful deaths, and Nichol himself is mounted on the Devil's back for "a journey into Spain." Virtuous Life, on the contrary, is reassured by God's Promise, and joined by Good Fame and Honour.[2]

[1] By Ulpian Fulwel. Dodsley, Vol. III. The play was printed in 1568.

[2] It will thus be seen that the play is to be grouped with the Morality *The Trial of Treasure* and the moral tragedy *The Nice Wanton* in probably owing something to French influence. For an account of the French plays of this type see p. 121, note 2, above.

The Prologue explains to his hearers why " our Author " has made this particular selection of title and subject :

> Sith pithy proverbs in our English tongue doth abound,
> Our author thought good such a one for to choose
> As may show good example, and mirth may eke be found,
> But no lascivious toys he purposeth for to use.

Then the play begins with a merry address to the audience by the Vice, Nichol Newfangle. Although Nichol is the embodiment of sin in general, he represents in a special way the fashionable, or newfangled, vices of the day. In narrating the history of his apprenticeship to Lucifer he tells the audience :

> All kinds of sciences he taught unto me :
> That unto the maintenance of pride might best agree.
> I learned to make gowns with long sleeves and wings :
> I learned to make ruffs like calves' chitterlings,
> Caps, hats, coats, with all kinds of apparels,
> And especially breeches as big as good barrels.
> Shoes, boots, buskins, with many pretty toys :
> All kinds of garments for men, women, and boys.
>
> .   .   .   .
>
> Nichol Newfangle was and is, and ever shall be :
> And there are but few that are not acquainted with me.

Lucifer joins his apprentice and greets him with pride and affection. Nichol meets these friendly advances at first with a good deal of chaffing on the subject of Lucifer's bottle-nose and ill-favored visage, but finally he sobers down and consents to hear his master's plan for retaining the allegiance of his followers on earth. Then Lucifer grows confidential and informs him :

> Thou knowest I am both proud and arrogant,
> And with the proud I will ever be conversant;
> I cannot abide to see men that are vicious
> Accompany themselves with such as be virtuous.
> Wherefore my mind is, sith thou thy part canst play,
> That thou adjoin like to like alway.

Nichol at first pretends to think that his master is exhorting him to live on a diet of leeks and onions, but the patient Devil again laboriously explains his real purpose; and then the apprentice bids him have no fear, since he is ready to play his part. Tom Collier is now seen approaching, and Lucifer steps aside to see how his plan will work.

Tom comes up and exchanges friendly greetings with Nichol. The latter asks for an account of the day's work, and Tom gleefully announces that for every bushel of coal he has sold he has delivered but three pecks. Nichol commends him for "as fit a companion for the devil as may be," and introduces him to Lucifer in pursuance of their motto. Tom accepts the introduction, joins in a song and dance with his new friend in token of amity, then retires to continue his dishonest trade. Lucifer commends his adroit apprentice, bestows his blessing upon him, and departs, leaving him to carry on the work of joining like to like.

Nichol is now joined by Tom Tosspot, who comes in angry and swearing because he can nowhere find a companion who does not exhort him to leave off his pride and blaspheming, instead of agreeing with him in friendly fashion. Catching sight of Nichol, he greets him as his friend and patron; and Nichol, for his part, promises to find the disgruntled Tom a companion "as fit for you as a pudding for a friar's mouth." Presently Ralph Roister appears on the scene, and is introduced to Tom as the promised mate. The new-made friends prepare to enlighten each other on the question of personal history; but Nichol, taking sudden offense at them for neglecting to remove their caps in the presence of their superior, pitches in and gives them a sound whipping. The two rogues become submissive at once and beg him to desist. This he consents to do after he has drubbed them to his heart's content. Then he orders Tom and Ralph to continue with their narratives, promising the farm "called Saint Thomas-a-Waterings or else Tyburn Hill,"[1] "that of Beggar's manor doth hold," to the one who proves himself the worse rogue. At the close of the hearing Nichol is unable to decide between two such unmixed scoundrels, so he judicially divides the prize between them.

The friends now receive a substantial addition to their company in the person of Hance, ironically addressed as "little bellied Hance" by the sportive Nichol. The newcomer is in an advanced condition of tipsiness. Attempting to dance, he sprawls over the floor instead, and finally decides to take the easier way and go to sleep. Then Philip Fleming, drunk and portly of waist as Hance himself, comes in looking for his drinking companion. He rouses Hance from his pleasant dream of being drowned in a barrel of beer, and urges him to return to the actual delights of the bottle. Nichol commends his disciples, and allows them all to depart for a drinking-bout, while he himself stays to receive two more favorite pupils, Cuthbert Cutpurse and Pierce Pickpurse. These rascals are highly praised for their success in their chosen trade, and Nichol generously informs them that they are to inherit a piece of property called "the land of the two-legged mare" (*i.e.*, the gallows). The two thieves are delighted, and are planning to order a feast in celebration of their good luck when Virtuous Life interrupts them with a soliloquy on the advantages of a clear conscience. Nichol invites him to join their merry company, but Virtuous Life is quite content with the approving fellowship of his undisturbed conscience. "My name," he proclaims loftily,

> is Virtuous Life, and in virtue is my delight.
> So Vice and virtue cannot together be united;
> But the one the other hath always spited.
> For as the water quencheth fire, and the flame doth suppress,
> So virtue hateth vice, and seeketh a redress.

[1] The two places chiefly used for execution, after the discontinuance of the Elms in Smithfield. — Hazlitt.

Nichol sees no prospect of a recruit in the person of Virtuous Life, so he retires, leading his two followers, and the audience is left for a while at the mercy of the incorruptible soliloquizer. At length the sermon is cut short by the entrance of Good Fame, God's Promise, and Honour, who have come to show their appreciation of Virtuous Life by joining themselves to him.

After the withdrawal of this virtuous troop, Nichol Newfangle reappears with a bag, a staff, a bottle, and two halters, with which to reward his followers. He is in high good humor over the success of his plans. His pupils have spent all their substance on the strength of his promises; and when Tom Tosspot and Ralph Roister come in he presents them with the bag and the bottle and tells them to go begging. They lament their simplicity in allowing themselves to be duped, and turn the tables on Nichol for a moment by throwing him down and beating him heartily; but this does not help their case, and at last they accept the inevitable result of their folly and go out to beg for a living.

Severity, the judge, now appears; and when Cuthbert Cutpurse and Pierce Pickpurse come on the stage seeking a refuge from the law, he detains them and sentences them to the gallows. Nichol puts the halters about their necks, thus fulfilling his earlier promise, and then turns them over to Hankin Hangman, who leads them forth to execution. Finally the Devil comes in, and Nichol Newfangle is compelled to mount on his back to "make a journey into Spain," while Virtuous Life and his companions appear and wind up the play by applying the obvious moral to the situation.

The author here chose to improve the lives of his audience by exhibiting vices to shun rather than virtues to emulate. We have in the play a whole troop of sinful and amusing persons to warn us by their careers that unauthorized gaiety cannot last forever, and one rather colorless abstraction to assure us by his experience that virtue, besides the oft-promised reward of its own radiant self, is enriched by various earthly emoluments well worth considering. This playwright, like many others, was willing to furnish his audience with the incentive for a good laugh, while occupied, in the main, with the sterner business of improving their lives.

A general comment may here be made with regard to the Morality playwright and his purpose in producing such a type of drama. It is too often indicated, in general terms, that the Morality was a purely religious production, and that the frowning author had but one desire in life, to herd his ignorant flock of listeners together on the straight and narrow path to Heaven. In some cases this judgment would undoubtedly be the correct one. The most earnest seeker for frivolous motives could hardly credit Bishop Bale with any lighter desire than this. Bishop Bale, to give him his full due while we are about it, went farther than this : he narrowed the path till it could accommodate none who did not start in it from the Protestant fold. But from Bishop Bale down to the author of *Like Will to Like, Quoth the Devil to the Collier* ranged a line of authors, in most of whom the desire to amuse and the desire to edify were mingled in varying proportions. This is not in the least contradictory to the statement in the introductory chapter that a *sine qua non* of the Morality is its avowed purpose of improving life ; but one must insist that the author, while accepting this as a technical requirement, followed his own natural bent in the direction of fun or of seriousness.

To return to the play under discussion, the nature of each character is easily determined. Virtuous Life, or Virtuous Living, personifies the abstraction that his name indicates. He might, by an almost imperceptible change of character, be the man of virtuous life, and accommodate himself to the action as well as he does in his present nature. Very possibly the author may have felt that one virtuous type figure would not be enough to oppose to the swarm of vicious ones, but was unwilling to bore himself or his audience with more than one, and consequently personified the godly life itself, which could apply to any number of people. God's Promise, Honour, and Good Fame personify the rewards which belong to an upright life. On the other side are Tom Tosspot, Tom Collier, Hance, Cuthbert Cutpurse, Ralph Roister, Philip Fleming, and Pierce Pickpurse, who are types of the people who follow vice and suffer for it. In some cases the name indicates the particular vice to which the character is addicted. When, for instance, Ralph Roister introduces himself to Tom Tosspot, the latter comments on the significance of their names:

> It should appear by your sayings that we are of one mind,
> For I know that roisters and tosspots come of one kind.[1]

But in such a case as that of Tom Collier, — the type of men who are dishonest in business relations, — we must go beyond the name to the actions. Nichol Newfangle is the Vice of the play, who represents "all sins generally." Evidently his particular designation, given instead of a regular Vice name, is to harmonize with the general tone of the names ranged on the side of evil. Lucifer requires no explanation, and Severity is simply the judge who appears at the close of the play to give the dupes of Nichol their deserts; it makes no difference whether we regard him as the severe judge or as the severity of the law, which punishes the wicked.

The interpretation is simple and unequivocal: Men who in this life practise vices and yield to the temptations of the Devil are fit companions only for each other and for the master whom they serve. Their pleasures are provided by Satan and his agents, and are of brief duration. In the end they pay the penalty by sorrow and disgrace, and have as a prospect for eternity the endless pains of hell, provided by the master whom they have followed on earth. The virtuous life, on the other hand, is entirely

---

[1] P. 320.

removed from these vices and sinful pleasures of the world, and is accompanied by the rewards which naturally belong to those who practise self-restraint and piety. To those who lead this life God's promises of prosperity and happiness are fulfilled, by substantial tokens of fame and honor in this world and by assurance of salvation in the world to come.

The Tyde Taryeth No Man,[1] by George Wapull, is much more serious in tone. There are scarcely any touches of humor such as abounded in the last play. Corage, the Vice who embodies all sins, and his more specialized co-workers, Hurtfull-helpe, Paynted-profite, and Fayned-furtheraunce, employ their time in urging people to cheat their neighbors, disobey their parents, and sacrifice all their scruples of conscience to the desire for worldly pleasure and advancement, since "*the tyde taryeth no man.*" But finally Faythfull-few asserts himself in the service of his master Christianitye, and employs the same text to persuade people to turn from the error of their ways while there is yet time. Thus the text, like that of *Like Will to Like*, is used in the service both of good and of evil, and both the plays serve as practical lessons to show that people who employ the Devil's sophistry in twisting good advice to wicked ends must suffer for it.

After the Prologue, Corage, the Vice, enters and gives the audience an insight into his methods of work. His general purpose is to procure souls for hell as he explains.

> I, Corage, do call
> Both great and small
> To the Barge of Sinne;
> Wherein they do wallow
> Tyll hell do them swallow:
> That is all they do win.

[1] *Illustrations of Early English Popular Literature,* edited by J. Payne Collier, London, 1864. The play was printed in 1576, but Collier conjectures that "the drama is of considerably older date than the year inserted on the title-page."

The minor Vices, Hurtfull-helpe, Paynted-profite, and Fayned-furtheraunce, join their leader, and the four discuss ways and means of ruining people.[1] These plans are for a time interrupted by the usual question of superiority among the Vices, and the question is settled by the superior physical force of Corage. Then they curtail their names to Helpe, Profite, and Furtheraunce, in order to make a good impression on people, and go out to perform their duties.

Corage, left behind as general manager, is presently joined by his friend Greedinesse. The latter is being momentarily hampered by a brief onslaught on the part of his conscience. A preacher of the gospel has encountered him on the street and has reproached him and his kind as evil members of the commonwealth. But Corage soon raises his friend's mind beyond the reach of petty embarrassments with a lecture on his favorite text, "The tyde taryeth no man," and persuades him that he must make money while he can and in any way that he can. Greedinesse he addresses by a name which the latter much prefers, and under which he commonly works, — Master Welthinesse, — except when he, Corage, forgets himself and lapses into the use of the correct name.

When Greedinesse is sent away, comforted and uplifted in spirit, Hurtfull-helpe comes in with No-good-Neighbourhood. The owner of this sinister name is eager to procure a tenement possessed by Greedinesse. Another man is occupying the tenement, but No-good-Neighbourhood is consumed with the desire to turn him out on the street and take possession himself. Corage informs him how this may best be done, and recommends him to the self-styled Furtheraunce, who comes in at this

---

[1] Here, as a natural enough result of the absence of a human hero to strive for, the Vice-motives are divided. Corage does his work, in the main, unselfishly, and for the general furtherance of wickedness. On the other hand, his followers, like the Vices in *Respublica*, declare that they are laboring for their own gain.

moment. At the counsel of his advisers No-good-Neighbourhood leaves off all but the last element of his name, and under the more attractive designation of Neighbourhood goes out, with Hurtfull-helpe and Fayned-furtheraunce, to obtain the coveted tenement.

The high seat of Corage is now approached by Willing-to-win-worship, a courtier who is in dire need of money. Corage impresses his favorite motto upon this new pupil, advising him not to be too nice in the selection of his paths toward courtly advancement. Hurtfull-helpe and Fayned-furtheraunce reappear. They are introduced to Willing-to-win-worship under their assumed names, and agree to further his ambitions on consideration of a fee.

When the courtly employer and his two servants depart on their errand, Corage is again visited by Greedinesse, whom he tells that Neighbourhood and the courtier are looking for him on matters of business. Greedinesse, scenting profit, hurries out to find them. Corage himself departs to look up some of his "schollers," and during his absence the tenant who has been ejected in favor of No-good-Neighbourhood comes in with bitter complaints on the hardness of the times. He wonders where he can find Christianitye, and decides to follow up this search as his one remaining hope of receiving fair treatment in the world.

When the unhappy tenant goes out, Corage reappears and resumes his seat as judicial adviser for the whole world. He is now approached by "the mayd, Willfull Wanton," who yearns for a husband, — apparently an unholy desire. Corage urges her to disobey her mother, who is virtuously opposed to the idea of marriage, and to get a husband at all costs, since "the tyde taryeth no man." Willfull Wanton departs, much emboldened by this advice. Then the three subordinates of Corage troop in to report progress and to exult over the gains from their lucrative traffic.

When the businesslike Corage has sent his helpers back to their duties, he is visited by Wastefullnesse, the husband of Wantonnesse, the former "mayd Willfull Wanton," now happy in the possession of a husband and a more satisfactory name. Corage reminds his caller that "the tyde taryeth no man," and advises him to be no niggard with his wealth. Wastefullnesse is exhibiting his confidence in the soundness of this advice when suddenly his wife, Wantonnesse, rushes in and casts bitter reproaches on him for his neglect of her. Corage, in the office of mediator, again applies the ever-ready motto, urging them to take their pleasure while they are young enough to enjoy it, and the husband and wife go away lovingly together.

The stage is now cleared for the interposition of a short scene which has only the most general connection with the rest of the play. The Sergeant is shown leading the Debtor off to jail. He shows a readiness to accept a bribe from his prisoner, but the Debtor refuses to free himself in this dishonest manner, and is hurried away to custody.

Christianitye now appears, bearing a sword with "Pollicy" written on one side and "God's word" on the other, also a shield with "Riches" on one side and "Fayth" on the other. He laments that through the greediness of people he is forced to show his sword and shield with the titles "Pollicy" and "Riches." Faythfull-few enters, greets Christianitye lovingly, and turns the titles, though Christianitye warns him: "You faithful in number are few." The experiment is no sooner tried than Greedinesse enters with his master Corage, and after a hot argument with Faythfull-few compels Christianitye to turn his weapons again. Then the whole company leaves the stage, Faythfull-few assuring his friend and master that he will strive to right his weapons in the near future.

Wastefullnesse comes in, poorly clad and bewailing the fact that he and his wife are compelled to separate and seek their livings. Dispayre joins him and urges him, in rather impressive language, to make an end of his life.

> Thy prodigall sinnes are so manifold
> That God of mercy doth thee utterly denay,
> Therefore, to ende thy life it is best.
> Thy calling for mercy is all but in vayne;
> By ending thy life thou shalt be at rest;
> But if longer thou live great shall be thy payne.

Wastefullnesse accepts the advice, and is on his way out to kill himself " with cord or with knyfe," when Faythfull-few rushes up and restrains him. Then the latter kneels down and prays with the unfortunate Wastefullnesse, and together they beseech God to banish Dispayre, who " flyeth " as the petition is offered up. Faythfull-few instructs Wastefullnesse to " scan " the motto "Tyde taryeth no man" "after God's will," and sends him back to his wife with fresh strength.

The decline of the Vices is now indicated by the mournful appearance of Corage, who enters weeping for the death of Greedinesse. Faythfull-few and Authority follow, looking for Corage, who makes violent efforts to escape. But Correction comes in to aid in the arrest, and to him the Vice is handed over for punishment. Christianitye now joins his friends; Faythfull-few turns his weapons to show " God's word " and " Fayth "; and the play ends with prayers on the part of Christianitye and Faythfull-few that the weapons may never again be reversed.

Some of the characters here, such as Fayned-furtheraunce and No-good-Neighbourhood, stagger under the weight of most oppressive names. Though we find in *Magnyfycence* such characters as Counterfet Countenaunce and Courtly Abusyon, and in the later Morality *All for Money* such pretentious figures as Prest-for-Pleasure and Learning-without-Money, the authors of English Moralities prefer, in general, simplicity of nomenclature.

However, if the author of *The Tyde Taryeth No Man* was acquainted — as it seems very probable that he was — with the earlier French Moralities, he could parallel his figures with such involved abstractions as Desperation-de-Pardon, Honte-de-dire-ses-pechies, Crainte-de-faire-penitence, and Esperance-de-longue-vie,[1] and could justly pride himself on his self-restraint.

But if the author of the present play is to be credited with a somewhat doubtful moderation in the length of names, he must at least be denounced as utterly reckless in assigning abstract names to type figures. Greedinesse, Wantonnesse, Wastefullnesse, and No-good-Neighbourhood, though abstractions in name, are in reality types of wrongdoers, each of whom is especially addicted to the kind of wrongdoing that his name implies : Greedinesse is the man actuated by greed of wealth, Wantonnesse is the wanton young woman who lusts for pleasure, Wastefullnesse is the careless and wasteful young man, and No-good-Neighbourhood is the bad neighbor. But since we are governed in our classifications by the internal evidence of the play, we must note a fragment of contradictory evidence as to the nature of the most important of these types, namely, Greedinesse.

As Corage is sitting in council, Greedinesse, his friend and disciple, enters in a rather perturbed state of mind. He has been reproached for his lack of good citizenship, and his drowsy conscience has almost been stirred by the reproach.

> As I walked along through the streate,
> By such wayes as mine affayres did lie,
> It was my chance with a preacher to meete,
> Whose company to have I did not deny :
> And as we two together did walke,
> Amongest other communication we had,
> The preacher brake out with reprocheable talk,
> Saying that we cittizens were all to bad.
> Some of us, he sayeth, are greedy guttes all,
> And evill members of the common welth.[2]

[1] In *L'Homme Pécheur* (acted 1509).   [2] P. 16.

Greedinesse, therefore, in his eagerness for gain, is an "evill member of the common welth," or, in the picturesque figurative phrase of the preacher, a "greedy gutte," the type of person that every well-informed American of to-day will easily recognize. Greedinesse again sounds a modern note in the ease with which he stills the half-audible murmurings of his conscience under the direction of the master Vice, Corage; and, to complete the comparison, Greedinesse assumes the name Welthinesse.

So far, then, Greedinesse is undeniably a type; but later in the play the author seems to become disturbed at having presented a figure with an abstract designation as a consistent type. Corage enters weeping for the death of his friend, and thus soliloquizes:

> Why, but is Greedinesse dead in good sadness?
> *(Reasoning with himself)*
> My thinkes these newes are not true which you tell,
> Yes, truly, he dyed in a great madnesse,
> And went with boate straight into Hell.
> Why, foole, Greedines will never dye,
> So long as covetous people do live.
>
> .   .   .   .
>
> I am sure he is dead, or one of his likenesse,
> For when he was buryed I stood by,
> And some sayd he dyed of the new sicknesse.[1]

This is a very curious soliloquy, and I am at a loss to explain it. It may be that the author took this method to explain what is more obvious without such a clumsy explanation, that is, that Greedinesse is not what his name suggests, but a type figure. He can hardly have intended that his audience should interpret this as a real doubt on the part of Corage. The Vices are never fooled as to the identity of the characters with whom they come in contact. But whatever purpose the above soliloquy may have been intended to serve, the conclusion is inevitable, — Greedinesse is an indefatigable seeker after wealth, who has come to a miserable end.

[1] P. 77.

The real personifications of evil are Corage, Hurtfull-helpe, Paynted-profite, and Fayned-furtheraunce. Corage, the leader, represents vice in general, while the other three are of an unusual kind, representing evil influences in the world instead of human vices. If we remove the qualifying words from each of the names — as the owners of the names do for themselves — we have left the names of the three influences which these characters seem to exert in favor of the human beings with whom they come in contact. The first represents the help that worldly-minded people seek in their efforts for advancement, the hurtfulness of which they do not realize; the second represents worldly profit, the evil of which is painted over, or disguised; and the third stands for earthly advancement, which, though a strong influence with people of mercenary minds, is only a snare to entrap them to their downfall. Hurtfull-helpe's own explanation of his tactics is worth quoting, as it indicates the regular method employed by Vices here and elsewhere to delude their human victims.

> If men in me hurtfullnesse should know,
> There are few or none that with me would deale:
> Therefore this word hurtfulle I never reveale.
> My name I fayne playne Helpe to be,
> Wherefore ech man for helpe doth come unto me.[1]

Christianitye is, of course, the chief representative of virtue, and Faythfull-few, a type figure, stands for the few Christians who remain true to their religion. Authority and Correction, who appear only to confirm the final overthrow of vice at the close of the play, represent the powers of good law and morality. Dispayre is the Agent of Retribution who appears frequently in the Moralities to punish type figures who have consorted too long with Vices.

There is no necessity now of going into details to outline the interpretation of the allegory step by step. The general meaning

[1] Pp. 8-9.

is that people who make worldly wealth and advancement their object in life are following a delusion. They struggle on, thinking it necessary to grasp opportunities as they come, when suddenly they are overtaken by death or give way to despair ; and it is fortunate for them if they are brought to their senses in time to turn to Christianity. In this mad rush for pleasure and advancement Christianity is neglected or, worse still, is employed for purposes of policy. But there are always a faithful few who follow religion sincerely and with faith ; and these few are able, when the law assists them, to overthrow the reign of vice and to cause their religion to be embraced.

In *All For Money*,[1] the last play of this class, the sole purpose is to show the power and the evil of money. The text is not cited in full, but one does not need to go far to find what is implied, — " The love of money is the root of all evil." The play is not so grimly earnest as the last Morality discussed. There is a good deal of rough humor in William's perplexity over the management of his two wives, in Sinne's teasing of Satan, and in the latter's " roaring and crieing " lest Sinne will desert him. There is also a pervasive satiric tone which allies the play closely with *The Three Ladies of London*, and which gives it a sort of relish almost completely lacking in *The Tyde Taryeth No Man*.

Some of the names here are more involved and more pretentious than the best — or worst — of those in *The Tyde Taryeth No Man*. Prest-for-Pleasure and Swift-to-Sinne are comparatively innocent ; Learning-without-Money and Money-without-Learning are conceptions that can be understood without much effort; but Neyther-Money-nor-Learning is nothing. That is evident. But what particular variety of nothing is he ? As a type figure he could be understood, but as a personified abstraction

[1] Ed. by Ernst Vogel in the *Shakespeare Jahrbuch*, XL. The play was written by T. Lupton, and was printed 1578.

he launches the imagination out into darkest space. And when we find a simple individual scarcely worth noticing bowed down under the title "William-with-the-two-Wives" we must conclude that the author consciously adopted the "French guise" and used long names for their own sake.[1]

The Prologue has a long preamble on the evils of money. From his point of view there is scarcely a vice or crime on the whole list that may not, in some way, be traced to the damning influence of pelf. However, he concludes rather obviously, money is not necessarily an evil in itself. It is an evil because we use it for evil purposes, and it could, conceivably, be a source of good, just as

> we may cut our necessaries and meate with our knyfe
> Wherewith many have cut their owne throtes and bereved them of their life.

After this cheerful simile has cleared away the lingering cobwebs of misapprehension, the Prologue winds up his speech by remarking that the "pleasant tragedie" that is to follow has been constructed because people are so greedy of money. He hopes that people may thereby amend their faults, then retires.

Theologie, Science, and Arte enter in succession, and each makes his solemn plaint that he is sought for money instead of for his own sake. After their departure Money comes in exulting that he is worshipped and served by all classes of men, from the lord to the apprentice. This potent ruler is joined by Adulation, who greets him with esteem and affection, and assures him that all his labors are for the sake of Money. While the two friends are exchanging confidences Money is suddenly taken sick. Mischievous Helpe comes in to wait on him, and with the aid of this attendant Money succeeds in vomiting up a full-grown son, Pleasure. The new-born Pleasure has hardly time to give an account of his place in the scheme of things when he, in his turn, becomes sick also, and obtains relief only

[1] See p. 192, above.

when, with the assistance of Prest-for-Pleasure, he vomits up a lusty offspring, Sinne. The line is not yet complete. Sinne is taken with violent pains, Swift-to-Sinne is hurriedly called in, and with his aid Sinne gives birth to Damnation.

It soon becomes evident that Sinne is the interesting member of this fertile family. In other words, he is the chief Vice of the play. The others retire and leave him to amuse the audience with an account of his influential position in the world of affairs. He is finally interrupted by Satan, who comes in shouting with joy over the enlargement of his kingdom through the efforts of Money and Pleasure. Sinne immediately takes a stand upon his dignity. Then, he infers,

> I and my son Damnation be no bodie with you,
> Sinne and Damnation belike bring a man to heaven!
> Is thy kingdom diminished through us, thinkest thou?
> . . . .
> Howe can Money and Pleasure bring men into hell
> Without Sinne and Damnation, Sir good face, me tell?

Since he is of no service he may as well retire. But here Satan sets up a lamentable roaring, and tearfully beseeches Sinne to remain with him lest his kingdom decay through his ancient enemy Jesus. Sinne has not the slightest intention of deserting Satan, but he has obtained a hold over the latter which he does not fail to utilize, when the mood seizes him, to the production of roars of dismay. The Devil calls in Pride and Gluttonie to help him conciliate the offended Sinne, who finally allows himself to be pacified, and consents to remain.

In the next scene there is a convocation of several not very interesting persons, Learning-with-Money, Learning-without-Money, Money-without-Learning, and Neyther-Money-nor-Learning. There is a great deal of explanation and discussion, but the chief feature of the scene is a debate between Learning-without-Money and Money-without-Learning on their respective. merits. The former makes use of his particular stock-in-trade to swamp his less intellectual rival with learned arguments, and Money-without-Learning is compelled to take refuge in the conviction,

> If I should diminishe my money but one grote,
> I should not be quiet these two days, I wote.

When this argumentative group retires, Money comes in, puffing with fatigue. He is so much in demand that he cannot overtake all his duties, and finds that he must have a helper. His grandson Sinne joins him, and, learning his need, proclaims that he has a friend

> who has such a minde and great love to money
> That he will doe anie thing for you by and by.

Then All-for-Money comes in, "apparelled like a ruler or magistrate," and receives his instructions. He is to take the place of Money, and the latter gives him explicit directions as to the persons he shall favor.

> What suters so ever come to crave your ayde,
> If they come from me let them not be delayde.
> Whatever their matter be, have thereto no regarde,
> For if they come from me they will you well rewarde.

All-for-Money promises to be faithful to his charge, and his patron departs, leaving him in the judgment-seat, with Sinne in attendance. Then a succession of people troop in and implore help from the magistrate, and he dispenses his favors strictly and consistently on the basis of recommendation from Money. Gregorie Graceless is in danger of hanging for his thefts, but he carries his token of the friendliness of Money, and he is sent away pardoned. William-with-the-two-Wives has married one woman for money and another for love, and now he wishes to be rid of the first one while retaining her goods. William has been recommended by Money, so the magistrate arranges to suborn witnesses who will swear falsely and rid the husband of his undesirable wife. Nichol-never-out-of-the-lawe comes in to complain of a poor wretch who has a bit of land which adjoins his own estate, and which he himself is anxious to have. On presenting his credentials Nichol is assured that he shall have the protection of the law in robbing his poor neighbor. Sir Lawrence Livingless, an ignorant priest who does not know " Greke, Ebrewe, nor Latin," is rewarded with a benefice on account of good standing with Money ; and for the same reason old Mother Croote gets the promise of a couple of witnesses to aid her in compelling a young man whom she loves to marry her. On the other hand justice is sternly meted out to Moneyless-and-Friendless, who has committed only the petty offense of taking a few ragged clothes off a hedge.

When All-for-Money has filled his purse he retires, accompanied by Sinne. Then, as a last reminder of the baleful results of the worship of money, Judas and Dives come in bewailing the state to which they are reduced by their love of wealth. In the midst of their complaints Damnation enters and drives them off to hell. Then Godly Admonition, Vertue, Humilitie, and Charitie end the play with the regular commendation of virtue.

The task now remains of sorting out the thirty-two characters, ranging from Theologie, Science, and Arte, to Judas, Dives, and Mother Croote. Lupton seems to have entered on his work with the determination to drag in every type, individual, and abstraction that might serve to add an extra fragment of testimony on the evils of money. As a consequence the majority of the thirty-two appear only once to say their say, and then disappear, while most of the action is carried on by about half-a-dozen figures.

Theologie, Science, and Arte need no explanation. They appear only once, make their moan, and retire. Money, Pleasure, Sinne, Pryde, and Gluttonie are the Vices of the play, while Damnation, the offspring of Sinne, is an Agent of Retribution. Adulation and Mischievous Helpe are also on the side of evil; they are not active Vices, but simply attendants upon Money. Vertue, Humilitie, and Charitie are the Virtues, and Godly Admonition represents a force on the side of goodness; but these four appear only at the close of the play to drive the moral home. There is no contest between Virtues and Vices, and no human hero to strive for; the play is simply a presentation of wickedness and its punishment. Consequently the Virtues and Vices are regarded, not as personal qualities, but in the wider sense of influences at work in the world.

Learning-with-Money, Learning-without-Money, Money-without-Learning, and Neyther-Money-nor-Learning are personified abstractions, not very consistently conceived, who are pressed into service for the sake of a scene which culminates in a debate on the comparative merits of money and learning. This ends the list of abstractions.

The last statement might possibly be challenged, since the important figure All-for-Money still remains. There is no help to be got from the name itself. In this respect All-for-Money is inscrutable. But his actions are, on the whole, those of a type figure rather than of a personified abstraction. He sits in the judgment-seat, "apparelled like a ruler or magistrate," and delivers his verdicts in favor of those who can pay most for them. This method of behavior would not harmonize with any abstraction suggested by the name, and we are safe enough in regarding All-for-Money as the type of corrupt rulers and magistrates.

Prest-for-Pleasure, Swift-to-Sinne, Moneyles-and-Friendles, and Moneyles are type figures, sufficiently described by their exhaustive titles to go without further comment. Gregorie Graceless, Sir Lawrence Livingless, William-with-the-two-Wives,[1] and

---

[1] I do not insist that William is to be narrowed down to the type of man that marries two wives. He must be given more scope than that; and, in any case, his descriptive title universalizes him more or less.

Nichol-never-out-of-the-Lawe are also types, less highly universalized than the others. Finally, Judas, Dives, and Mother Croote range themselves at the foot of the symbolic ladder on the plane of individualization.

The following interpretation must, of course, be merely a series of remarks connected only by their bearing on the text, and having no real logical sequence or organization: When money becomes the great object of life all sorts of evils result. Theology, science, and art, which should be studied for their own sakes, are converted into means for obtaining wealth, and people forget that learning without money is far more desirable than money without learning. Wealth procures pleasures which are sinful and which lead to eternal damnation. The rulers and magistrates are infected with these mercenary desires, and use their power simply as a means for amassing wealth, with the result that judgments are given in favor of those who can pay most for them, while the poor man is ruthlessly punished for the smallest offenses. People should remember the fate of Judas and of Dives, who in this life obtained money at the expense of Christian virtue and are now suffering in hell for it. To avoid such an end we must listen to God's admonition, and practise virtue, humility, and charity in our lives.

CHAPTER VII

MORALITIES DEALING WITH THE SUMMONS
OF DEATH

The Summons of Death is made the motive in only two plays, *The Pryde of Lyfe* and *Everyman,* though it appears in *The Castle of Perseverance,*[1] that great storehouse of Morality motives, and also in the nineteenth play of the Coventry Cycle (*The Slaughter of the Innocents*).[2] Of course there is no telling how many plays of this class may have been written, acted, and forgotten; but judging by the numbers of each class that have come down to us, — which should preserve the original ratio fairly well, — one naturally asks why a motive which is made so tremendously effective in *Everyman* should have been so little in vogue. But our standards of effectiveness do not necessarily coincide with those of the playwright and audience of the fifteenth and sixteenth centuries. The Morality is primarily a bit of practical teaching, designed to warn men, by precept and by example, from a life of viciousness, and to lead them to a life of sobriety and virtue. Death and the life beyond enter into the discussion comparatively seldom; the playwright assumes, with some show of reason, that if the present life is well conducted the life beyond the grave will look after itself. I fancy, too, that the extreme solemnity of death scenes did not much appeal to the average spectator, but that he preferred to leave the play with a pleasant and renewable determination to live in virtue rather than with a sombre realization of the imminence of death.

[1] See p. 63, above.   [2] See p. 30, above.

The Pryde of Lyfe[1] remains now only as a fragment, but
fortunately this fragment consists of the first part of the play;
and the unusually long and descriptive prologue outlines the
action from beginning to end. The hero is presented in two
aspects; first, allegorically, as a king, accompanied by his queen
and subjects, who is finally vanquished by a rival king; second,
literally, as the typical human being, with typical qualities, who
at length must succumb to death.[2]

When the Prologue has outlined the play, the Kyng of Lyfe
enters and exults in his strength and power. He is ruler over
all lands, and no one dares to oppose him. His two soldiers,
Streinth and Hele, flatter him and confirm him in this Herod-
like opinion of himself. But his queen, who is wiser than he,
begs him to think of mortality:

> thinke, thou haddist beginninge,
> Qwhen thou were i-bore:
> & bot thou mak god endinge
> thi sowle is fforlore.

This strikes the King as being the merest foolishness. He
upbraids his queen for her fanciful language, and demands to
know if she wishes his death so that she may " have a new."
The Queen, however, holds stoutly to her point. She insists on
the power of Deth, the great conqueror, and on the perishable-
ness of things of this world. The King then turns confidently
to his two soldiers, and asks their opinion of his power to combat this rival monarch:

> streinth & hele, qwat sey ye,
> my kinde, kornin knightes?
> schal deth be lord ouer me
> & reve me of mightes?

[1] Edited by Alois Brandl in *Quellen des weltlichen Dramas in England*.
The date of the play is not known, but it is usually placed about as early as
the *Castle of Perseverance*.

[2] Cf. *New Custom* (p. 46, etc.) for the same sort of treatment.

They assure him that Deth shall not harm him while they are in his service. Then, for a further bolstering up of his pride, he sends for Mirth, his messenger, and lays the case before him. Mirth answers with even more assurance than the two soldiers, and for this he is warmly commended by the King, who promises to advance him and give him "the erldom of kente."

The Queen then secretly despatches Mirth for the Bishop, to save her lord. The Bishop comes at Mirth's bidding and preaches a sermon on the vices of the day, ending with a special warning to the King; but the latter rewards his services with railing and scorn, and finally orders him home. The Bishop goes with a last warning that Deth will come very soon and deal to the King his death-wound.

The King now determines to settle the question of supremacy by an actual encounter with this mighty Deth. He summons Mirth and sends him with a challenge

> Of deth & of his maistrye
> Qwher he durst com in sighte,
> Ogeynis me & my meyne
> with fforce & armes to ffighte.

Mirth starts off confidently, and here the manuscript comes to an abrupt end. But the sequel, as indicated by the Prologue, is this : Deth comes to the land, slays people right and left, and finally encounters the Kyng of Lyfe in "a sterne strife." The outcome of the encounter is that Deth drives the King to the earth and gives him his mortal wound. Then an intercession scene is indicated for the close of the play, where "oure lady mylde" prays her " son so mylde " for the soul of the dead King.

Rex, or the Kyng of Lyfe, is the representative of mankind, — the human hero, who always figures where this motive is used. Regina cannot be shown to serve any special purpose allegorically. When we regard the literal aspect of the play she is simply the thoughtful wife of a reckless and boastful king;

but when we return to the allegory she cannot be regarded as the typical wife, nor, on the other hand, does she stand for wisdom or prudence. It is, I think, simply a case of an author's having two purposes in mind : one to construct an allegory of life and death, the other to present an over-confident king, like Herod, with his natural companions ; and the latter purpose comes in at times and crowds out the former. Regina could easily be taken as the type of wise companion or counsellor, though there is nothing in the presentation that will warrant attaching more significance to her than I have indicated. Episcopus, or the Bishop, is merely a bishop or, if you like, a type of the spiritual adviser.

Streinth, Hele (Health), and Mirth, the servants of the human hero, represent human qualities. They are not on the side either of vice or of virtue, and it is not necessary that personifications should be on either in this class of plays, where there is no struggle to win the hero to a life of virtue or of vice. Streinth and Hele require no explanation, but Mirth is not quite so obvious a character. He stands, apparently, for high spirits, the joy of living which accompanies health and strength. Deth completes the list of figures in the play.

The interpretation is necessarily much broken up by the incomplete state of the manuscript, but the remaining portion can be explained thus : Man, exulting in his health and strength, laughs at the idea of death. His high spirits make him feel that he could ward off death by his own power. It is in vain that he is warned by friends and spiritual advisers that death comes to all men sooner or later ; and finally his pride becomes so great that he rails at and abuses anyone who dares to suggest such an idea to him. In a spirit of mirth he wantonly runs a mortal risk, and (to proceed by the flickering light of the prologue), after a hard struggle in which his boasted health, strength, and spirits avail him nothing, he succumbs. He has no merit of his own to save him from eternal punishment for his pride on earth, and it is only by the intercession of the Virgin Mary with her Son that his soul is received into heaven.

The other play of this class is *Everyman*,[1] the best known of all the Moralities, — or, to dispense with understatements, the only Morality that is generally known. *Everyman* is to be grouped with *The Castle of Perseverance*, and, as far as one can judge, with *The Pryde of Lyfe*, by the tone of restrained pathos, by the power to excite the emotions of pity and terror, which these three plays possess in common, and which mark them off from all other English Moralities. And among these three there is no question of supremacy. *The Castle of Perseverance* is marred, from this point of view, by a good deal of claptrap and roaring of devils; *The Pryde of Lyfe* presents a king who at first repels our sympathy by his extravagant boasting; but *Everyman* is sombre and restrained from the beginning in both speech and action, and the hero, as he goes to obey the summons of Death, takes on a human interest and a tragic pathos that make him unique among Morality figures.

After a short summary of the action by the Messenger, God speaks alone, lamenting the condition of men and the poor return they make Him for His sacrifice. They are so led astray by worldly riches that He must now deal out justice to them. Having thus decided He calls Death, " His mighty messenger," and instructs him to go to Everyman with a summons to depart on a pilgrimage, taking a "sure reckoning" with him. Death delivers his message, and Everyman is at first completely nonplussed by the strangeness of the demand. But the messenger tells him explicitly what he must hasten to do.

> On thee thou must take a long journey,
> Therefore thy book of count with thee thou bring,
> For turn again thou cannot by no way :
> And look thou be sure of thy reckoning ;

---

[1] Dodsley, Vol. I. The play was printed before 1531, but is of uncertain date.

For before God thou shalt answer and show
Thy many bad deeds, and good but a few,
How thou hast spent thy life, and in what wise,
Before the chief lord of paradise.

Everyman confesses that he is not ready to yield a reckoning on such short notice, but thinks that if he had "twelve year" in which to make preparation he could get his accounts perfectly clear. Death, however, will listen to no such stipulations, and denies even the humble request for a respite until the morrow. Then Everyman inquires piteously if he will be allowed to "come again shortly," providing he makes this pilgrimage and delivers his reckoning. "What!" exclaims Death, "Weenest thou thy life is given thee, and thy worldly goods also?" "I had weened so, verily," answers Everyman. "Nay, nay," Death assures him,

it was but lend thee;
For, as soon as thou art gone,
Another awhile shall have it, and then go therefro,
Even as thou hast done.

So Everyman, bowed down with grief, resigns himself to the stern necessity of complying with the summons of Death, and seeks about for friends to accompany him on this dreaded pilgrimage. He first repairs to Fellowship, who marvels at his appearance of sorrow, and demands heartily to know what he can do for his friend. Everyman tells him of Death's order, and beseeches him to come on the lonely journey. But this is not what Fellowship expected. He flatly refuses to take the pilgrimage. "And yet" he adds,

if thou wilt eat and drink, and make good cheer,
Or haunt to women the lusty company,
I would not forsake you.

Leaving the fickle Fellowship to his pleasures, Everyman turns to Kindred and Cousin, comforting himself that here, at least, he will find constant friends, "for kind will creep where it may not go." Kindred and Cousin greet him lovingly and urge him to make any request that he may have in mind; and Cousin adds, "wot ye well, we will live and die together." Thus reassured, Everyman asks them to go with him on his long journey and help him to render his account. But Kindred declines, offering to send his maid instead, and Cousin is seized with a sudden cramp in the toe. Everyman turns away from them almost in despair. There is now but one left of all the friends who have accompanied him thus far in life. He reflects:

> Yet in my mind a thing there is:
> All my life I have loved riches;
> If that my Goods now help me might,
> It would make my heart full light.

Goods appears on the summons and assures his friend that he can bring him remedy for any sorrow or adversity in the world. Everyman replies that his sorrow is not of this world, but is caused by the necessity of yielding an account "before the highest Jupiter of all"; and, since money "maketh all right that is wrong," he has come for his friend Goods to accompany him before the seat of God. "Nay, nay, Everyman," answers Goods, "I sing another song; I follow no man in such voyages." He explains to the dismayed Everyman that it would only make things worse for him if they should go together. Since he, Goods, has made the account "blotted and blind" he is hardly the one to call upon now to make it clear. And, he continues, he does not belong to Everyman, but was only lent to him for a while. "I had weened otherwise," answers Everyman with pathetic simplicity, and in utter despair turns to Good Deeds, whom he has neglected for years. She answers him weakly:

> Here I lie cold in the ground;
> Thy sins have me so sore bound
> That I cannot stir.

Everyman begs her for counsel in his sore need, and she tells him that, though she is too weak to perform the journey herself, she has a sister called Knowledge who will be true to him and assist him to make the dread reckoning. Knowledge enters, promises to abide with him, and leads him to Confession, who gives him a scourge called Penance. Everyman confesses his sins with grief and uses the scourge on his body, after which Good Deeds is able to stand up and go with him. In preparation for the journey Knowledge gives him the garment of sorrow, called Contrition, and the sisters direct him to summon Discretion, Strength, Beauty, and Five Wits to counsel him upon the way. He assembles these counsellors, and they all agree to go, promising to stand by their master forever.

Thus the whole company proceeds on the pilgrimage, with Everyman leading. But soon he becomes so faint that he can walk no farther, and must creep into a cave to rest; whereat Beauty starts to leave him and, to his despairing appeal to her, answers that she would not remain " and thou wouldst give me all the gold in thy chest." Strength also asserts, " The game liketh me not at all," and takes his departure, followed by Discretion. Last of all, Five Wits decides to leave, untouched by Everyman's final appeal, " I took you for my best friend."

Of all his earthly companions only Knowledge and Good Deeds now remain ; and Knowledge warns him that, although she will not forsake him before death " for no manner of danger," yet she can follow him no further. Everyman grows weaker every moment, and at last, commending his spirit into the hands of God, he dies. Knowledge hears the singing of angels, and rejoices that Everyman's soul has been received into bliss. Then an angel appears and summons Good Deeds to follow the soul of her master to heaven.

Everyman, Fellowship, Kindred, and Cousin, the type figures of the play, having been discussed thoroughly in an earlier chapter,[1] need no further comment here. Beauty, Strength, Knowledge, Discretion, and Five Wits are personifications of a different order. Goods represents earthly riches; Good Deeds, the charitable acts performed by Man during life; and Confession, the sacrament of confession and absolution. None of the other figures needs explanation.

The play is an allegory of mankind in the presence of death. Man, seeing that his end is near, realizes with deep sorrow that his worldly possessions and the friends and kinsmen whom he loved so deeply must be left behind. He knows that he must yield a reckoning, before the throne of God, of his life here on earth; and though he has performed good deeds, yet his sins have been so many that they overbalance the good. His only reasonable course now is to make full confession of his sins and pray for absolution. Having performed this he undergoes penance and is filled with sorrow and contrition for the evil he has done. Thus his spirit is purified, and the good deeds of his life stand out more clearly. As he approaches death his strength, his intelligence, and lastly his faculties desert him. The soul leaves the body, and, by virtue of the good deeds done on earth, is received into heaven.

[1] See pp. 5–8, above.

CHAPTER VIII

MORALITIES DEALING WITH RELIGIOUS AND
POLITICAL CONTROVERSY

Several of the Moralities already considered have shown strong controversial tendencies, but the fact that they are modelled after conventional Morality schemes — the controversial element coming in only as a secondary consideration — made it more reasonable to treat them under the classes to which those schemes belong. But there are three plays (strictly speaking, two plays and a half-play) which, while conforming in all essentials to the general definition of the Morality, are avowedly and primarily controversial in tone. Their sole aim is to expose and correct national abuses. All the other Moralities make it their chief aim to preach morality to mankind in general, though several of them have also a satiric bearing on national affairs. But the three plays of the present class have nothing to do with a general inculcation of morality, and would only be hampered by adopting the conventional schemes which presuppose this purpose. They have to do with national problems of religion and politics, and employ great freedom of allegorical plot in order to exhibit these problems in all possible aspects. These three plays are *The Satyre of the Thrie Estaites*, Part II (a complete play in itself), *King Johan*, and *Respublica*.

The Pleasant Satyre of the Thrie Estaites has already been treated in part.[1] The first section of the play presents the human hero, who goes through the regular stages of State of Goodness, Fall from Grace, Life in Sin, and Final Conversion.

---

[1] See pp. 87 ff., above.

This section having been treated in its regular place with Class I, b, it now remains to discuss the second part of the play, which follows a different scheme, or rather dispenses altogether with a conventional scheme and devotes itself to a vigorous attack on the political and religious evils of Scotland shortly before the Reformation, with suggestions for reform.

In Part II the human hero, Rex Humanitas, drops into insignificance. He takes his seat with the parliament, and when his voice is heard it is on the side of right; but with his final conversion at the close of Part I he ceased to be an important figure. Our interest from now on is centered upon the wranglings of the "thrie estaites," including the various statements of national abuses which, as a matter of fact, had much to do with the religious revolution which was soon to follow.

The action begins with a proclamation of parliament by Diligence. Then the three estates, represented by Spiritualitie, Temporalitie, and the Merchand, come walking in backwards, led by their Vices. They address the King and take their seats, together with Gude Counsell and Correctioun. Then the King makes a short speech, indicating that parliament is assembled for the purpose of reforming abuses and bringing oppressors to punishment "with help and counsell of King Correctioun." Spiritualitie speaks up hastily and warns the king against any sudden reforms. "The peopill of this Regioun," he argues, "may nocht indure extreme correctioun." Then, with a stern rebuke to the lords for attempting to hinder the progress of reform, Correctioun sends Diligence out to proclaim that it is the King's will that all who are in any way oppressed shall come and make their grievance known.

At this invitation Johne the Common-weill rushes eagerly forward, shouting:

> Out of my gait, for God's saik let me ga:
> Tell me againe, gude Master, quhat ye say,

and when Diligence repeats his offer he responds fervently:

> Thankit be Christ, that buir the crown of thorne,
> For I was never sa blyth sen I was borne.

Diligence leads him over to the King, who learns his name, and
then enquires why he carries so sad a face. Johne replies that
it is because the three estates go backwards. The King has
heard this report before, and is anxious to know the names of
the Vices who lead the estates. Johne, who is perfectly familiar
with them, proceeds to explain:

> Thair canker cullours, I ken them be the heads:
> As for our reverent fathers of Spiritualitie,
> They ar led be Covetice and cairles Sensualitie.
> And as ye se Temporalitie has neid of correctioun,
> Quhilk hes lang tyme bene led be Publick Oppressioun:
> Loe! quhair the loun lyis lurkand at his back;
> Get up, I think to se thy craig gar ane raip crack.
> Loe! heir is Falset, and Dissait, weill I ken,
> Leiders of the Merchants and sillie crafts-men.

Johne demands that these Vices be put out, and Correctioun
orders the sergeant to lead them to the stocks. Then the doors
are closed and the session begins, with Johne the Common-weill
and Pauper guarding the doors. Gude Counsell states the main
grievance of Scotland, and Johne follows him up vigorously with
a more detailed account of the ignorance and oppressions of
the clergy. Correctioun then orders the three estates to embrace Johne and to promise him friendship and protection for
the future. Temporalitie and the Merchand consent, but Spiritualitie refuses, thinking it unwise " in sic maters for to conclude
ouir haistilie." Then come Johne's more important charges of
sensuality, ignorance, and corruption among the spiritual lords.
Spiritualitie insults him and calls him a liar, and demands that
he shall be thrown out; but he holds stoutly to his indictment,
and is backed up by Pauper and by Gude Counsell, who reads

from Paul's epistle to Timothy on the subject. Veritie and Chastitie come up and add their accusations against the "Spirituall Stait," and Veritie concludes:

> My prudent Lords, I say, that pure craftsmen,
> Abufe sum Prelats are mair for to commend:
> Gar examine them, and sa ye sall sune ken
> How thay, in vertew, Bischops dois transcend.

Then the Tailzour and the Sowtar are brought in and questioned about their trades. They answer intelligently, showing that they understand their vocations, whereas the spiritual lords have demonstrated that they are entirely ignorant concerning theirs. Gude Counsell breaks out into passionate appeal:

> O Lord, my God, this is an mervelous thing,
> How sic misordour in this realme sould ring.
> Sowtars and Tailzeours, thay are far mair expert
> In thair pure craft, and in thair handie art,
> Nor ar our Prelatis in thair vocatioun:
> I pray yow, Sirs, mak reformatioun.

Our attention is now distracted for a moment from the wrangling of the three estates by the appearance of Common Thift. He has heard of the promised corrections, and is in a pitiful state of fear and anxiety to escape. As he passes the stocks he is greeted by his old friend and master Oppressioun, who is there detained. Oppressioun persuades him to take his place in the stocks for half an hour, while he shall go to procure relief for them both from Temporalitie. When the transference has taken place Oppressioun starts off gaily, hinting that it will be a long while before he and Common Thift will meet again; so the unfortunate Thift is left to bemoan the uneven distribution of honor among thieves.

We return again to the doings in parliament. Diligence brings in three "famous Clarks," who are welcomed by the King and instructed about preaching by Correctioun. The spiritual lords are now questioned concerning their work. Spiritualitie, answering first, shows that his conception of the ghostly duties refers to the maintaining of "concubeins" and the heaping up of wealth for his illegitimate children, but has not the remotest connection with the spiritual welfare of his people. Correctioun remarks:

> I wein'd your office had bene for til preich,
> And God's law to the peopill teich.

The Abbot, the Person, and the Priores, when questioned, show the same zeal for pleasure and profound ignorance of duty. Correctioun tells the Doctour (one of the three Clarks) to preach a short sermon on the duties of the clergy, and the Doctour complies, to the complete mystification of Spiritualitie and his friends.

The lords of the spiritual state are now despoiled of their robes, which are given to the three Clarks. The Priores is also stripped of her habit, and it is found that she has "ane kirtill of silk" under it. A friar is spied whispering in the ear of the Prelate. He also is seized and stripped, and it is discovered that he is Flatterie in masquerade. Then Johne the Common-weill is gorgeously clothed and given a seat in parliament, after which the Vices are taken out of the stocks and led to the gallows, where they are all hanged except Flatterie, who is banished from Scotland.

The play proper is now ended, but there still remains the Interlude of the Sermon of Folie, who comes in with "Folie Hattis" to sell. The King spies him and sends Diligence to summon him to the royal presence. Folie holds off the messenger for a while, but finally goes to the King and explains his identity. Then he hangs his hats on the pulpit and gets up to preach a sermon on fools and folly. He enumerates the different kinds of fools "dwelland in eurie cuntrie," and winds up with a disquisition on the folly of kings and emperors in making war on each other. Diligence, concluding the Interlude, apologizes for the tediousness of the play, and commends the audience to the protection of Christ.

There are, it may be seen, a few important changes in the rôles played in this second part of the play. The subordination of Rex has already been noticed. There is no further use for Wantonnes, Placebo, and Solace, who in the first part represented only the personal desires of the hero for pleasure. They were converted into characters representing innocent desires for pleasure, and, in any case, would have no function in a satire of purely national abuses ; so, except for a brief appearance at the beginning of the action, we see no more of them. But the most important change is the introduction of Johne the Commonweill, sometimes referred to simply as "the Commonweill." He is the type-representative of the common people, and, in the political aspect which the play has now assumed, becomes the chief figure. There is mention made of a new Vice, Covetice (covetousness), who combines with "cairles Sensualitie" to lead Spiritualitie into parliament and then disappears so far as the play is concerned. Publick Oppressioun, another Vice, leads Temporalitie into parliament, and appears later in the play. Common Thift, probably best regarded as an abstract figure representing thievery, appears toward the close of the play in an unimportant rôle. The Priores comes on to participate in the downfall of the Catholic Church ; and finally, during the exposure of the "Lords of the Spirituall Stait," three "famous Clarks" are brought in to exemplify the superiority of Protestant learning and virtue to Catholic ignorance and corruption. The most important of all these changes are the introduction of Johne the Common-weill, the practical disappearance of Wantonnes, Placebo, and Solace, and the subordination of Rex Humanitas as a dramatic figure.

The action, being interpreted, runs thus: The Catholic Church is responsible for many of the worst evils of the time. The spiritual lords are sensual and covetous; they care for nothing but personal gain and pleasure, and are ignorant of their simplest duties. The temporal lords are scarcely better. They band together for the oppression of the common people; and as for the merchants, they practise their trade with dishonesty and deceit. What is needed is a complete renovation. The Catholic dignitaries should be exposed and driven out of office, and replaced by learned doctors of the Protestant faith, who are zealous and mindful of their duties. The common people, who form the backbone of a realm, should be relieved from the oppression of the rich and given a voice in the government of the country. Then the land will be freed from oppression, dishonesty, and ignorance, and will flourish under the rule of liberty.

Kynge Johan,[1] the next play to be considered, is listed sometimes as a Chronicle Play, sometimes as a Tragedy, sometimes as a Morality, and sometimes as a sort of amphibious creation. But, whatever the play may have been in a former edition,[2] one

[1] Written by John Bale. The text used here is that in Manly, Vol. I. Fleay (p. 62) comments on the date and production: "King Johan, two plays in one, was edited by Collier from a MS. in the Duke of Devonshire's library, for the Camden Society, in 1838. This MS. was formerly in the possession of the municipal body of Ipswich, where the plays, beyond doubt, must have been performed. From p. 66, l. 13, the MS. is in the handwriting of Bishop Bale, who died in 1563, and as it contains a distinct statement (p. 102) that it was produced under Queen Elizabeth it must date between 1558 and 1563. She was at Ipswich 1561, Aug. 5–10, and at no other time. The concluding prayer shows that the plays were acted before her: and there can be no doubt that it was on this occasion."

[2] The MS. spelling varies, showing that Bale's alterations were made on a transcript of an older play, but this does not necessarily indicate a different authorship. Fleay concludes (p. 62) that "as Bale, in his own list of his dramatic works, mentions one *in idiomate materno de Joanne de Anglorum Rege*, and no other play on John of so early a date is anywhere heard of, it is almost certain that the original play, as well as the fashioned one, was by him. This is confirmed by internal evidence of style."

thing seems clear from the evidence of the text as it now stands, that is, that *Kynge Johan* is a Morality, though with an historical protagonist, who, by the way, is idealized until he becomes, to all intents and purposes, the type of a good or just ruler. All the other characters in the play are unexceptionable from the point of view of the Morality, and the fact that some of them pose at times as well-known historical figures does not affect the situation. The Vices are Vices from beginning to end of the play, even though, for greater effectiveness in their vicious work, they agree with each other in one section of the play to proclaim themselves personages of high rank in the Church. In almost every English Morality the Vices resort to the trick of changing their names for added effectiveness; and to say, for instance, that Private Wealth is the historical Cardinal Pandulph simply because in part of the play he agrees to call himself Cardinal Pandulph, is on a par with saying that the Seven Deadly Sins are really seven dramatic Virtues because when they attempt to seduce Man they usually proclaim themselves to be Virtues. It is evident that a thread of history runs through the play from beginning to end, but this historical thread could be removed in a few moments and the play would remain, in texture, exactly as it is now; whereas any attempt to remove the allegorical element would result in the complete dismemberment of the play.

Of course *Kynge Johan* is not an absolutely pure Morality, since one of the chief characters, Kynge Johan himself, is a real historical figure. But Kynge Johan is only in a half-sense the hero of the play, since, if he were wholly so, the play should end as a tragedy with his death. Nor does the action proceed with historical events as in a Chronicle Play, but advances, after the orthodox fashion of Moralities, to a triumphant and satisfactory conclusion with the complete overthrow of the

Vices and the establishment of peace and right. The death
of Johan, then, which would be the logical culmination of
the play if it were a Tragedy or a Chronicle Play, is only an
incident — though an important one — in the play as it stands.
Kynge Johan, in fact, comes nearer filling all the conditions
for a pure Morality than does *The Life and Repentance of
Marie Magdalene*.[1]

The play has a good deal of that peculiarly venomous anti-
Catholic invective of which Bale was the undisputed master.
For a deliberately planned, climactic insult it would take some
ingenuity to beat a conversation that takes place between Sedwyson and Dyssymulacyon when these two worthies pause in
their labors to work out a scheme of relationship.

> *Dys.* I have ever loved both the and thy condycyon.
> *Sed.* Thow must nedes, I trowe, for we cum of ij bretherne:
> Yf thu remember, owr fathers were on mans chylderne, —
> Thow comyst of Falsed and I of Prevy Treason.
> *Dys.* Than Infydelyte owr grandfather ys by reason.
> *Sed.* Mary, that ys trewe, and his begynner Antycrist,
> The great Pope of Rome, or fyrst veyne popysh prist.[2]

Sedwyson's characterization of his progenitor as the "fyrst
veyne popysh prist" indicates a fault in this play which has
already been discussed in the case of another Morality.[3] In the
absence of Virtues to maintain the right, a Vice will sometimes
grow exceedingly solicitous that the audience should understand
the full nature of the villainy that is being planned, and will
make an explanation that sounds like a remorseful confession.
At one point Sedwyson, who is the chief Vice, sends Dyssymulacyon to bring in Pryvat Welth and Usurpyd Power, and when
they come he explains to his audience the allegorical signification

---

[1] See p. 111, above.   [2] P. 548.
[3] *Marie Magdalene.* See p. 111, above.

of what is going on. The explanation, so far as tone is concerned, would be much more in keeping with a Virtue.

> Surs, marke well this gere, for now yt begynnyth to worke:
> False Dyssymulacion doth bryng in Privat Welth:
> And Usurpyd Power, which is more ferce than a Turke,
> Cummeth in by hym to decaye all spyrytuall helth:
> Than I by them bothe, as clere experyence telth:
> We iiij by ower crafts Kyng Johan wyll so subdwe,
> That for iijC yers all Englond shall yt rewe,[1]

and Dyssymulacion adds:

> Of the clergy, frynds, report lyke as ye se,
> That ther Privat Welth cummyth ever in by me.[1]

This fault — from an artistic point of view — of explaining the allegorical signification of an action, is tolerably common in the Moralities, especially in those with strong religious tendencies. The pleasure to be derived from allegory consists largely in the feeling that one is grasping a meaning which is merely implied; and when a composer of allegory, more anxious for the eternal salvation of his hearers than for their amusement, adopts the position of interpreter, he insults the understanding of any hearer who is quick-witted enough to grasp the meaning for himself.

Kynge Johan opens the play with a soliloquy showing his intention to rule his country well, to work justice, and to act in accordance with the will of God. He is then joined by the widow Ynglond, who is in sore distress from the abuses of the clergy. She asks Johan for justice from these despoilers of her peace, and he is very sympathetic. Before they can make any plans, however, Sedwyson intrudes himself and falls to cracking lewd jokes about the suggestiveness of the pair's being alone. Johan sternly orders him out, but he retorts

[1] P. 552.

confidently, "I shall abyde in Ynglond,[1] magry yowr harte," and adds that, through the Pope, he is able " to subdewe bothe kyng and keyser." He persists in his ribaldry, and abuses Ynglond at every opportunity. However, Ynglond goes on patiently reciting her wrongs to the king, and explaining the vile practices of the Pope and his followers, who have driven her husband, God, out of the country. Johan promises to help her, and she goes out. Then Sedwyson goes on in his mocking way to explain himself to the king. He makes no attempt to play the usual Vice's rôle of deceit and concealment of identity, but boldly asserts his power, and maintains that all Johan's subjects are on his side. Then, in spite of Johan's efforts to detain him for punishment, he hurries out on his business, and Nobelyte comes in.

The king is very much disturbed at Sedwyson's claim that he has the sympathy of the people of the realm, and he immediately confronts Nobelyte with his suspicions; but the latter assures him that he has always hated Sedwyson " for his iniquite." Johan is somewhat mollified, but still expresses doubts.

> A clere tokyn that is of trew nobelyte;
> But I pray to God we fynde yt not other-wyse.
> Yt was never well syns the clargy wrowght by practyse,
> And left the Scripture for mens ymagynacyons,
> Dyvydyng them-selvys in so many congrygacyons
> Of monkes, chanons, and fryers, of dyvers colors and facyons.

Clargy now puts in an appearance, and by his insolent demands at once provokes a hot argument with the King. Then Syvyll Order appears, and joins sides with the King in the argument against Popery, as upheld by Clargy; and Nobelyte also

---

[1] The name " Ynglond," it may be seen, is rather equivocally employed. Johan, in his opening speech, announces that he is " Kyng of Ynglond." Then the personified Ynglond comes in as a widow, and, in her presence, Sedwyson announces that he " shall abyde in Ynglond." It is, of course, the old story of confusion between literal and allegorical statement.

sympathizes with the King, though his defective intellect does not permit him to go beyond commending his leader when the latter makes a good point. At length Johan and Syvyll Order retire, and Nobelyte makes an abortive attempt to carry on the argument, but is soon brought to admit:

> I am unlernyt: my wytts are sone confowndyd.

Then he and Clargy part company, and Clargy sets out "to sewe un-to Rome for the Churches lyberte."

In the next scene Sedwyson comes in to await the appearance of friends "from the stues." He does not have to wait long. In a few moments Dyssymulacyon enters, singing the litany, and the two friends fall into a discussion on the state of Popery in England. They agree that something must speedily be done to better conditions, as the "abbeys go downe every-where"; and Dyssymulacyon promises to get a child of his own bringing up to help Sedwyson in his efforts. Sedwyson is anxious to know who this child is, and his friend informs him:

> Mary, Pryvat Welth; now hayve I tolde the what.
> I made hym a monke and a perfyt cloysterer,
> And in the abbeye he began fyrst celerer,
> Than pryor, than abbote of a thousand pownd land, no wors,
> Now he is a bysshope and rydeth with an hondryd hors,
> And, as I here say, he is lyke to be a Cardynall.

When Pryvat Welth comes, Dyssymulacyon adds, he will bring Usurpyd Power with him, "and than the gam is ower." Dyssymulacyon is despatched for his son, who in turn brings his friend along with him; and Sedwyson, with a keen eye to the allegorical significance of the scene, persuades Usurpyd Power to retire with him for a moment and then bear him in upon his back,

> That yt may be sayde that, fyrst, Dyssymulacyon,
> Browght in Privat Welth to every Cristen nacion,
> And that Privat Welth browght in Usurpid Power,
> And he Sedycyon, in cytye, towne, and tower.

The assembled company enter into a long discussion on the ways and means of maintaining popery in the land, and in the end they disguise themselves; Usurpyd Power as the Pope, Pryvat Welth as a Cardinal, and Sedwyson as a monk; while Dyssymulacyon explains to the audience that they are preparing to punish Johan for rebelling against Holy Church. The so-called Pope changes the names of his disguised friends to complete the deception. Pryvat Welth becomes Pandulphus, Sedwyson becomes Stephen Langton, and Dyssymulacyon becomes Raymundus. They all set out to compass the destruction of the King, and the Interpretour comes in to give a foretaste of coming events.

In the next act Sedwyson and Nobelyte come in conversing,[1] and Nobelyte grieves over the controversy now raging between the King and the Church. Sedwyson speaks warmly in favor of the Church, and in the end Nobelyte kneels down for his blessing. After promising complete submission to the Church, Nobelyte goes out, and Sedwyson is joined by Clargy and Syvyll Order. Sedwyson unfolds to them his plans for bringing Johan into subjection to the Church, and they all retire.

Johan now appears, lamenting that he is so persecuted by the Church for doing what the welfare of his country demands. Pryvat Welth comes in "lyke a Cardinall," and commands Johan, in the Pope's name, to make peace with the Church on the Church's terms. Johan refuses indignantly, and Pryvat Welth curses him in the name of the Pope. Syvyll Order and Nobelyte enter, but they refuse to converse on terms of friendship with the King, since he is now "a man defylyd." Johan is left alone; but soon the widow Ynglond comes in

---

[1] There is a notable inconsistency in this scene. Sedwyson, who has been named Stephen Langton, here speaks of himself as Good Perfectyon, a messenger from the Pope. He has no reason for giving this name before Nobelyte, and this is probably a feature of the original play overlooked in the process of remaking.

with her son Commynalte, who is blind, "for want of knowlage in Christes lyvely veryte," as he explains. Ynglond reminds Johan of his promise to relieve her distress, but he answers mournfully that his hands are tied and he can do nothing for her.

Pryvat Welth (or Pandulphus, as he now calls himself) approaches the group and orders Commynalte out to wait on his captains Nobelyte and Clargy, who are preparing to join the French king against their country. Commynalte goes meekly, but Ynglond disowns him for it, and refuses to leave the King. After some arguments, accompanied by threats on the part of Pryvat Welth, Johan gives up the crown rather than involve his country in war. Then Treason comes in, arrayed as a priest, and joins forces with the other enemies of the King.

Johan and Ynglond go out, and Dyssymulacyon joins Sedwyson with a cup of poison which he plans to give to Johan. He is determined to put this scheme through at all costs, and says that he will drink half the poison himself if such a step is necessary to throw the King off his guard. Then when Johan reappears, with the faithful Ynglond still in attendance, he introduces himself under the new name Simon of Swynsett, and offers him the drink. Johan is extremely thirsty, but also a bit suspicious, and he demands that the supposed Simon shall first drink half the contents of the cup. The demand is complied with, and Johan takes what is left. Then the poison begins to work on Dyssymulacyon, and he staggers out in a dying condition, calling for his friend Sedwyson. Johan himself is soon overcome, and is supported out by the grief-stricken Ynglond.

Veryte now appears and assures the audience of Johan's honesty and loyalty to his country. Though he is dead his noble acts still live, and his Christian zeal is declared by his expulsion of the Jews from the country. Nobelyte, Clargy, and Syvyll Order enter; and Verity rebukes them all roundly for their cruelty to the King, finally reducing them to sorrow and contrition. Imperyall Majestye approaches, Veryte reports to him that he has performed his commands, and then the two go on to harangue the repentant culprits, who, to compensate for their wickedness, promise to exile the Pope and his followers from the country and to defend the supremacy of Imperyall Majestye. Sedwyson joins them and argues violently in behalf of the Pope, but in the end he is sent out, under the guard of Syvyll Order, to be hanged. Then Imperyall Majestye, Nobelyte, and Clargy give each other assurances of fidelity, lay plans for establishing the true religion, and end the play with a prayer for the Queen.

Most of the characters are easy to interpret. Sedwyson, Pryvat Welth, Dyssymulacyon, Usurpyd Power, and Treason are personifications — the Vices of the play. Veryte and Imperyall Majestye are the Virtues, and the latter stands for kingly power. Syvyll Order is more mysterious. He defines his position thus :

> Ye know very well, to set all thynges in order
> I have moche ado, and many thynges passe fro me,
> For yowr common-welth, and that in every border
> For offyces, for londes, for lawe and for lyberte,
> And for transgressors I appoynt the penalte;
> That cytes and townes maye stand in quiotose peace,
> That all theft and murder, with other vyce, maye seace.[1]

That is, he may be a personification standing for national justice, or a type representing the administrators of justice. Since he receives his directions from Johan in company with Clargy and Nobelyte, — two type figures like Spiritualitie and Temporalitie in the *Thrie Estaites*, — and turns against Johan when the latter is excommunicated, he had best be regarded as a type figure standing for administrators of justice. Johan is consistently in the right throughout the play, and it would be

[1] P. 538.

unreasonable to suppose that national justice could ever be opposed to him. Commynalte is a type standing for the common people, like Johne the Common-weill in the *Thrie Estaites*. Ynglond is a symbolic figure representing England, and Kynge Johan is the historical king, idealized to represent the good king who is beset by treacherous foes.

The play in its historical aspect needs no explanation. Allegorically it may be thus interpreted: In the past England has been well-nigh ruined by internal strife, caused by the Romish Church. The spiritual lords made it their aim to amass private fortunes, practised dissimulation, and usurped the power belonging to the king. They did their utmost to raise sedition in the land, not stopping even at treason. The common people sympathized with the king in his efforts to bring peace to the land, but they were rendered ignorant by their lack of religious instruction, and could not be of much service. The nobles and judges were well-meaning and tried to serve their king faithfully, but the Church had such power over them that when it pronounced a curse upon the king they did not dare to stir in his defence. Thus kingly authority was rendered of no avail, and the country was plunged in misery for three hundred years. But now the beneficent power of the throne, assisted by the enlightened knowledge of God's truth as introduced by the Protestant faith, has restored the country to peace and happiness, and the old vices of the Catholic Church have lost their power in England.

The final play of this class is " A merye enterlude entitled *Respublica*, made in the yeare of oure Lorde 1553, and the firste year of the mooste prosperous Reigne of our moste gracious Soveraigne, Quene Marye the first." [1] After having Protestant abuse dinned into our ears through the last two plays it is a

---

[1] Edited by Leonard A. Magnus for the Early English Text Society, London, 1905. The editor conjectures that the author was Nicholas Udall.

relief to hear at last a word from the other side. But the author, though his sympathies at least were on the side of the Catholic Queen Mary, was no Bishop Bale, and he contented himself with taking a general view, through the allegorical telescope, of England's condition when his "moste gracious Soveraigne Quene Marye" came to the rescue. There is no direct attempt to fasten blame upon the Protestant Church. The vices "held up to scorn" are national vices, and we are only to infer that they were allowed full scope, before Mary's time, owing to the laxity of Protestant rule.

We have a special debt of gratitude to pay to the author — whoever he may have been — for putting into the mouth of his Prologue an unusually concise statement of the purpose of his play; which statement, when broadened, will be found to suggest many of the theories which have been insisted on at some length throughout this work. The Prologue states:

> the Name of our playe ys Respublica certaine:
> oure meaninge ys (I say not, as by plaine story,
> but as yt were in figure by an allegorye)
> to shewe that all commen weales Ruin and decaye
> from tyme to tyme hath been, ys, and shalbe alwaie,
> whan Insolence, Flaterie, Opression,
> and Avarice have the Rewle in their possession.[1]

That is, though the play has its special application to the social conditions in England at the accession of Queen Mary, it is universalized, by the allegorical method, into a depiction of the causes which bring on the ruin of a commonwealth. This is the first and last time we encounter an open avowal of the employment of allegory.

Respublica just misses the technical structure of the class representing the struggle of Vices and Virtues for the possession of man. The Vices, Avarice, Insolence, Oppression, and

[1] P. 1.

Adulation, all find it necessary to get into the service of the widow Respublica in order to carry on their schemes. But their schemes are merely for self-aggrandizement,—by which we are to infer the selfish schemings of politicians and men in power. They make no attempt to corrupt Respublica, and, in fact, avoid her company except when they feel that it is time to patch up another report of the good work they are doing. In other words, the entry into her service is only the stepping-stone toward the fulfilling of their own schemes of personal aggrandizement. The regular Vices of Class I, b, do not work for themselves,[1]— except when in humorous by-play they refer to having robbed houses and picked pockets in order to get spending money for the taverns and stews. Their single aim is to get into the hero's favor, and no personal or selfish motive enters into consideration. But in this play and the one last treated the case is entirely different. In *Kynge Johan* the Vices worked for their own evil interests, and arrayed themselves openly against Johan because he understood them and opposed those interests; in the present play the Vices have their own interests uppermost, and array themselves against Respublica, not openly, since that would defeat their aims, but secretly, to deceive her and to enrich themselves at her expense. Thus they fail to make the appeal of their brethren in Class I, b, who frequently win our sympathy by their hearty devotion to the cause.

The important conclusion to be drawn from this is that in the plays of Class I, b, the evil figures simply represent vices which assail the heart of man, while in the present class the evil figures, though primarily representing national vices, also

[1] There are slight exceptions to this rule in the case of some Vices in *Magnyfycence* and in the *Satyre of the Thrie Estaites*. These selfish Vices have been discussed above in the treatment of these Moralities. They were rendered necessary by the underlying satirical bearing of the plays. In so far as *Magnyfycence* and the *Satyre* employ this kind of Vices they are directly related to the plays of this last class.

connote the idea of corrupt personages who practise these vices
to the detriment of the nation.[1]

The Prologue beseeches the indulgence of his hearers, and
outlines the play to follow. Then the first act begins with a
soliloquy by Avarice, the chief Vice, who discloses his plans for
amassing wealth. He has long been awaiting the chance to
feather his nest in view of old age,[2] and now the chance has
come. He will introduce himself to the wealthy Dame Respublica, who wastes and throws away enough to fill his purse. But,
since he would not be welcome if his name were known, he
decides to disguise himself and change his name to Policie.
He hopes no one will blame him for looking out for his own
interests. One must spend money daily, and then there is always
the danger of thieves. But at the mention of thieves a sudden
fear strikes to his heart. " Owte, alas," he wails, " I feare I left
my Cofer Open." The audience is suddenly deserted, while
Avarice rushes out in an agony of doubt and fear.

Insolence, Oppressyon, and Adulacion come in singing, and
Adulacion praises the voice of Insolence as equal to that of
an angel. Insolence is not much moved by this flattery, but
demands to know " what availeth that to highe dignitiee."
Oppression roughly breaks in, agreeing that it avails " not a
strawe," so far as he can see. But Adulacion is not lightly
to be shaken from his determination to admire. He assures
Insolence that he is as fit to rule the land as he is to sing a
song, and here Oppression takes common ground with him.

[1] It is to be noted that in the *Satyre of the Thrie Estaites*, Part II, these corrupt personages are represented more directly by type figures. This is really
the ideal way of presenting this motive, since it dispenses with the necessity
of making the connection between the vices which are personified and the
persons who practise the vices.

[2] This, of course, is the regular attitude, not of a personified vice, but of a
typical avaricious man. The personified vice of avarice has but one consistent
function — to influence an individual, or a type figure, to the arousing of
avaricious desires. This inconsistency appears throughout the play.

Insolence does not object to this prospect of power and afflu-ence, but they all agree that their "fownder Avarice" must be consulted before any steps are taken.

While they are conversing Avarice comes back, complaining bitterly of thieves, and congratulating himself that he got to his coffers in time to save them. He is so intent on his own thoughts that the three others have great difficulty in gaining his ear; and when he does notice them at last he flies into a rage and accuses them of being the thieves who tried to rob him half-an-hour before. But they finally succeed in allaying his suspicions. He becomes partially mollified, and consents to join them in the struggle for success and wealth, though the slightest occasion is still enough to arouse his suspicions again. He discloses the fact that Respublica, "the ladie of Estate," is in great trouble over the decaying of her fortunes, and would welcome anyone who could bring her a prospect of relief. Furthermore, he promises to introduce them to her so that they can work together and all succeed in getting a share of her estate. It is first necessary that they shall all find more attractive names; and Avarice, who has already prepared his disguise, suggests Authority as a new name for Insolence, Ref-ormation for Oppression, and Honesty for Adulation. Adula-tion has great difficulty in getting his new name fixed in his mind, but he finally succeeds. Then Avarice turns his own gown inside out, "for theise gaping purses maie in no wyse be seen," and at last they are ready for the introduction to Respublica.

In the second act Respublica comes in bewailing the muta-bility of fortune in the state. She knows not how it is, but good government always seems to bring prosperity; and now her own fortunes are ebbing, — ergo, what she needs is good gov-ernment. Avarice approaches, so intent again upon the question of his money-bags that he does not at first notice the downcast

Respublica; but, suddenly catching sight of her, he recollects himself with a start, and introduces himself as " Maister Policie." Respublica welcomes him eagerly, and implores his aid, which he readily grants, promising to bring, in addition, his three friends, Authority, Reformation, and Honesty. Avarice calls in the proffered friends and introduces them, with some serious blunders on the part of Adulation, who finds it very difficult to repress his real nature. A compact is made, and then Respublica retires to give her new counsellors an opportunity to consult among themselves for the good of her estate. Adulation, who is much perturbed by the effort he has just made at self-repression, insists on having a song "to lighten our hartes." Then they retire happily to their new work.

The third act introduces Respublica rejoicing in her new hopes of prosperity. She wonders, however, what Master Policie has been doing, since he has not yet made any report of his work. Adulation enters and assures her that he and his fellow-workers have been toiling night and day to improve her estate. Then, somewhat to the confusion of Adulation, they are joined by a friend of Respublica's, People, who is an honest and rather shrewd fellow, with a great affection for Respublica and a lurking suspicion of her new counsellors. People tells sorrowfully of his poverty and affliction, but protests his love for Respublica, and she in turn assures him of her constant affection. Adulation breaks in with loud avowals of his own good intentions, but he is regarded very coldly by the honest People. Then Respublica and People retire to let Adulation consult with his friends, who are soon to arrive. Presently Avarice enters, again busied with his ever-present reflections on his money-bags. He is soon followed by Oppression, and later by Insolence. The newly-arrived workers have been very busy in their absence, and have rich fruits to show for their toil in the shape of bishoprics and lands. Adulation, whose ambitions have not soared as high as they might have, is strongly censured for having procured only "three hundred pound by the yeare and one manior place."

In Act IV Respublica comes on alone, very ill at ease because People is still unhappy and oppressed. Somehow the new management is not producing the golden results that it promised at first. She is joined by the unhappy People, and then by Avarice, who excuses himself for his long absence on the plea that he has been immersed in "depe studies" to find a way of increasing his patroness's wealth. But People has got beyond even the pretence of accepting Avarice's explanations. "That lye," he responds, "ere this is flowen as ferre hens as Polle steple." Avarice asks, and is granted, permission to bring in his brother counsellors. They are assembled, and all combine to bear down the arguments of People. Respublica is stupid and gullible, as usual, and about the only suggestion she contributes to the argument is, "Undoubtedly, I fele many thinges are amisse." But People argues stoutly against the present abuses in the Church, which are falsely called reformations. Avarice and his friends maintain that these apparent abuses will really work for the good of People in the long run if he will only have patience to wait; and at this argument People is mollified and consents to give the reforms a chance. Respublica, delighted at the prospect of amity, retires to give the others a chance to settle things peaceably among themselves. The moment she disappears the Vices turn furiously upon People, revile him as a peasant and a lout, and order him home. People bows beneath the storm and prepares to get out of the way, but he proffers one last request: "One worde erche goe. Yele geve volke leave to thinke?" "No, marie, will we not," retorts Oppression, "nor to looke, but winke."

In the last act Mercy enters with a speech in praise of God, and announces that she is sent from God to aid Respublica. While she speaks Respublica approaches in deep distress, and praying to God for help. Mercy goes up to comfort her, and while they are together Avarice enters at another part of the stage. Here he is presently joined by Adulation, who announces that "there is newe stertt up, a ladye cald Veritee." Avarice is much disturbed by the report, and draws Adulation aside to warn him that they must be on their guard against Mercy and Truth, who are their bitter enemies. While they are occupied in their asides Truth joins the two women at the other part of the stage. In a few minutes Justice and Peace follow, and now the four sisters, Mercy, Truth, Justice, and Peace plan a "blysfull renovacion" of Respublica's estate. Respublica, whose eyes are at last opened to the real state of her affairs, turns to Avarice and dismisses him, in spite of his loud protestations of innocence. Then she calls People, and he enters and tells her that things are looking up with him.

The women now retire. In a few moments Oppression, Insolence, and Adulation come in, and, encountering People, begin promptly to load him with abuse. But they receive an abrupt check from Avarice, who comes racing in to warn them of the plot that is on foot. Before they can get away the four sisters come in with Respublica and accuse them. They can still lie as readily as ever, but when the cloak of Avarice is turned and his money-bags disclosed, their real characters are revealed. Then the sisters turn the culprits over to People to be guarded.

Finally Nemesis enters, and, after reassuring Respublica and People, confronts the Vices with her knowledge of their crimes. They make a last despairing attempt to escape punishment by shifting the blame on each other; but their accuser sternly commends them to People to be closely guarded until the day for their trial. Nemesis again promises Respublica and People to restore them to their former state of happiness, and the play is ended.

The characters here are absolutely unequivocal. Avarice, Insolence, Oppression, and Adulation represent national vices. Misericordia, Veritas, Justicia, and Pax, the Four Daughters of God, are virtues representing the power and influence of God making themselves felt in the land. Nemesis, though in a special sense Queen Mary, is allegorically an Agent of Retribution. Respublica is symbolic of the country, like Ynglond in *Kynge Johan;* and People, "representing the poor Commontie," is the familiar type figure that we have encountered in all these political Moralities.

The interpretation is equally simple and unequivocal: When a commonwealth falls under misrule an opportunity is given to all the baser national impulses, avarice, oppression, insolence, and adulation. The common people are the ones who must bear these ills, while the persons higher in authority are enabled to gratify their avarice at the common expense. The country is reduced to despair. But a just punishment is in store for those who thus oppress the land for their own gains. When a good ruler succeeds to power he quickly apprehends and punishes the oppressors, and brings comfort to the people; then mercy and truth, righteousness and peace, become the mainsprings of national feeling.

CHAPTER IX

CONTEMPORARY PLAYS WITH MORALITY FEATURES

We have now to take a brief survey of a few sixteenth-century plays which conform in some respects to the requirements of the Morality, without belonging primarily to that class. The discussion in the first chapter of this work has shown the reasons upon which this distinction is based, so that very little more than a brief outline of each play to be considered now will suffice to show the necessity for discarding it. The three essentials of the Morality, to repeat from my definition of Chapter I, are didactic purpose, the presentation of personified abstractions and universalized types as *dramatis personae*, and allegorical structure.

The Preaty Interlude Called Nice Wanton[1] has been discussed in part in Chapter I. It presents the same motive which enters into the construction of *Like Will to Like*[2]; that is, the contrast of two lives, or two sets of lives, with poetic justice meted out at the end of the play. The outline, in brief, is this:

After the Messenger, or Prologue, outlines the play, Barnabas comes in and discusses the distribution of virtue among the different members of his family. It is plain to the youthful mind of Barnabas that he himself has been generously treated in this respect, while his brother and sister, Ismael and Dalila, have been woefully stinted. Apparently the mother, also, is not

[1] Manly, Vol. I. Fleay, p. 32, states that the play was acted at court by the Paul's choir boys on August 7, 1559. He thinks the author may have been Thomas Ingeland.

[2] See note 2, p. 180, above.

so good as she might be, for she settles the family quarrels by the simple expedient of beating Barnabas and petting her "tender tidlynges," Ismael and Dalila. The brother and sister appear, and fully justify Barnabas's account of them by replying with abuse and ridicule when he urges them to go to school with him. Barnabas departs alone for school, and Ismael and Dalila throw away their books and decide to go in for a life of pleasure.

In the next scene a neighbor, Eulalia, comes in to warn Xantippe that two of her children, Ismael and Dalila, are laying themselves open to grievous censure. She urges the mother to "chastyce them for it," but Xantippe receives the advice in the usual spirit of ingratitude evinced by mothers on such occasions. Thereupon Eulalia departs, and shortly after Xantippe leaves the stage clear for the presentation of Iniquitie, Ismael, and Dalila in the well-known dice-throwing scene. Dalila joins forces with Iniquitie, and they make short work of the brother's purse. Ismael goes out to replenish his purse by robbing some one, and Iniquitie and Dalila break into a violent quarrel because he accuses her of keeping back part of the common winnings. She leaves in a rage; and Iniquitie, after commenting on the wickedness of the brother and sister, departs also.

After "a long interval" Dalila reappears, ragged and disfigured by disease. Presently Barnabas joins her. At first he fails to recognize his sister in the tattered creature before him; but when she discloses her name he remarks characteristically that the outcome is just what might have been expected. She begs him to intercede for Ismael, who is to be tried for his life; and Barnabas, promising to do what he can for them both, leads his sister away to feed and clothe her.

Then follows the scene in which the unfortunate Ismael is tried, before Daniel the judge, for "felony, burglary, and murdre." Iniquitie is present, and tries unavailingly to purchase the prisoner's freedom by bribing the judge. Ismael is condemned to be hanged, but before being led away he accuses Iniquitie of leading him into the life of sin. Then Daniel orders that Iniquitie be imprisoned also, and the latter is led out by a halter, defying his captors to injure him.

In the final scene Worldly Shame appears, rejoicing in the late turn of events. Dalila is dead of her disease, and Ismael is hanging in chains. Xantippe comes in and, hearing his account, attempts to kill herself. But Barnabas returns just in time to save her. He comforts her by the assurance that Dalila repented before her death, and adds that he has heard the same of Ismael. Xantippe retires in a more resigned frame of mind; and Barnabas, after exhausting the significance of his family's career, ends the play with prayers for the Queen.

The point of contact between this play and the Morality is the element of moral didacticism, — the aim to teach a lesson for the guidance of life. But even this is a good deal obscured by the fact that *The Nice Wanton* deals with individual human beings. The Prologue reminds his hearers that "He that spareth the rod, the chyld doth hate," and indicates that the purpose of the play is to show that

> If chyldren be noseled in idlenes and yll
> And brought up therin, it is hard to restrayne
> And draw them from naturall wont euyll,
> As here in thys interlude ye shall se playne.

But, since Barnabas, Ismael, and Dalila have all been brought up by the same mother, they should all have gone astray, unless we are to suppose that Xantippe unintentionally drove Barnabas into the paths of virtue by employing the rod on his person because she disliked him. Even in the latter case the play would be contradicting the moral, "He that spareth the rod, the chyld doth hate." On the whole, it seems necessary to conclude that the author believed strongly in the efficacy of the rod irrespective of the motives behind the rod. But enough has been said to show that the working out of the lesson has been confused by the employment of individual persons, who may turn out good or bad irrespective of parentage or training.

The play contains no type figures. There are two personified abstractions, Iniquitie and Worldly Shame. The latter appears only once, and here he is not employed in allegorical action, but merely comments on events which have taken place. Iniquitie is a more important figure. He is prominent in the chief scene of the play, — the dice-throwing scene. But here the action is not allegorical. Iniquitie is undoubtedly intended as the personification of vice, but as far as the action is concerned he might just as well be another sinner like Ismael or Dalila. He does not induce them to a life of sin (the allegorical way of depicting vice as entering the heart) but merely joins them, at one stage of their career, in the capacity of boon companion. Evidently he is given his far-reaching abstract name in order that the dice-throwing scene may be more strongly suggestive of the wickedness of Ismael and Dalila than if they were shown simply with a fellow-sinner.

The Nice Wanton thus coincides with the Moralities in that its aim (though vaguely realized) is to teach a direct lesson for the guidance of life. It does not employ the sort of characters proper to a Morality, and it is not allegorical in structure.

The Disobedient Child[1] has also been shortly discussed in Chapter I. The author here announces the same purpose that we find animating the play of *The Nice Wanton*, *i.e.*, to show the evil results of a failure to employ the all-sufficient rod of correction upon children. The working out of this purpose in

[1] By Thomas Ingelend. Fleay, *History of the Stage*, p. 32, states that the play was produced at court, by Leicester's servants, Christmas, 1560–1561. But in his *Biographical Chronicle*, I, 307, he says it was "a revised interlude of the time of Edward VI" and "was probably acted at Court, 6th March 1560–1. . . . If so, it was acted by the Paul's boys. . . . There is no evidence that interludes of the morality species were ever acted at Court by men players." It is edited in Dodsley, Vol. II.

The Disobedient Child is less convincing even than in *The Nice Wanton*. The Rich Man (whom the action shows to be some particular man, who happens to be rich, and whose name is withheld for no particular reason) takes it into his head that marrying is the unpardonable sin. His son commits this sin, and is disowned forever by his righteously indignant father, who warns his compeers, the fathers and rich men of the audience, that

> we parents must have a regard
> Our children in time for to subdue,
> Or else we shall have them ever untoward,
> Yea, spiteful, disdainful, naught, and untrue.
> And let us them thrust alway to the school,
> Whereby at their books they may be kept under;
> And so we shall shortly their courage cool,
> And bring them to honesty, virtue, and nurture.[1]

The avowed purpose of the play, then, is to show the danger of neglecting discipline when the child is young; but the lesson which the action seems to enforce is: if a young man insists on being married he must pay the bitter penalty of a ruined life, without hope of forgiveness.

The outline, in brief, is this: The son complains to his father of the severity of school life. The father urges him to keep on, but he refuses and finally discloses the fact that he is yearning for a wife. At this the father flies into a rage. "Why," he exclaims,

> foolish idiot, thou goest about a wife,
> Which is a burthen and yoke all thy life.

But the son is not to be shaken from his purpose, and the father disowns him.

In the next scene the two cooks, male and female, come in to prepare for the feast. They give the latest information about the approaching nuptials, and then retire as the young man comes in with his prospective bride. After some love-making on the

[1] P. 280.

part of the enamored pair, the priest comes in and marries them. When the wedding-party retires new light is thrown on the marriage question by a long denunciatory soliloquy on the part of the father, who quotes from Hipponax and Ovid to support his views.

The sad fulfillment of these prophetic utterances is seen presently, when the wife comes in beating her husband and ordering him to work. The wretched husband goes to work, but the beating continues. When the possibilities of corporal punishment are exhausted and the husband lies prostrate on the ground with a broken head, the gentle wife retires, followed at some distance by her timorous and remorseful mate. Then the Devil comes on in high spirits to announce the success of his earthly schemes, which culminate in marriage. Finally the son repairs to his father for help. He is sincerely repentant, but the evil deed has been accomplished, and happiness is irretrievable. The father sends him back to his wife, to drag out his days in the misery which he has brought upon himself.

The only aspect of this play which brings it into relation with the Moralities is its avowed purpose of teaching a lesson. The action is not allegorical, and the characters are merely individuals with their names withheld, as the Prologue's explanation will show :

> In the city of London there was a rich man,
> Who, loving his son most tenderly,[1] etc.

The Disobedient Child, then, should be classified merely as a *tendenz* play.

The Interlude of the Virtuous and Godly Queen Hester[2] is a biblical play with a few allegorical figures introduced in an unimportant scene. The plot runs as follows :

[1] P. 267.

[2] Edited in *Anonymous Plays, 2nd Series*, by John Farmer. The play was first printed in 1561. Fleay, p. 66, states that it was "beyond doubt a play acted by the Chapel children publicly by way of retaliation for their inhibition at Court in 1560."

King Assverus listens to a discussion among his three gentlemen as to what should be the object of greatest honor. One of these gentlemen is Aman, who proves himself so skillful in argument that he is appointed the King's chief counsellor. Presently Assverus decides to be married, and he sends Aman to gather the wisest and most beautiful maidens of the kingdom, in order that the best possible selection may be made. Mardocheus, the Jew, hears of the King's intention, and brings forward his niece as a candidate for the royal favor. When the maidens, then, are assembled before the King, Hester is among them; and her wit and beauty so captivate Assverus that he chooses her for his queen.

Then comes the scene which connects this play with the Morality group. Pride enters, poorly clad. He explains that he has had to lay aside his fine clothes because Aman will not allow any man but himself to go well dressed, and wishes to have a monopoly of pride.[1] Adulation joins him, and complains in like manner that Aman will permit no one but himself to deal in adulation, or flattery. Finally, they are reinforced by Ambition, who adds his complaint in the same key. As a last resort in their extremity, the three Vices decide to resign everything to Aman, "to the intent," as Ambition expresses it, "that Sathan may love him well." Having surrendered their respective personalities to their master exponent, these Vices drop out of sight for the rest of the action.

In the next scene Hardydardy approaches Aman, and by the charm of his witty conversation persuades the latter to engage him as servant. In the course of their conversation Hardydardy refers to the bequest of Pride, Adulation, and Ambition; but Aman understands this only as a merry jest on the part of his entertaining follower.

[1] The chief characteristic of the allegorical figure Pride is, here and elsewhere, love of finery.

The play proceeds with the scriptural story of Aman's attempt to have all the Jews killed, the frustration of this plan by Hester, and the condemnation of Aman. Hardydardy is present at the banquet where Aman's villainy is exposed. He exults in the downfall of his master, and comments to Assverus on the justice by which Aman is to be hanged on the gallows that he himself has prepared for Mardocheus.

This brief outline is sufficient to show how slight is the Morality element in the play. The aim is to present a dramatic rendering of a well-known biblical narrative, not to teach a lesson for the guidance of life. The structure is not allegorical, and the characters proper to an allegorical action that do appear are kept so much in the background that they might be omitted without essentially affecting the play.

The method of developing Aman into the master spirit of pride, adulation, and ambition is quite unique. Apparently the author did not wish to encumber the main action of his play with allegorical machinery, and consequently introduced the three Vices, Pride, Adulation, and Ambition, in their separate scene, as an easy way of showing the wickedness of Aman and the extent to which his evil desires had carried him. The regular allegorical way of depicting this would be to have the three Vices apply to him for service, be admitted, and then proceed to guide his life by their counsels. But the opposite way is taken: Aman does so much of the work usually performed by the Vices that the Vices themselves are thrown out of employment; and all they can do in revenge is to give him so much of their natures that he will inevitably overreach himself.

Hardydardy is a colorless sort of figure. He is, of course, the technical representative of the chief Vice of the Morality, but here he plays only the part of fool, or jester. His entry into the service of Aman was probably understood, in a dim way, as being symbolic of the complete occupation of Aman's heart by

" all sins generally," but this is not expressed in the play. It is merely suggested by Hardydardy's general air of maliciousness, and his unfeigned joy when Aman is brought to a sudden end in the midst of his crime.

The short interlude of *Johan the Evangelist* [1] must be noticed in passing, as it is carried on partly by the sort of characters proper to a Morality. The action begins with a discussion between a godly person named Irisdision and a pleasure-loving person named Eugenio. Irisdision gives an allegorical description of two paths — one leading to good and the other to evil — by which a man may travel. Eugenio is affected, but, waiving the question of allegorical paths, he decides to go out and have his fun while he may. The pair retire in different directions, and Johan the Evangelist appropriates the empty stage. He pompously introduces the audience to himself, preaches a short sermon, and retires with the promise that he "wyll hastely agayne be here." Then Actio comes in, complaining that some-one has wakened him before his time by throwing water upon him. Eugenio returns, and is greeted by Actio as an old friend. Some witticisms are exchanged, and then Eugenio tells of a sermon he heard by a good man (apparently Johan), who spoke of everlasting life and happiness. The two friends decide to walk abroad and partake of such enjoyments as occasion may offer, but Eugenio is determined that they shall return "by pryme" to hear the next sermon from Johan.

The next to appear is Evell Counsayle, who is presently joined by Idelnesse. Evell Counsayle is anxious to find a master, and is prepared to perform any service of a wicked nature that may be demanded of him. He learns that the hobby

---

[1] In the Malone Society Reprints. The editor (p. vi) suggests the possibility of a date before 1557 for the play. It was discovered in quarto form, in 1906, and was purchased by the British Museum. The quarto is undated, but the catalogue of the British Museum assigns the edition to about 1565 on grounds of typography.

of Idelnesse is to corrupt other men's wives; so he announces that he is peculiarly fitted to assist an employer in such work. Then the two go about their business, hastened on their way by an apprehension that they may be disturbed by the sermonizer "that layde fyrst In principio togyther." Their places are taken by Actio and Eugenio, who return discussing their recent adventures. Presently they see Johan approaching, and pause to hear the forthcoming "sermonysacyon." Johan opens his discourse with the parable of the Pharisee and the publican, and then proceeds with a stern denunciation of sin. The two listeners are converted on the spot, and Johan concludes the play with admonitions to his recruits.

It is hardly necessary to comment on the formlessness of the play. It is neither Morality nor biblical tale, and if anyone feels impelled to classify it he had better content himself with calling it an "Interlude," which would indicate that it is probably a play. The characters that concern us here are Evell Counsayle and Idlenesse. Their conversation makes it almost certain that Idlenesse is a type figure representing the idle man, and that Evell Counsayle is the abstract personification of the tendencies towards mischief such as Satan still finds for idle hands to do. The rest of the characters are individuals. As for the purpose of the play, it is strongly moral in tone; but there is not the slightest attempt (or, if there is, it cannot be detected) to teach one connected lesson for the guidance of life.

In *Kyng Daryus* [1] the Morality features are much more evident. The play is about equally divided between Morality and Bible History, and the two elements are completely separated, the only semblance of contact being in one speech at the end of the action. The outline, in brief, is as follows:

---

[1] Edited by Alois Brandl in *Quellen des weltlichen Dramas in England vor Shakespeare.* The play was registered October, 1565. Fleay, p. 59, states: "This was probably an old interlude, revived possibly at Christmas 1563–4."

After the Prolocutor outlines the action to follow, Iniquytie, the chief Vice, enters looking for some friends to converse with. No one joins him, and he works himself up into a condition of extreme irritability, so that when the virtuous Charyte appears he is made the target for a fusillade of abusive language. Charyte protects himself behind the ever-present bulwark of scriptural quotation, but finally becomes disgusted with his opponent's language and leaves. Then appear Importunyte and Parcyalytie, two minor Vices. The irascible Iniquytie is suspicious of them at first, but relents when he learns their names, and receives them as his followers.

Their conference is interrupted by Equytie, and a furious altercation follows. The three Vices use all the threats and abusive language at their command, and are almost driven to despair when Equytie stoutly holds his ground, since they realize that their power will be lost if they cannot drive him out. Equytie makes several long speeches to them with great calmness and presence of mind, and expounds the Scriptures freely. At last he kneels down and prays, then goes out leisurely with a last disdainful speech to his excited opponents. The three Vices sing a song and retire from the stage.

Agreable and Preparatus, the two servants of King Daryus, enter, and are soon followed by the King with his counsellors Perplexitie and Curyosytie. Daryus sends the two servants to bid a company to his feast. Presently Aethopia, Percia, Juda, and Media come in, partake gratefully of the feast, and retire. Then the King and his counsellors also depart.

Iniquytie returns, trolling a merry song, and is at once joined by his two followers. They settle down to a discussion of their ancestry, and Iniquytie informs them that the Pope is his father. But this pleasant interchange of family histories is interrupted by Equytie, who comes prepared to renew the recent argument. In the ensuing quarrel Iniquytie, as his followers think, shows too much disposition to reason with Equytie, and they leave in disgust. Iniquytie is placed at a decided disadvantage when his opponent is reinforced by Constancy and Charytie. A long and bitter exchange of insults follows, with occasional attempts on the part of the Virtues to convert the incorrigible Iniquytie. Finally, according to the stage direction, " somebody must cast fyre to Iniquytie," who rushes out shrieking,

> Nay, I go to the devil, I fere.

The Virtues give thanks to God, sing a song of triumph over the destruction of Iniquytie, and retire.

King Daryus comes in and despatches his two servants for his counsellors. When the counsellors appear he explains to them that he has overheard an argument among his three chamber-servants, and has collected pieces of paper on which they have written down certain mysterious statements. The three servants, Stipator primus, Stipator secundus, and Zoro-babell, are summoned and made to explain their written state-ments. Stipator primus argues for the strength of wine, Stipator secundus for the strength of the king, and Zorobabell for the strength of women. Zorobabell is triumphant, and is taken into the King's favor. Then, before they leave the stage, he petitions for the rebuilding of Jerusalem.

Constancy comes forward with a speech maintaining that Zorobabell was victorious through him, while the other two servants were flatterers. Equytie and Charytie join him, and the three conclude the play with prayers for Queen Elizabeth and her counsellors.

The only point of contact, then, between the Morality and the biblical parts of the play is the speech of Constancy referring to his services to Zorobabell. There is an indirect relation, how-ever, in the fact that the Morality scenes are symbolic of the strife going on at the court between right and wrong, equity and iniquity, culminating in the victory of Zorobabell. The Morality element, also, is very interesting in itself. It could be lifted bodily out of the play in which it is now but a secondary element, and placed alone as a complete Morality on the theme, Conflict between Virtues and Vices for Supremacy. As there is no mention of any prize to be striven for, it would be an example of Class I, a, in its purity.

Horestes,[1] an historical play by John Pickering, is of interest in this discussion mainly on account of the presence of a Vice (denominated almost entirely throughout the play as "the Vyce") who poses at various times as Pacience, Courrage, and Revenge. Judging from his actions in the play, and by the fact that he is once introduced, in a long speech, as Revenge, it seems probable that he was intended to personify the spirit of revenge. A few other personified abstractions also appear, in unimportant rôles.

The play begins with a long conversation in which the Vice disguises himself under the name Pacience. He encounters two rustics, Hodge and Rusticus, and by judiciously playing them off against each other involves them at last in a game of fisticuffs. While they are thus busily engaged he steals in quietly, and impartially bestows a few stinging buffets. Then he takes to his heels and leaves the amazed rustics to patch up the quarrel at their own convenience.

In the next scene Horestes comes on, lamenting the murder of his father and the shameful conduct of his mother, Clytemnestra, who has brought about the death of her husband, and is now with her guilty lover and accomplice, Egistus. He is undecided as to whether he should avenge his father's death. But at this point the Vice approaches, announcing himself as

---

[1] Edited by Brandl in *Quellen des weltlichen Dramas*, etc. The play was published in 1567 by William Griffith. There is no entry of it in the Stationers' Register.

Courrage, the messenger of the gods, and says that the gods have decreed that Horestes shall make war on his mother and her accomplices. This advice is seconded by King Idumeus, who first gets the opinion of his servant Councell. Before Horestes departs on this mission, Dame Nature attempts to dissuade him from this cruel action against his mother, but in vain. He wages war against Clytemnestra and Egistus and slays them both, backed up by the counsels of the Vice, who now appears frankly as Revenge.

Menelaus, the brother of the slain Clytemnestra, now proceeds against Horestes; but, after a conference, he sees that the latter has had good reasons for avenging his dead father, whereupon he forgives him and bestows on him the hand of his daughter Hermione. They retire, and Revenge appears in a downcast mood, and equipped for a journey, since his influence in the country has come to an end. He bestows characteristic advice upon the audience and takes his leave.

Finally, Horestes comes in with his bride Hermione. Truth and Dewtey place a crown on his head, and conclude the play with speeches on their usefulness in the kingdom.

Horestes would have nothing in common with the Moralities except for the fact that a few of its characters are personified abstractions. These characters are unimportant here. Even the Vice, Revenge, could easily be spared. He is not responsible for any of the important actions of the play, but simply appears to influence persons who are already in the mood for revenge.

The "tragicall history" of *Cambyses* [1] is frequently mentioned in connection with the Moralities, but it has so little in common with them that it will not be necessary to go into an outline of

[1] The play was written by Thomas Preston, Fellow of King's College, and afterwards Master of Trinity Hall, in Cambridge. It was licensed to John Allde in 1569–70, but was written some years earlier. The text used is that in Dodsley, Vol. IV.

the plot. Ambidexter is the Vice, technically speaking. As a matter of fact he is simply a double-faced rascal who provides most of what amusement there is in a very sanguinary play, and performs one important act of maliciousness. He goes to young Smirdis, brother of the murderous King Cambyses, and proposes to him a plan for supplanting his brother in the popular favor. Then he proceeds to Cambyses and informs him that Smirdis is working to overthrow him in order that he himself may enjoy the kingdom. The obvious result follows. Cambyses goes out to see to the death of Smirdis. Ambidexter is in high glee at this outcome, and confides to the audience :

Thereby you may perceive I use to play with each hand.[1]

Several personifications appear for brief intervals throughout the play. They are, however, not only unessential, but unimportant to the last degree. Shame appears once in a short interval in the action to address the audience in deprecation of the wickedness of Cambyses. Commons' Cry makes a brief plaint to the King on the miseries of the people, then Commons' Complaint continues the strain, backed up by Proof and Trial. Execution, Cruelty, and Murder are employed by the king to enforce his frequent demands on the lives of his relatives and friends. Attendance and Diligence are simply a pair of followers who appear with young Smirdis during the brief period between the arousing of his ambition and his death. Preparation is a figure, common to many plays of the period, whose duty it is to prepare feasts.

Not one of these allegorical figures has any important place in the action. They could all be supplanted by such characters as First Lord, Second Lord, First Murderer, Second Murderer, and so on. *Cambyses* is, then, a " tragicall history," displaying a few minor characters borrowed from allegory.

[1] P. 215.

Appius and Virginia[1] is announced on the title-page as a "Tragicall Comedie," but perhaps it would seem less paradoxical, from the point of view of modern expression, to speak of it as a "tragicall history," like *Cambyses*, with some allegorical figures introduced. It is, from our point of view, a much more important play than *Cambyses*. In the latter there was no attempt to show that the play was produced to teach a single lesson for the guidance of life; but in *Appius and Virginia*, as I have shown before,[2] there is such an attempt. Some of the allegorical figures here, also, are of more importance in the plot than are any of those in *Cambyses*, as the following outline will show.

The Prologue makes a speech in praise of chastity. Then Virginius comes in with his wife, Mater, and his daughter, Virginia. They converse on the advantages of domestic happiness and affection, then solemnly depart. Haphazard, the Vice, enters with a long and somewhat incoherent speech, showing, in a general way, that he is in the world for no good purpose. He soon has a pair of tangible objects for his merry jests. Mansipulus and Mansipula, two servants, join him, and presently he takes occasion to bestow a sound drubbing upon the person of the former. Subservus comes, they all sing together, and then retire amicably.

The serious part of the play begins now with a soliloquy from Judge Appius on his madness for Virginia. Haphazard joins him with a plan by which he may obtain the object of his desire. Conscience, with a burning candle, and Justice, with a sword, come to warn him, but he decides to accept the advice of

---

[1] The title on the old edition runs as follows: "A new Tragicall Comedie of Apius and Virginia. Wherein is lively expressed a rare example of the virtue of Chastitie by Virginias Constancy in wishing rather to be slaine at her owne Fathers handes, then to be dishonored of the wicked Judge Apius. By R. B. Imprinted at London by William How for Richard Ihones. 1575." The text used here is that in Dodsley, Vol. IV.

[2] See p. 13 of this work.

Haphazard. He retires, full of his new purpose, and Conscience and Justice appear alone for a few minutes to comment sorrowfully upon the probable outcome of events.

Appius, following the advice of Haphazard, now instructs his friend Claudius to accuse Virginius of stealing a thrall of his, a young child (*i.e.*, Virginia), and bringing her up as his own daughter. Haphazard, who is present, urges them on, and goes out with Claudius to see that the base scheme is carried through. Conscience, hidden behind a curtain, makes a last faint appeal to Appius, but is not heeded.

After another comic scene with Haphazard and the servants, Virginius comes in wondering why Appius has neglected him of late. His curiosity is soon appeased when Appius and Claudius come in with their trumped-up accusation. They give him stern orders to deliver up Virginia to her rightful master, then leave him to mourn the sudden calamity to his house. Virginia enters and learns the sad news. She is determined, however, to retain her chastity, and requests her father to take her life at once. He complies, somewhat unnecessarily cutting off her head on the stage. Then he prepares to end his grief by suicide; but Comfort arrives on the scene and persuades him instead to proceed with his daughter's head to Appius, and get comfort in seeing the bad end in store for the tyrant.

In the next scene Appius comes in accompanied by Haphazard, who amuses his master by talking nonsense, which seems, however, to have a sinister suggestion of impending disaster. They are suddenly joined by Virginius, who bears the head of his daughter. He denounces the tyrant sternly, and Justice and Reward follow close on his heels to avenge him. Justice approaches Appius with the warning, " Thy reward is ready here, by Justice now allotted," and Reward proclaims :

Thy just reward is deadly death; wherefore come, wend away:
To death I straight will do thy corpse: then lust shall have his prey.

Appius is handed over to Virginius, who takes him to prison and returns in time to become the custodian also of Haphazard, who has been sentenced in the meantime by Justice and Reward. Finally, Fame enters with Doctrina and Memory, who bear a tomb. Memory writes on the tomb; and Fame, Justice, and Reward all proclaim that they will continue to treat virgins and their persecutors according to their deserts.

It is evident that *Appius and Virginia* has much more in common with the Moralities than have most of the plays we have considered in this chapter. Many of its characters are personified abstractions, and the author takes pains to insist that he is teaching one particular lesson for the guidance of life. Haphazard, who may be taken for the representative of "all sins generally," originates the scheme by which Appius is to corrupt Virginia, and in the end the tyrant is punished, and the Vice overthrown, by the abstractions Justice and Reward. But a closer study of the play shows that this allegorical element is merely grafted on to give a superficial explanation of actions that really result from the characteristics of the different human beings taking part, and that are sufficiently motivated without the introduction of these abstract figures. The allegorical structure is lacking, and again the conclusion is indicated that one consistent lesson for the guidance of life cannot be made the sole point in any other dramatic structure. The author proclaims that his play teaches virgins to value honor more than life, but the play does not teach this any more than it does any one of half-a-dozen other lessons. Human beings with individual characteristics cannot, except by the most unusual kind of accident, lend themselves, in action, to the illustration of one unequivocal lesson for the edification of their fellow-sinners.

Finally, we have one play, written late in the period, which exhibits the allegorical structure and allegorical figures, but which falls short of being a Morality because there is no attempt to teach a single connected lesson for the guidance of life. This is *The Three Lords and Three Ladies of London*.[1] It is a sequel to *The Three Ladies of London*, and has already come in for some slight discussion in the treatment of the latter play;[2] but it is still necessary to present an outline of the somewhat involved action.

The three lords of London, Policy, Pomp, and Pleasure, come to sue for the hands of Lucre, Conscience, and Love, who are in prison.[3] They argue over the coming distribution of the ladies, each exhibiting great anxiety that Lucre may be the one to fall to his share. They apply to Judge Nemo for their brides, and he sends Sorrow to bring them from prison. After a scene in which Fraud, Dissimulation, Simony, Usury, and Simplicity foregather and recount their adventures since their last meeting, Sorrow leads in the three ladies and places them on three stones that have been set in place for them. The first stone is marked " Remorse," the second " Charity," and the third " Care." Fraud, Dissimulation, Simony, and Usury, the former retainers of Lucre, now apply for a renewal of her favor, but she rejects them all, and they make a hasty exit as Judge Nemo reappears with the three lords of London. Falsehood and Double-Dealing enter at about the same time, and address themselves to Love, but Nemo steps forward and drives them out. Honest Industry, Pure Zeal, and Sincerity now take the three ladies in charge, and lead them out to change their prison rags for seemly apparel.

After a comic scene in which Fraud, disguised as a Frenchman, persuades Simplicity to invest ten shillings with him in return for some jewelry which he claims to be worth ten pounds, Nemo enters with the three lords, who are still wrangling for the possession of Lucre. Determined to marry off all three of his protégées, Nemo resorts to a bit of pious fraud. He goes

---

[1] Edited in Dodsley, Vol. VI. The play was printed in 1592, but was probably written a couple of years earlier.

[2] See p. 51, above.   [3] See conclusion of *The Three Ladies of London*.

out and leads in Conscience clothed in white, proclaiming that she is Lucre. The lords admire her beauty, and Pleasure, in particular, falls so violently in love that he remains constant even after the deception is uncovered. A sudden interruption comes at this point. Diligence comes running in to warn them that a Spanish host has come to conquer the land, aiming their hostilities chiefly at the three lords of London, and with intent to carry off the three ladies into bondage. The three lords retire to prepare for the combat.

While the lords, behind the scenes, are girding on their armor, Usury appears with the luckless Simplicity, and threatens to imprison him for attempting to sell his (Usury's) jewelry. Fraud comes in and gets Simplicity off with only the loss of the jewelry, which is forfeited. Fraud, Dissimulation, and Simony now decide to go over to the invading army, and urge Usury to join them; but Usury has misgivings about proving traitor to his own country. Simony argues: " 'T is not our native country, thou knowest. I, Simony, am a Roman : Dissimulation, a mongrel — half an Italian, half a Dutchman : Fraud so, too — half French and half Scottish; and thy parents were both Jews, though thou wert born in London, and here, Usury, thou art cried out against by the preachers. Join with us, man, to better thy state, for in Spain preaching toucheth us not." But Usury has made up his mind that he is better off in London than anywhere else, and he is not to be moved from this position.

The three lords of London now appear, dressed for war and accompanied by their pages; and, advancing from the opposite side of the stage, come the three lords of Spain : Pride, with his page Shame; Ambition, with his page Treachery; and Tyranny, with his page Terror. Fealty, the English herald, advances to parley with the Spanish herald Shealty.[1] Then there

---

[1] Policy explains that *shealty* is an Irish word signifying " liberty," but that it should mean " remissness," or " looseness."

are two or three symbolic encounters, in which the London lords, with much patriotic comment, beat down the shields and the lance-points of the Spanish lords. The latter can offer only railing and abuse in return for their symbolic drubbing, and in the end they are put to flight.

Judge Nemo now leads in his trio of London ladies, who advance to greet their victorious lords. Lucre makes up to Pomp, Love to Policy, and Conscience to Pleasure. A triple wedding is decided upon, after which the ladies retire. Then the lords are applied to by Fraud, Dissimulation, and Usury, who are still patiently seeking service. But Policy takes Usury and puts a mark on him — a little " x " in the middle of a great " C." Then the three rascals are driven out.

Nemo, still acting the part of gentleman usher, brings in Desire, Delight, and Devotion, the three lords of Lincoln, who hope to prove attractive in the eyes of the three ladies of London. But their suit is not to be granted. Nemo decides that the London ladies must not be separated from the London lords, and, in rather doubtful compensation, he presents the lords of Lincoln with the three stones marked " Care," " Remorse," and " Charity."

In the final scene the triple wedding is celebrated with great ceremony. In the crowd of onlookers is Simplicity, who suddenly espies his enemy Fraud in disguise. He raises a great hue and cry, and the two are brought before Pleasure, who ordains that Fraud shall be bound, and that Simplicity, for his revenge, shall be allowed to thrust at him with a torch. But when the preparations are made Simplicity starts off in the wrong direction with his torch, and Fraud slips away in the crowd. So, in merry fashion, the play is ended.

This involved allegorical structure is employed, not to bring out, step by step, a lesson useful for its application to life, but mainly to show the superiority of England over other countries, and of London over other parts of England. It has the outward form, but not the animating spirit, of the Morality. The characters, while they are individually proper to the Morality, are combined, not with a view to subordinating them to one central action with a moral import, but for the purpose of presenting a series of scenes which would express the complacent mood of the London audience.

In all of the plays considered in this chapter we have found elements common to the Moralities, and even the brief discussions that have been accorded these plays will be sufficient to show that the experiment of combining Morality elements with Comedy, History, and Tragedy was not a success. It would be possible to include here a few other plays from the second half of the sixteenth century, and also a few artificial revivals from the seventeenth century; but we have now considered all the sixteenth-century plays that could by any chance be mistaken for Moralities, and to consider examples from the seventeenth century would be little more pertinent to our discussion than to consider *Everywoman* and other so-called Moralities of a recent date. The Morality as a serious type of drama withdrew gradually from the stage as the sixteenth century proceeded toward its glorious closing decade, and by 1600 its place on the boards was completely occupied, not by a lineal descendant, but by a youthful and vigorous usurper, the drama of real life.

CHAPTER X

THE MORALITIES CONSIDERED IN RELATION TO THEIR ORIGINAL AUDIENCE

It is so frequently asserted of the Moralities that they were dull, dreary, and lifeless, that these adjectives have become the stock epithets of the literary historian when he turns aside for a momentary inspection of these unfortunate plays. Undoubtedly this ill report is due in no small degree to the unhappy taste displayed by the Morality in its selection of a name. While we may find ourselves approving highly of the conditions in life which are the results or the natural accompaniments of morality, we feel something peculiarly unlovely in the connotations of the term itself. One natural result is that we have an instinctive repugnance for the dramas that display this ugly brand so openly. It would not be much worse for them if they were termed, instead, " Respectability plays."

But, while the name itself is equivalent to a warning to pass by on the other side, there are two characteristics, more organically connected with the plays, that are just as displeasing. These are *allegory* and *homily*. I should like, then, before bidding my subject farewell, to consider briefly what defence may be made for the employment of these two devices in the Moralities.

In the first place, it is quite safe to assume that the modern reader has a deep-seated abhorrence of the term " allegory." He occasionally finds himself reading with interest literature that belongs to the allegorical category, but that is because he finds in this literature some quality, apart from allegory, that charms or interests him. *The Pilgrim's Progress* and the first two cantos of *The Faerie Queene* still have their wide circles of readers, in spite of the allegorical framework on which they are constructed. In *The Faerie Queene* the reader allows himself to be conducted, to the sound of Spenser's exquisite music, into the charmed country of mediaeval romance, and there he is thrilled with the interest that belongs to the vicissitudes of wandering knights and fair ladies. If the knights and ladies were designated by abstract or type names (in accordance with the strict tenets of allegory) instead of by names that are merely suggestive, the reader would find his interest seriously hampered. But, as it is, he can ignore the allegory as completely as if it were, as Mrs. Malaprop supposed, " on the banks of the Nile." The commendation regularly accorded to Bunyan's masterpiece indicates the same sort of explanation for the interest which it still arouses. *The Pilgrim's Progress*, it is said, is to all intents and purposes a story of real life, and may be read and enjoyed as such. The allegorical framework, we are assured, can be ignored, and we can regard Christian and Hopeful as individual human beings of flesh and blood, travelling in strange lands, and encountering sundry adventures with a great variety of other interesting human beings composed of equally solid flesh and crimson blood. This explanation is perfectly applicable to the work. While Bunyan carefully designated his characters by abstract and type names, he at the same time characterized them as individual human beings ; and thus his allegory approached so near to the confines of literal narrative that his readers, starting where he stopped, can with the slightest effort complete the journey by themselves, crossing the debatable land between allegorical and literal, and establishing themselves securely and happily on the open ground of literal narrative. I shall show presently that exactly this same condition, though from a different cause, was frequently brought about when the Moralities were presented on the stage.

Bunyan wrote another work, *The Holy War*, in which the action all takes place in the remote and murky forest of allegory. The scheme is worked out with infinitely more pains than in *The Pilgrim's Progress*, but we no longer care to subject ourselves to the intellectual labor of translating *The Holy War* into literal terms.

I hope not to be understood as implying here a contradiction to a remark, made in my Preface, that the finest Moralities are those which cling most consistently to the allegorical scheme. A piece of literature cannot be a work of art simply by virtue of being consistently allegorical. In allegory, as in other forms of literature, the measure of success must be estimated by interest and effectiveness. Neither of these qualities can exist long if the reader is compelled to make swift and recurrent transitions from allegorical action to abstract statement. In the Moralities, with their well-recognized and comparatively simple conventional schemes, the action is rarely so involved as to become confusing; but in spite of this, the author, for reasons which I shall specify later, frequently compels his actors to pause and deliver an apparently uncalled-for explanation of actions that seem in themselves obvious. This compels the reader or spectator to move rapidly from one atmosphere to another, and the interest, which should be continuous, is broken. But if, on the other hand, the allegory becomes so involved as to be meaningless without an understanding of the interpretation underlying the allegorical action — and this is the case in *The Holy War* — the reader is compelled on his own account to pause and get his bearings; and the interest is again, for the time at least, diverted from the allegorical narrative itself.

The finest allegory, then, is that which maintains an interest in itself, and for its own sake, and which does not request or compel the reader to close his eyes, even for a moment, in order to puzzle out its connection with the actual meaning. To this

end an allegory should be consistent, and it should be comparatively simple, not dealing with remote or unfamiliar ideas. The
underlying meaning may flow along with it so smoothly that the
reader will subconsciously perceive it, or it may be entirely ignored at the moment, to be "recollected in tranquillity" at a
later time. In this class are the two Moralities to which I
accorded special praise in my Preface, — *Everyman* and the
Play of Wit and Science.

The injustice done to allegory to-day is in the tacit assumption
that all allegory is bad allegory, — that it is dull if we accept it
as it is, and irritating if we try to translate it into literal terms.
We are more interested, we say, in the spectacle of our flesh-
and-blood fellow-creatures as they battle with temptations, make
love to each other, and pass through the fire and flood of strange
adventure. The "bloodless abstractions" of allegory are remote
from the life we love to contemplate. They make no appeal to
our sympathies, and we prefer to employ our intellects in a more
practical way. There is, I think, a real reason for this feeling
of irritation in the fact that in modern literature we frequently
encounter works which are robbed of much of their human
interest by the occasional introduction of allegory. Such a device is, indeed, intensely irritating, and quite warrants a reader
in desiring to curse allegory out of existence. In parts of Tenny-
son's *Idylls of the King* we feel that a brave story of love and
chivalry is being pruned down to make space for a bit of lifeless
allegory quite out of place in such surroundings; and we naturally look upon the allegory with the resentment that an intruder
inspires. In such an environment it is, of course, unnatural. If
it is to be effective, it must move by itself, and not in conjunc-
tion with pictures of supposed reality. The plays that I have
considered in the preceding chapter are, in every case, seriously
hampered by the grafting-on of allegorical characters and actions
to their main scheme of literal presentation.

When, however, an allegory fulfills the rather simple conditions that I have laid down, it may be quite as interesting and absorbing as a narrative or representation of real life. The effect, as a matter of fact, is much the same. While more is meant than meets either the eye or the ear, no guide-book is necessary or desirable for the purpose of ascertaining what that more is. The attention is centered on the action itself, and the action charms and interests in proportion to the skill of its presentation. We should approach a consideration of the absolute merits of the Moralities with this sympathetic realization, and with the recollection that the Moralities were in their day not read, but acted. This latter fact had, undoubtedly, a great influence in preserving the proper attitude towards allegory on the part of the audience. If, then, we would consider the question of excellence in the case of the Moralities, we should try to ascertain the contemporary point of view.

In the first place, we must remember that, for the potential spectators of the Moralities, the classifying term had none of the unpleasant connotations that it has for us, and that the literary method for which the term stands had for them the comfortable associations of an accepted convention. Their ancestors for generations had regarded human problems through the medium of allegory, and had been keenly interested in the medium itself. The time had not yet arrived for relegating allegory as a means of amusement and intellectual recreation to the dust-bin of literary tradition, and they came to the spectacle with unprejudiced minds.

In the second place, it is obviously unfair to dismiss the *dramatis personae* of the Moralities as a set of dreary abstractions, going through a series of lifeless dialogues merely to bring out a moral. They could not have been dreary abstractions to the people who saw them on the stage, or, needless to say, they would not have appeared in play after play for more than two hundred years. In the Morality of *Mankind* the spectators are called upon to pay "red royals" in return for the pleasure of witnessing the performance, and there is no indication that they could enjoy it more cheaply in other cases. Thus, since Moralities continued to be acted, the spectators continued to sacrifice their royals for the sake of beholding them, and consequently the spectacle must have afforded them a considerable amount of satisfaction. What fascination, then, could the Morality have possessed which it is now so hard for us to detect?

The question of comparative excellence among the Moralities I have discussed from time to time in the preceding pages. At present I am concerned with refuting the wholesale condemnation of plays of this type. Now, judged purely as literature to read, the Moralities are, I think, underestimated in most literary histories. For a long time the convention has been to dismiss them with the remark that they are dull, homiletic, and lifeless; and a glance at the lists of *dramatis personae* seems to bear out this remark. A play presenting a set of characters designated as Mankind, Riot, Charity, Humility, Pride, and Lechery hardly gives promise of interesting dialogue or exciting action. But, if one reads doggedly on in order to discover what such a play actually contains, one will probably discover that the more vicious of these apparently chilly abstractions indulge in a good deal of coarse but frequently amusing repartee; that they exhibit a surprising amount of virility in opposing their natural enemies in the open field, and a fine if reprehensible subtlety in hatching their plots under cover; and that a good deal of excitement and suspense is aroused in the outcome of the strife between the lewd fellows and their virtuous opponents to supplant each other in the favor and companionship of Mankind. The patient reader, thus encouraged to peruse other plays, will also find that Riot, Pride, and the like are often characterized as distinct personalities, and that they exhibit amusing idiosyncrasies which add materially to the interest without detracting from the consistency of the allegory. If all this can be found in the Moralities, the actual state of the case is very different from the popular belief that each allegorical character, labelled with his name, appears in his appropriate scene, makes his appropriate speech, and retires.

If the reader who has made the discoveries outlined above then goes on to consider that the plays which he has found so much above the expectation raised by the lists of *dramatis personae* were written, not to be read, but to be acted, he will probably come to the conclusion that the spectators did not pay down their good " red royals " for nought. He will, in that case, be arriving at what I conceive to be the only just conclusion, reached by the only reasonable method. No criticism of the Moralities can be definitive which ignores the fact that they were presented to contemporaries as acted performances.

Our own contemporaries were somewhat surprised, a few years ago, to discover that *Everyman* was tremendously effective on the stage. The general situation in the play (man in the presence of death) is, to be sure, one that by its inherent tragic intensity might be supposed to appeal to people of all times. But the criticism that is applied to Moralities in general will apply just as readily to the play of *Everyman*. When the summons comes to the type that represents mankind to present his account before the throne of God, this type-person proceeds to several other type-persons and to personifications of abstract qualities, with the request that they accompany him. Would not this situation, we might ask, be made infinitely more effective if we had, instead, an individual person surrounded in his last moments by his friends, and striving pathetically to prepare for death by the same methods that have enabled him to live his life ? And is not the allegorical method unbearably artificial and lifeless as a medium for depicting so important a crisis ?

These questions might easily be answered to the discredit of *Everyman* if it had remained simply a printed text. But those who have seen it on the stage realize that such an estimate would be entirely unfair. When the play was acted, the characters, instead of being dreary types and abstractions, were at once individualized and humanized; and the same transformation once took place in the case of every one of the other Moralities which are now so hastily judged on the basis of the printed copy.

There is no evidence that the play of *Everyman* was especially popular in the days when Moralities held the stage. On the other hand, there is pretty good evidence that the kind of Morality of which *Everyman* is the exemplar was not very popular. Of the thirty-one Moralities that have come down to us, only two are constructed on the scheme presenting the Summons of Death, while in the popular class presenting the Conflict between Virtues and Vices are listed twenty-four out of the thirty-one. Some of the probable reasons for this proportion I have already discussed.[1] Suffice it now to say that in the dramatic spectacle of two opposing bands intent upon victory at all costs, and usually with a very tangible and important prize as the meed of victory, the spectator of the Morality period probably found the excitement and interest that the theatregoer always demands in return for his money. When these so-called "bloodless abstractions" appeared on the stage, they had to bestir themselves vigorously if they would maintain the field against their natural foes. The plays exhibit now one party, now the other, in the ascendant; and these ups and downs are accompanied by many a subtle plot and many a stern encounter. The suspense aroused and the excitement stimulated in the minds of the spectators would, as always, depend largely on the combined skill of the playwright and the actors; but the potentialities were inherent in the Morality itself.

[1] See p. 202, above.

I referred, a few pages back, to the fact that the allegory of *The Pilgrim's Progress* approaches so near to the borders of concrete narrative that its readers frequently forget that they are following an allegory; and then went on to mention that the same result, from a different cause, was apparently produced in the acting of the Moralities. This cause I have, as I think, just indicated. In some of the Moralities we find that speeches are introduced in which the actors call attention to the allegorical signification of their actions. This apparently resulted from the knowledge, on the part of the playwright, that his audience was prone to center its interest in the very human and exciting action on the stage. If the playwright happened to be a person of stern moral purpose, he would naturally be anxious that his audience should not lose sight of the excellent lesson inculcated, and he would take this precaution to ensure their souls' welfare. The occasional device, then, of breaking the allegory to call attention to its meaning is a most interesting bit of testimony that the spectators, without this device, were likely to be seduced by the excitement of the action into regarding the play as a purely human spectacle.

Again, the scheme presenting the Conflict between Virtues and Vices has wide possibilities of humor; and this was another reason for its great popularity. In *Everyman* there is not a glint of humor, except in the situation where the fickle Cosyn suddenly develops the cramp in his toe which conveniently prevents him from accompanying Everyman on his pilgrimage. The *motif* of such a play is the most solemn within the range of human experience. No humorous possibilities are inherent in the scheme. Humor could be introduced only in isolated scenes of the kind that are inserted in Shakespearean tragedy to relieve the intolerable strain of the main action. And in such a play as *Everyman*, where the action is, from the very nature of the situation, swift and brief, no spectator could wish to have the main allegorical scheme interrupted by disconnected scenes of humor that would be grotesquely out of place.[1] But the popular Conflict scheme, on the other hand, includes a list of characters that lend themselves naturally to humorous dialogue and situation. These are the Vices, the jovial scoundrels who are the natural opponents of the Virtues, and who are actuated by a burning zeal to maintain friendly relations with Man. When these abstract personifications of vice foregather in private to lay plans and compare experiences, they frequently become, for the time being, types representing mortals who lead reprehensible lives. In this capacity they entertain themselves, and incidentally the audience, with many a merry anecdote of the lives they lead; indulge in sallies of repartee which are often coarse, but, from the point of view of the contemporary spectator, always amusing; and frequently proceed from repartee to active trials of strength and skill. Then, when they advance to the real business of conquering or supplanting their enemies, the Virtues, they frequently resort to subterfuges and practical jokes which would delight an age that still detected humor in such things.

The merry quips, gibes, and practical jokes of these representatives of vice might seem at first to be out of harmony with the spirit of a play which is in its scheme allegorical, and which has for its avowed object the inculcation of morality. But such is not necessarily the case. As to their fitness in an allegorical scheme, it is to be noted that personified vices, if they are to be consistently characterized, are best characterized by having carnal conversation and ungodly acts attributed to them. Now, while such acts and such conversation are not in strict

[1] The allegory is so interrupted in Lyndsay's *Satyre of the Thrie Estaites*. But here the scheme is of a very different kind, and, from the nature of the situation, moves slowly. Besides, the *Satyre* is of excessive length, and could not be viewed at a continuous session. Consequently, the isolated humorous Interludes are introduced for the purpose of allowing the spectators to depart occasionally for purposes carefully specified by the Prologue.

accord with the severe tenets of good behavior, they are often undeniably amusing, and are eminently in harmony with the characters of reprehensible persons and personified vices. As to their fitness in a play written to encourage morality, we are to remember that one orthodox way of persuading people to be good is to teach them to shun evil. The Morality playwright was sensible enough to realize that Vice is not always a monster of frightful mien, but that he frequently appears as a very amusing and companionable creature. But he never committed the blunder of allowing his audience to depart with the conviction that vice is, after all, more pleasant than virtue. The true natures of the seemingly attractive personifications of evil were always laid bare, and the spectator discovered, or was confirmed in the impression, that while vice is at first sight "pleasant to each man's intent," its ways lead down to hell.

In our hasty strictures on the Morality, which, we say, was written with a moral and not with a dramatic purpose, we overlook the fact that writers of the drama from beginning to end have argued for the moral effect of their productions. During the most corrupt period of the English drama, the writers of comedy still contended that they were exhibiting vices and follies to be shunned, that they attacked immorality by showing it to be foolish and harmful. One may well question whether these dramatists did not occasionally introduce their scenes of folly and vice, not in a fury of moral zeal, but rather from a politic desire to amuse the audience; but, at least, they were employing the sound argument that men may be taught virtue by being warned against vice. They realized, what the Morality playwright realized long before them, that a play, to inculcate morality, does not necessarily exhibit only persons who preach morality, and that it is not perforce heavy and solemn, but will be more successful in a variety of ways if it is frequently the opposite.

This leads to the second point proposed for consideration in this chapter, — the presence of homily in the Moralities. The whole purpose in this concluding discussion is to give reasons for the belief that the plays in question were not merely moral disquisitions, moulded in a dramatic form that was dull and uninteresting, and foisted upon an unwilling audience, but that they were plays conforming to a literary scheme that had long been in favor, and were written in a way that was pleasing to the audience upon whose verdict their success depended. Now, along with the humorous scenes that have just been discussed, there appears, in all of the Moralities, a good deal of homiletic moralizing and religious instruction. That is, the playwright carried out his avowed purpose of inculcating morality not merely in the negative but also in the positive way. The same sort of defence, however, that I have made for allegory as a dramatic method suited to the times, can also, I think, be made for the frequent presence of the dramatic homily.

In the Moralities most of the really dramatic effects are produced by the champions of vice, occasionally reinforced by the representative of mankind in a state of depravity. These are the actors who deal in lively sallies of wit, formulate subtle schemes and deep-laid plots, and exhibit exciting rapidity of action. In addition to this, they are frequently characterized in amusing and interesting ways. But with the actors representing virtues the case is very different. They, as a rule, do justify the familiar defining phrase " bloodless abstractions," and one is led to suspect that the critics have taken the word "morality" too literally, and have supposed that the Virtues are the only important actors. These personifications of commendable qualities are often very slightly characterized. They are never consciously amusing, and are never entertaining in our sense of the word. When they are not engaged in administering lofty rebukes to their opponents, they conceive it to be their business to impart moral and religious instruction, in the form of long speeches, to the dramatic representative of mankind, or to the audience. But they return to the stage so often, and remain there so much of the time, that we should do well to inquire whether or not they were *personae gratae* to the playgoers.

It cannot be premised too often or too emphatically that when men are engaged in serving the public the broad lines of their work are laid down by that public itself. Many of our contemporaries applaud vigorously from their exalted station in the theatre when a noble sentiment is uttered from the stage; but they would give a very different expression of personal feeling if they were treated, instead, to a long homiletic speech on the advisability of preparing for death, or on Saint Paul's explanation of the scheme of redemption. For this reason among others we hear many beautiful sentiments when we attend the theatre, but practically no homiletic speeches. If, on the other hand, the plays of another period are consistent and regular in their introduction of such speeches, we may be sure that the latter found favor in the eyes of those whose patronage supported the stage.

It is well known that the poetic homily was an established literary form before and during the time when Moralities were being produced. Outside of the classic literature of this period, which is itself frequently homiletic in form, there was a large body of more popular poetry (part of which has been preserved) that consisted of religious instruction and moral exhortation. In addition to this, the public had been accustomed, for generations before the appearance of the Moralities, to receiving religious instruction through the medium of the drama as embodied in the Miracle plays. The Moralities, therefore, were simply employing what was a well-recognized and acceptable tradition in both poetry and drama when they in turn exhibited a tendency to moralize and instruct; and the spectators, apparently, had no suspicion of the great truth, which it remained for later ages to discover, that moral and religious matters are in harmony, not with the pleasures and employments of the week, but only with the quiet retirement of the seventh day and the house of prayer.

It is not an easy matter to make out a convincing case for the inherent excellence of a type of play that has been persistently decried in the pages of many standard works. And this task is rendered all the more difficult since the type presents many characteristics which, while they were undeniably suited to contemporary tastes and needs, become merely dull and irksome when they confront the readers and critics of to-day. My appeal for a juster estimate of the Moralities must be to the student whose literary sympathies are not wholly bound up with that which makes an immediate and obvious appeal to the present, but who can still find merit in a form of dramatic entertainment that seems to have possessed, in its own day, the power to please as well as to instruct.

LIST OF AUTHORITIES AND EDITIONS

BATES, KATHARINE LEE. The English Religious Drama. New York, 1893.

BRANDL, ALOIS. Quellen des weltlichen Dramas in England vor Shakespeare. Ein Ergänzungsband zu Dodsley's Old English Plays. (Quellen und Forschungen, LXXX.) Strassburg, 1898.

CARPENTER, FREDERIC IVES. The Life and Repentance of Marie Magdalene, by Lewis Wager. Chicago, 1904.

CHAMBERS, E. K. The Mediaeval Stage. 2 vols. Oxford, 1903.

COLLIER, J. P. The History of English Dramatic Poetry to the Time of Shakespeare. London, 1879.

COLLIER, J. P. Illustrations of Early English Popular Literature. London, 1864.

COURTHOPE, W. J. A History of English Poetry, Vols. I and II. London, 1895–1897.

CREIZENACH, WILHELM. Geschichte des neueren Dramas. Vols. I–III. Halle, 1893–1903.

CUSHMAN, L. W. The Devil and the Vice in the English Dramatic Literature before Shakespeare. Halle, 1900.

DODSLEY, R. A Select Collection of Old Plays. Chronologically arranged, revised and enlarged by W. C. Hazlitt. 4th ed., 15 vols. London, 1874–1876.

ELLIS, F. S. The Golden Legend; or, Lives of the Saints, as Englished by W. Caxton. London, 1900. (Temple Classics.)

FARMER, JOHN STEPHEN. Anonymous Plays. Series 1–4. London, 1905–1908.

FARMER, JOHN STEPHEN. The Dramatic Writings of John Bale. London, 1907.

FARMER, JOHN STEPHEN. Recently Recovered "Lost" Tudor Plays. London, 1907.

FARMER, JOHN STEPHEN. The Tudor Facsimile Texts. London, 1907.

FLEAY, F. G. History of the Stage. London, 1890.

FURNIVALL, F. J. The Digby Plays, with an Incomplete Morality of *Wisdom, Who is Christ*. 1882. (New Shakspere Society, Series VII, 1; reissued for Early English Text Society, 1896.)

FURNIVALL, F. J., and POLLARD, ALFRED W. The Macro Plays. Early English Text Society, London, 1904.

GAYLEY, CHARLES MILLS. Representative English Comedies. London, 1903.

GAYLEY, CHARLES MILLS. Plays of our Forefathers. New York, 1907.

HALLIWELL, J. O. Ludus Coventriae. A Collection of Mysteries, formerly represented at Coventry on the Feast of Corpus Christi. Shakespeare Society, London, 1841.

HERFORD, C. H. The Literary Relations of England and Germany in the Sixteenth Century. Cambridge, 1886.

HONE, W. Ancient Mysteries described, especially the English Miracle Plays, founded on Apocryphal New Testament Story, extant among the unpublished Manuscripts in the British Museum. London, 1823.

Jahrbuch des deutschen Shakespeare-Gesellschaft. 45 vols. 1865–1909.

KOELBING, ARTHUR. Zur Characteristik John Skeltons. Stuttgart, 1904.

LAING, DAVID. The Poetical Works of Sir David Lyndsay. 3 vols. Edinburgh, 1879.

MAGNUS, LEONARD. Respublica. Early English Text Society, London, 1894.

Malone Society Reprints. London, 1907.

MANLY, J. M. Specimens of the Pre-Shaksperean Drama, Vols. I and II. Boston, 1897.

PETIT DE JULLEVILLE, LOUIS. Les Mystères. 2 vols. Paris, 1880. (Part of Histoire du théâtre en France.)

PETIT DE JULLEVILLE, LOUIS. La Comédie et les mœurs en France au moyen âge. Paris, 1886.

PETIT DE JULLEVILLE, LOUIS. Répertoire du théâtre comique en France au moyen âge. Paris, 1886.

PETIT DE JULLEVILLE, LOUIS. Les Comédiens en France au moyen âge. Paris, 1889.

POLLARD, A. W. English Miracle Plays, Moralities, and Interludes. Oxford, 1890.

RAINE, J. The Towneley Mysteries. With preface by J. Hunter and glossary by J. Gordon. 1836. (Surtees Society, III.)

RAMSAY, ROBERT LEE. Skelton's " Magnyfycence." Early English Text Society, London, 1908.

Romania: recueil trimestriel consacré à l'étude des langues et des littératures romanes. 37 vols. 1872–1908.

SMITH, LUCY TOULMIN. The Plays performed by the Crafts or Mysteries of York on the Day of Corpus Christi. Oxford, 1885.

SYMONDS, JOHN ADDINGTON. Shakspeare's Predecessors in the English Drama. London, 1884.

TEN BRINK, BERNHARD. Geschichte des englischen Litteratur. Berlin and Strassburg, 1877–1893.

TRAVER, HOPE. The Four Daughters of God. Philadelphia, 1907.

WARD, A. W. A History of English Dramatic Literature. 2d ed. 3 vols. London, 1899.

WRIGHT, THOMAS. The Chester Plays. 2 vols. 1843. (Shakespeare Society.)

INDEX

275

N